W9-ARE-224

LIFE STYLES
IN THE
BLACK GHETTO

LIFE STYLES
IN THE
BLACK GHETTO

William McCord

John Howard

Bernard Friedberg

Edwin Harwood

W · W · NORTON & COMPANY · INC ·

NEW YORK

WINGATE COLLEGE LIBRARY
WINGATE, N. C.

Copyright © 1969 by W. W. Norton & Company, Inc.

Library of Congress Catalog Card No. 69–18479

ALL RIGHTS RESERVED
Published simultaneously in Canada by
George J. McLeod Limited, Toronto

PRINTED IN THE UNITED STATES OF AMERICA

2 3 4 5 6 7 8 9 0

Contents

47633

6 *Contents*

Introduction

"The problem of the twentieth century is the problem of the color line," W. E. B. DuBois predicted at the turn of the century, "the relation of the darker to the lighter races of man in Asia and Africa, in America and the islands of the sea."

The trend of contemporary affairs—the emergence of China, the development of new nations in Africa, and the domestic crisis of America—has amply borne out Du Bois's prophecy. Although we recognize the interrelation of these events (black nationalists, for example, look to Africa for inspiration), we have chosen in this volume to examine "the problem of the color line" as it exists in our nation.

We have further limited ourselves to an analysis of the urban Negro, for undoubtedly the most significant change in American Negro life has been the unprecedentedly rapid and sweeping Negro migration to the cities. This change has had many effects: housing segregation has actually increased because of urban migration; the move to the cities (as sociologist Lee Rainwater has pointed out) may well have contributed to the break-up of Negro families; and, as Thomas Pettigrew has noted, urbanization has entailed *more* school segregation. And then, of course, there are the riots—that apparently distinctive characteristic of American cities in the 1960's.

This concern with the urban Negro is neither new nor unique. Ideologists, demagogues, a Presidential commission—and many fine scholars—have addressed themselves to assessing the condition of city Negroes and proposing solutions to the nation's greatest internal problem.

Why, then, should we issue still another set of opinions about the ghetto Negro? Essentially, because we believe that we can present new evidence based on unique experiences. We must admit, however, that our data merely confirms—or, in a few cases, conflicts with—existing studies, and we must sadly confess that one book can hardly affect the policies of a nation or the hearts of its people. We can only hope that the power of the pen is greater than that of the shotgun.

Even this hope may prove fatuous, however, when one reviews the political climate of America at mid-century. The Chief of Police of Houston, for example, greeted the admirable 1968 report of the President's Commission on Civil Disorder by commenting that the riot commission "and other slobbering groups" offer "an open invitation to engage in riots." The chief probably reflected the sentiments of most white Americans.

We hope to change the minds of some of these people. Our claim to offer new evidence gains some credence from these facts:

• Several of us have had the instructive, frightening experience of directly observing the riots in Watts (1965), Houston, Oakland, Newark, and Detroit (1967), and Orangeburg, South Carolina (1968). We interviewed, with necessary alacrity, some 150 people during these times when "rivers of blood" flowed. We have also had the contrasting opportunity of observing an incident (and interviewing 120 participants) which might have resulted in a riot, but did not. Actually being in a riot—seeing, for example, a man fifty feet from you felled by a shot—teaches one more than any public-opinion poll, textbook, or report can.

• We have attempted to submit our subjective impressions to the slightly more rigorous test of interviewing 1,185 urban Negroes in three American cities. These interviews were conducted by fellow Negroes in the homes, bars, barber shops, and streets of the ghetto. They reflect what people *say* they think, but clearly history may soon prove our findings inaccurate. In 1964, for example, Gary Marx conducted a well-designed comparative study of American Negroes. In *Protest and Prejudice* he reported that the great majority opposed violence; during our research (1966-68) we discovered that a majority of Negroes—whether in a southern city or in Watts—sanctioned the use of violence under certain conditions. Such anomalies do not invalidate either piece of research. The problem is that social scientists cannot keep up with the pace of history. As Martin Duberman, a Princeton historian, pointed out in *The New York Times* in 1968:

At present, the Negro mood seems to me too mercurial, and our techniques for measuring it too uncertain, for anyone to pronounce on the matter with confidence. One problem is that any given individual in the black population probably contains within himself a variety of conflicting emotions. He may feel friendly toward a Jewish civil rights worker and fury toward a Jewish grocery store owner; pleased that his salary has gone up and outraged that he continues to be paid less than his white counterpart; proud to be an American but also proud of the new African states where blacks fully control their own destinies.

Thus, our data should be regarded as merely one more link in a chain of evidence which some future historian may use in attempting to understand "the Negro mood" of the 1960's. Nonetheless, because of the pressing nature of the problem, we believe that Americans should know the temper of the ghetto—now.

• In an attempt to gain a less ephemeral knowledge of the ghetto, we have further interviewed another 620 people who represent different responses to ghetto life. Chosen because of their actual behavior and/or reputation in the community, these Negroes exhibit different life styles. They range from the apathetic to the militant, from the skid-row bum to the affluent, from the head of a numbers racket to ministers. Anyone acquainted with such classics as *Black Bourgeoisie* or *Black Metropolis* will recognize some of these people, for the historical constraints of the ghetto allow only a limited number of ways to survive.

• Finally, we have attempted to unify the sociological and psychological approaches to the problem by examining the collective responses of urban Negroes to their condition and the reaction of the "white establishment" to these movements. Here we have based our comments on interviews with indigenous leaders of the Negro ghetto as well as white mayors, detectives, and businessmen.

We, the authors and staff who have produced this book, come from a diversity of backgrounds and convictions. Some of us are Negro, some are white; some come from the North, others from the South; we range in political beliefs from "radical" through "conservative." These differences prevent us, of course, from coming to any unanimous, authoritative "solution" to the problems facing contemporary America. Nonetheless, we hope our varied shadings and opinions have allowed us to examine ethnic conflict in as objective a way as possible. As Kenneth Clark has written, "The new American dilemma is one of power. The dilemma is a confrontation between those forces which impel a society to change and those who seek to maintain the past." We have tried realistically, and sometimes sadly, to explore the consequences of this tragic confrontation.

WILLIAM MCCORD

Syracuse, New York, 1968

Acknowledgements

This report on the urban Negro—from its inception in the bloodshed of Watts to its completion—took four years of work, of anger, and of anguish. Naturally, when one dives into the maelstrom of contemporary events, one is caught in a riptide of conflicting forces. In real terms: Should authors shield a fleeing activist from police? Should one warn rioting students that they are about to be mauled by a police raid? How do you respond to a charge of being "Trotskyite" after reporting the statistics on exploitation cited in this book? We had to make all of these decisions.

Many people demonstrated a concern and loyalty far beyond the normal. We wish to thank particularly Hifa Rezak, Deni Seinfeld, Macey Reasoner, Anita Kasdorf, and Betty Hunt, who gave invaluable assistance in helping to direct the gathering of material and also aided in the collation and analysis of the data. Robert Stout and Charles Young skillfully guided the statistical analysis of the data.

Generous grants from the Texas Department of Mental Health, consultation assistance from the National Institute of Mental Health, and financial aid from the Rice University Center for the Study of Social Change (administering grants from the Office of Naval Research and the United States Department of Justice) made the research possible.

Through the auspices of the mayor's office in Houston, the authors were allowed to talk with leaders of local governments and police departments in Los Angeles, San Francisco, and Oakland. In every case, the authors were given valuable information and much hospitality.

Douglass Price-Williams, chairman of the Psychology Department at Rice University, originally analyzed the data on Negro opinions and the sections on the "activist" and the "achiever." Blair Justice, of the Houston mayor's office, allowed the use of his questionnaire in Watts and aided in the discussion of the data. Chandler Davidson and Christopher Knipp were extremely helpful in constructively criticizing the manuscript.

We owe a special debt, of course, to the various teams of interviewers who spent great energy and took more than the usual interest in their work.

In different form, sections of this book have appeared in *The New York Times Sunday Magazine*, *Trans-Action*, *The New Leader*, and the *American Behavioral Scientist*. The authors would like to express their appreciation for permission to republish parts of the book.

PART I

THE NEGRO AND THE CITY

In this section we offer some background material on the condition of urban Negroes. On a theoretical level, Edwin Harwood outlines the process of urbanization among American Negroes in both its demographic and cultural aspects. Harwood devotes his attention to the generation of Negroes being raised in the northern urban ghettos and takes a close look at the differential response of white European and American Negro migrants to the city.

In the following two chapters, Bernard Friedberg, John Howard, and William McCord describe the specific conditions in Houston and in Watts, two of the three cities in which the greater part of our interviews were conducted. Although we realize that they cannot be considered "typical" of every city in the United States, we feel that neither can any other city. Each one, in spite of many similarities with other cities, has its own particular combination of factors, its own special "ambience." Nevertheless, rather than attempt to give an overall view of all urban ghettos, we have decided to concentrate on Houston and Watts.

Friedberg gives, first, a brief account of Houston's Negro population in terms of housing, education, employment, etc., and then examines in greater detail the racial tension that resulted in the Texas Southern University uprising in 1967—what led up to it, the ingredients, the reaction of Houston's white population and civil authorities, the prospects for the future.

In the chapter on Watts, Howard and McCord (who conducted on-the-spot interviews during the actual rioting) explore the motivations behind the infamous 1965 riot and the events leading up to it, and offer an appraisal of the post-riot situation in Los Angeles.

CHAPTER 1

URBANISM AS A WAY OF NEGRO LIFE

Edwin Harwood

In the 1920's Negroes began entering the industrial cities of the North in sizable numbers. They were, however, still an insignificant proportion of the population in these cities and were clearly not as conspicuous a segment of the urban lower classes as the European immigrants who had preceded them in much larger numbers. Since the European newcomers and their descendants still faced major problems in adjusting to an urban-industrial society, they were naturally of more interest to settlement-house workers, social researchers, and politicians. At that time they, not the Negroes, were the problem and were the ones who figured in the statistics on crime, destitution, and family disorganization. In fact, in some cities the older Negro settlements were better established and better off economically than many of the foreign-born colonies. The situation, however, began to change when large numbers of unskilled southern Negroes went north to seek wartime jobs in industry during 1917 and 1918.

To understand the problems encountered in the urban Negro ghettos that have grown up since that time, it may help to com-

WINGATE COLLEGE LIBRARY
WINGATE, N. C.

pare the differences between the Negro's adaptation to urban
life and the patterns of adjustment of earlier generations. Neither the findings of the sociologists working in the 1920's nor
the data from more recent studies justifies the assumption that
rural white or Negro Americans have a pattern of adjustment
similar to the acculturation process of foreign settlers.

POVERTY VS. CULTURAL CONFLICT

First of all, poverty did not have the same impact on European
immigrants as it has had on rural American immigrants to the
ghetto. The European immigrants were poor in their countries
or origin; on the whole, they were much better off in American
cities, notwithstanding the hard conditions of slum living and
unskilled labor. Consequently, the personal and social disorganization of the foreign-born was not so much the result of poverty or discrimination as of the conflict between their traditional peasant values and the more rationalistic secular ethos of
an urban-industrial culture. It was a problem of cultural assimilation, not economics. Many immigrants, however—eventually
most—actively sought the rewards that could only be obtained
through participation in the larger society. Creative energies
that would have been dissipated under the "oppressive communal order" of peasant society could develop more fully in the
American urban setting.[1] Today's descendants of the immigrant ghettos run the cities, police them, and profit from their
vigorous industrial growth.

Today, with the exception of a few groups (mainly Latin
Americans), slum residents are largely native Americans. Even
before they arrive in the cities, many are already prepared for
urban living standards by nationwide communications media
and the patterns of mass consumption common to an industrial
society, and thus the cultural hiatus occasioned by a change
from rural to urban residence is not as great as it was for the
Europeans.

It is also important to note that the foreign-born had fewer of the basic amenities of life than today's slum dwellers—and certainly no systematic welfare services.[2] Paradoxically, economic poverty has become a public issue among welfare professionals and social critics in part because things have been getting better. As our society has developed the resources to combat poverty with some hope of success, and as the growing affluence in other sectors of the society has made the poverty that still exists both more conspicuous and less acceptable, poverty has become a proper and realistic matter for attention. And this may also partially explain why cultural conflict rather than economic poverty was so prominent in discussions of slum problems fifty years ago, when poverty was much greater. What little could be done for the immigrant poor was done by working-class politicians who understood—much better, I think, than some civic leaders understand today—what their poor constituents wanted. Thus there was an informal organization of welfare distribution carried out at the local political level, but nothing that could be called a "program." Middle-class reformers and volunteer social workers were no match for city politicians who had jobs and cash to distribute as well as coal and turkeys.[3]

The social pathology of the urban Negro community has always seemed to be more strongly linked to the urban Negro's economic plight than to cultural conflict. When we consider Frazier's study of the urban Negro, *The Negro Family in Chicago*, the importance of economic factors stands out, in spite of the fact that he stressed cultural conflicts in his theory. Frazier found that the well-adjusted Negro families were those that had experienced economic mobility into the working and lower-middle classes. The disorganized areas of Chicago's Black Belt—the areas with a high proportion of broken homes, illegitimacy, and other disorders—were inhabited largely by lower-class Negroes, many of them recent newcomers from the South. Only in the middle-class and stable working-class district, where the Negro was economically secure and had come to adopt the normative patterns of the larger urban society, did Frazier find an increase in family stability and the kind of interest in Negro communal institutions that indicated stable social organization.[4]

Frazier recognized that stability in family and community life was facilitated by the Negro's adoption of the standards of the larger society and by his integration into the professional and occupational life of the city. He argued that the better-adjusted Negro families were "selected" by virtue of their moral fortitude for higher economic status, and he did not see economic advancement as a necessary prerequisite for family stability. This allowed him to discount the importance of such economic factors as steady employment with some opportunity for mobility and social stability. Only in a footnote in his study did he cite data which show the important relation between Negro unemployment and the incidence of Negro family desertion.[5]

Frazier, and some other influential sociologists of his era, believed that the breakdown of rural cultural traditions explained the Negro's plight and that it was not primarily caused by economic discrimination or employment at unsteady menial jobs. If some Negro families were able to escape disorganization, it was because they were able to instill a strong sense of discipline in their members; of course, these families achieved upward mobility.

Those who would disagree with Frazier, insisting that the root causes of Negro disorganization are economic, have been able to muster an impressive array of factual data. Negroes have been shown to have, in relation to other ethnic minorities, higher rates of personal disorganization, which are in large part the result of severe economic handicaps imposed upon large numbers of urban Negro males. Unstable employment at low-paying jobs greatly restricted their opportunity to move into the stable working class.[6] Partly because of these economic handicaps in the cities and partly because of a slave system in the South that deprived Negro males of a basic human right to continuous family life and family authority, Negro males had a much more difficult time keeping their families together in the city. Negro men were certainly not alone in facing economic discrimination in the northern cities. The Irish encountered

plenty of it a century ago; indeed, for a while Negroes were preferred to Irish workers in some instances.[7] Negro families, however, were less able to withstand these pressures. When Frazier
uses the term "black peasant" in referring to the unsophisti-
cated rural Negro he fails to see that at least the European
peasants enjoyed the basic right to a stable family life even
when they lived under the most oppressive manorial system, as
was the case in Ireland. In this most fundamental respect, the
Negro migrants were not like the European peasants.

The Irish arrived with family traditions, parish-church organizations, and associations devoted to the cause of national libera-
tion. They had ward heelers and elective officials who had come
up from within their ranks and who saw to it that able-bodied
male constituents were kept employed. Indeed, the political
power that the Irish mustered in the large eastern cities has no
parallel within the Negro communities. This enabled the Irish
to stablize their economic situation and even overcome discrimination against Irish workers. The ability to grant franchises,
tax concessions, and public-works contracts gave the Irish politician a control over the Irish urban fate that no other immigrant
bloc ever achieved to the same extent through the political
offices of the city. Spokesmen for "reverse discrimination" or
even "black power" could, if they wished, point for justification
to an old American political tradition which, if not exactly hal-
lowed, was a recognized fact of life in many cities for a long
time. Since the Irish and other ethnic blocs used political
power to achieve a kind of reverse discrimination in their favor,
it seems perverse to deny to Negroes these avenues for self-
fulfillment and mobility. But, unfortunately, the era of the
political machine is past. "Black-power" advocates, moreover,
are as hostile to machine politics as the white middle classes.[8]

INFORMAL SOCIAL ROLES AND NETWORKS

Surveying contemporary studies of Negro lower-class life, we
see that Frazier's empirical generalizations, based on the

research he did in the late 1920's, still hold considerable interest despite our doubts about the theory he used to explain them. Negro family disorganization in the cities has persisted and, given the higher fertility rates of Negro females in the past twenty years, poses greater problems. The social and personal disorganization of lower-class Negro communities is viewed correctly as a by-product of years of economic discrimination. Contemporary research studies are realistic in yet another sense: they show that Negroes have developed strategies which, given the restrictions of their urban environment, help them to cope with these pressures. Negro migrants, like the Europeans who preceded them, developed social roles and institutions that allowed them to cope with the more formal and impersonal institutions of the American city. For example, the matrifocal family of the lower-class Negro community helps the Negro female raise a family in the absence of a male breadwinner. It is a defense against social isolation as well as an attempt to insure against economic insecurity.

Negro migrants, then, were not totally without resources to resist the disintegrating pressures of urban societies, although it might be argued that their strategies for survival have not proven as adequate for long-range social stability and economic upward mobility as those of the European immigrants.

In *Black Metropolis*, the most comprehensive study of Negro community life, Cayton and Drake discuss the strengths of lower-class ghetto life as well as the disorganization produced by economic discrimination. Because they note how male unemployment contributed to Negro family disorganization, their study is contemporary in a way that Frazier's is not. However, they emphasize the solidarity and the opportunities for meaningful satisfactions that the lower-class Negro enjoyed in the ghetto.[9] In a recent article, Drake reaffirms this point of view, showing that the current tendency to highlight the disorganization of the Negro ghetto has not changed his earlier point of view: "For the masses of the ghetto dwellers this is a warm and familiar milieu, preferable to the sanitary coldness of middle-class neighborhoods and a counterpart to the communities of the foreign-born, each of which has its own distinctive sub-cultural flavor."[10]

Researchers who have taken the time to study slum social organization in great detail have found that slum inhabitants possess considerable informal social organization. William F. Whyte's classic study of Italian street-corner men in Boston showed that the decline of traditional institutions such as the family and the church—only in the sense of a weakening of their control over individual members of the community—was offset by the emergence of neighborhood gangs, clubs, and political leadership. Slum inhabitants were not demoralized or lacking in the normative codes that regulate individual behavior; in fact, they participated in the larger urban society through these intermediate forms of social organization, and they had as much social solidarity as other urban groups.[11]

However, Elliot Liebow's recent study, *Tally's Corner*, raises some doubts about the degree of solidarity enjoyed by lower-class Negroes, even where intimate friendships are concerned.[12] Liebow found that the mobility and transience of urban Negro males made for shallow friendships; relationships between men were further complicated by a kind of "open season" attitude toward both married and single women, which meant that distrust between men could easily develop over women. This would not have occurred with Whyte's Italians, who had strong convictions about the sanctity of marriage and made a clear distinction between "good" and "bad" girls. The interpersonal distrust that surrounds the institution of the family in the ghetto—if it can be called an "institution"—gets grafted onto other informal groupings, including the street-corner clique of acquaintances. This factor, along with the greater transiency of urban Negroes, makes for greater instability of primary-group relations. We cannot assume that all lower-class slum dwellers enjoy the same stability in their formal social organization. Some European groups, the Italians and Jews, for example, experienced very little personal disorganization in their adaptation to the American city. Other groups, such as the Poles, experienced much more disorder. (W. I. Thomas became interested in the Poles principally because of the extreme personal disorganization he observed among them.)

COMMUNAL ORGANIZATIONS

When we shift our attention from the informal social networks of the Negro slum to more formal kinds of associations, the differences between Negroes and other ethnic groups appear to be even greater. With the exception of the churches, the Negro lower classes were not involved in strong communal organizations to the same extent as the Jews, Poles, or Italians. The formal voluntary associations helped to bridge the gap between the lower and the middle classes among the immigrants, making it possible for the more successful and articulate to provide leadership for the community as a whole. Perhaps, as Oscar Handlin suggests, because the acculturation problems of the Negro were not so acute as those of the immigrant there seemed less need for private voluntary organizations.[13] In addition, the Negro middle class, unlike the upwardly mobile Jews, never established a strong foothold in small-business enterprises, which would have generated capital for strengthening communal-service and welfare organizations. Although members of the Negro middle class organized very early to combat racial discrimination with the help of influential whites, this effort was primarily in their own behalf. Their aim, to borrow James Q. Wilson's distinction, was class status rather than general racial welfare.

OTHER FACTORS AFFECTING GHETTO LIFE

There are other important differences between the contemporary urban Negro and the immigrants that have little to do with cultural background or differences in the amount of discrimination suffered. The fact that Negro migration occurred after the bulk of European migration has been recognized as a factor, related as it is to changes in the American economy and in the political structure of American cities which affected the ability of the Negro to adjust only because he happened to be the latecomer to the city. Some of these trends spell improvement for the Negro migrant in relation to the foreign-born newcomer.

The contagious diseases that felled many immigrants in the slums have been largely controlled, along with the abysmal sanitation conditions which aided the spread of disease. Slum housing has improved over what it was fifty years ago—not because of conscious efforts at upkeep and rehabilitation but simply because there is an increase in the supply of central-city housing vacated by city dwellers fleeing to the suburbs. More slum children are attending high schools, and more of them are graduating. There has even been a rise in the real earning power of unskilled and semiskilled workers since the period of the greatest influx of foreign immigrants. We must conclude that Negroes who are able to find employment and stay employed, especially in the light- and heavy-manufacturing industries, are better off economically than the foreign-born worker was. Of course, the Negro's relative share in the economy may appear even smaller than before because of the tremendous increase in the earning power of other groups and the rapid expansion of the middle-income stratum over the past fifty years, thus causing a greater sense of what sociologists call "relative deprivation." James Q. Wilson has aptly termed this the "psychological urban problem":

> As more affluent suburbs spring up, with neat lawns and good schools, the apparent gap between the quality of life in the central city and at the periphery increases. The suburbanites, adjusting rapidly to residential comfort, become more discontented with the conditions that surround the places where they work in the central city, even though these conditions are also (on the average) improving. Those city dwellers who cannot, for reasons of income or race, move to the suburbs,

grow increasingly envious of those who can; the prizes of worldly success are held up before their eyes but out of their reach.[14]

On the other hand, Negroes face inconveniences today that the foreign-born did not have to put up with. The renewal of transitional neighborhoods in the central cities has prevented some Negroes from acquiring housing of fairly good quality that they would have obtained in the normal course of events. City-planning and good-government rhetoric has so dominated the public's view of this problem that we tend to scoff at the idea that anything but harm could come from the earlier unplanned, spontaneous residential changes—what ecologists refer to as the "invasion and succession" of neighborhoods. Nevertheless, in the face of social discrimination and low income, this was the only way the minorities could increase their housing supply. Today, conservation and renewal of these transitional areas not only prevent the "natural" accretion of transitional housing to the Negroes' housing supply, but they may actually reduce the housing stock. Negroes in the more deteriorated sections of an upgraded district are forced to leave because they cannot afford the rents of the new housing units.[15] The irony of it all is that without proper relocation procedures and control over the displaced population, the impact of these changes on other residential areas is often less subject to prediction and control than under the old "natural" processes. Urban renewal and public housing often mean inadequate relocation for Negroes. Much of the public housing seems to generate as many problems as it solves, not to mention civic controversies that are costly in time, energy, and good will. It is often difficult to find tenants willing to move into housing projects in some cities. And if housing projects had to compete on the open market with the tenement housing available, they would quite likely fare even worse.[16]

The ghettoized lower-class Negro also has greater difficulty in getting to work. When the Europeans came to the city, most of the industrial and commercial firms that could absorb them in large numbers were located near the city's core, often in the same slums where the immigrant workers lived, which made it relatively easy for him to find a good job and get from home to work. Today, many of the industrial enterprises that pay relatively good salaries for unskilled and semiskilled workers have moved to the suburban regions, thereby greatly increasing the transportation problems of the low-income Negro population confined to the center of the city. Left behind are the marginal enterprises—restaurants, laundries, or service industries—that cannot afford to pay the same wages as the suburban manufacturing concerns.

Frequently overlooked in studies of the Negro ghetto is the changed political culture and organization of the American city, especially in the Midwest and on the eastern seaboard. Whatever we may feel about the political machine and bossism, the machine did provide both avenues for mobility and resources for welfare which, although inadequate from the standpoint of today's standards, were fairly well suited to the needs of the lower-class population. Indeed, the kinds of petty harassments characteristic of bureaucratic welfare professionals who, given the restrictions they work under, cannot help but appear priggish on occasion, may even make the old welfare system of the machine shine a bit by comparison. The old ward heeler was a member of the working class himself, knew his constituents well and, most important, did not keep books or check up on people. He was not really providing charity, but buying a vote. You did him a service and you had every right to ask him a favor.

In seeing to it that widows were fed, paupers buried, and the community entertained, sometimes with picnics and festivals, the machine politicians established bonds of solidarity with the immigrants which in turn helped to reinforce other bases of community solidarity. In a way, the machine was, as William F. Whyte points out, a guardian of the public peace. In allowing fines and tickets to be fixed, in giving in to the minor infringements of the law, numbers playing, and other petty vices, the slum dwellers were allowed to do things that middle-class society, had it been in control, would never have tolerated. At times, machine politicians and racketeers co-operated to see to it that the kinds of violent disorders and tensions, which would have galvanized the civic-minded middle classes to action, were kept in check.[17]

"Personalizing" the law may have made the public peace easier to enforce. The evidence that has been accumulated from a number of sources indicates that the growing efficiency and impartiality of police and governmental agencies may actually lead to an increase of tensions in the ghetto and an increasing feeling of alienation from city political authorities.[18]

Cities in which the politicians have become civic statesmen and look first to the demands of middle-class civic and business interests may not involve their lower classes in urban politics on a grass-roots basis as the older machines were able to do. If what we mean by the term "democracy" is a political system that provides channels for the expression of diverse needs, especially for lower-class people who lack the alternative channels open to the higher social classes, then many good-government reforms that have taken "politics" out of city administration must be judged undemocratic. What they accomplish, as Banfield and Wilson argue, is a transfer of political power to the middle and upper-middle classes, a situation which numerical voting strength alone would not have achieved.[19] I think the increasingly explosive tensions of the ghetto are in part the result of a growing political alienation of their lower-class residents. (Chicago is perhaps a notable exception. There the political machine does function in the Negro community along the old lines, although it, too, is undergoing change.[20]) In many cities today there is no adequate substitute for the "politicians" who at one time insured that the everyday frictions between agents of the government and ghetto residents were kept to a minimum. A politics of exchange and compromise—the machine style—is likely to be replaced by a politics of ideology, and the leaders of this new style are likely to exploit and encourage violent tensions rather than subdue them.

GHETTO ATTITUDES AFTER DETROIT

The pattern of racial rioting of the last few years in American cities seems only to reaffirm the diagnosis of the Negro problem that many reasonable men have put forth—namely, that it can be attributed to the pressures of poverty and discrimination. According to this interpretation, Negroes have become confirmed in the belief that American society is fair only to others and never to themselves. But we should note how relative the sense of deprivation is. A riot-torn Newark street is described in a weekly magazine as "scabrous." Compared with the cramped and filthy tenement alleys of fifty years ago, it would appear prosperous, at least before the riot. James Q. Wilson makes a good point when he describes the urban problem as being in part a "psychological" one. Negroes compare their situation not to the descriptions of the immigrants' slums available in archives and textbooks on urban problems, but to the society around them. Films and television open to large numbers a view of wealth that seems so easy to come by because it is enjoyed with such ease and taken so much for granted. What the family shows on TV portray is not the hard-working father of the lower middle class, the American ideal until the 1950's, but increasingly upper-middle-class families where lush family consumption is portrayed, but never the hard work necessary to afford it.

There also has arisen a greater tendency in our society to be critical of the constraints of law and order. Attacks on agents of authority and the legal basis of institutions are no longer confined to the pamphlets of sectarian radicals; the tendency has spread to much wider circles, including groups that were once staunch defenders of social order and bourgeois legal arrangements. When schoolteachers, professors, even clergymen take to the streets—for higher pay, action for the poor, peace abroad, whatever the issues—others quickly learn the lesson. Even if it is not in view of their own apartments, they can see it all on TV—massive demonstrations of disobedience by people wearing suits and ties, by people who enjoy the esteem of the larger society! Such activities, along with a tendency to view collective actions and disorders as a response to *structural* weaknesses of the society, provide ammunition to those who threaten violent disorder. As the will to resist illegal pressures breaks down, these radicals increasingly realize that the ballot and the courts are not essential in persuading a reluctant city council or state assembly to take action on whatever it is they want at the moment. They can take their case into the streets, where they will find the media more than willing to publicize their cause. As Morris Janowitz points out, the media have helped legitimize rioting by spreading the "language of rationalization of violence" that has become popular in certain intellectual circles.[21]

Finally, in addition to all the socioeconomic conditions that seem related to the malaise of the Negro ghetto, we should not overlook the importance of psychological factors. We have already noted that the Negro ghetto family is distinguished from the foreign immigrant family by its greater vulnerability to disorganization, which means that the entire social organization of the Negro slum is less stable than were those inhabited by foreign immigrants. What this has meant concretely is the growth of female-headed households, poor not simply because of discrimination, though that has certainly contributed to the problem, but because there is no male breadwinner and the mothers are too burdened with children to hold jobs. But added to the economic problem this presents, there is an emotional factor: how many Negro boys raised without fathers lack an internalized set of ethical controls, a functioning superego? Negro males who are brought up primarily by mothers and other female relatives pick up from them their hostility toward the males who are not there or, if they are, are not doing worth-while work in society. In such an environment it must be difficult to develop a constructive masculine self-image and the ambivalent self-image that does emerge can only be resolved in ways destructive both to the self and the society, through bold and violent activities that are only superficially masculine. If this analysis is correct, then the Negro youth who hurls a brick or an insult at the white cop is not just reacting in anger to white society, but on another level is discharging aggression toward the father who "let him down" and females whose hostility toward inadequate men raised doubts about his own sense of masculinity.

To understand all of the factors at work, however, it will help to look at the specific, often different, conditions that characterize an urban ghetto. Let us begin with Houston—a sprawling metropolis exhibiting an admixture of the South, the Midwest, and the West.

REFERENCES

1. For a discussion of these trends in the Jewish community, see Louis Wirth's *The Ghetto* (Chicago: University of Chicago Press, 1928), pp. 241–61.

2. Compare Oscar Handlin's description of the dismal tenements of the Boston Irish in *Boston's Immigrants* with contemporary accounts of residential slum conditions. For a brief appraisal of the historical trend toward better housing for slum residents, see James Q. Wilson, "The War on Cities," *The Public Interest*, No. 3, Spring 1966, pp. 31–32.

3. As Jane Addams noted with regret; see "The Class Basis of the Reform Ideal" in Edward C. Banfield, ed., *Urban Government* (New York: The Free Press, 1965), p. 207.

4. E. Franklin Frazier, *The Negro Family in Chicago* (Chicago: University of Chicago Press, 1932), pp. 120–21, 249–52, *passim*.

5. *Ibid.*, p. 149n. Frazier cites the statistic and leaves it at that.

6. Lee Rainwater, "Crucible of Identity: The Negro Lower-Class Family," *Daedalus*, Winter 1966, pp. 172–211; Daniel Patrick Moynihan, "Employment, Income and the Ordeal of the Negro Family," *Daedalus*, Fall 1965, pp. 758–69. Moynihan suggests that we may have gone too far in emphasizing the independent role of economic factors in explaining Negro disorganization. He believes that in the case of many Negro

families, psychological impairment may have been so great as to preclude a satisfactory adjustment even under the best of economic circumstances.

7. See Robert Ernst, *Immigrant Life in New York City, 1825–1863* (New York: King's Crown Press, Columbia University, 1949), pp. 66–68.

8. For a comprehensive and insightful discussion of these trends, see Edward C. Banfield and James Q. Wilson, *City Politics* (Cambridge, Mass.: Harvard University Press, 1965), pp. 115–27. This alienation of ideological white and Negro leaders from this type of political arrangement has been discussed in detail by Wilson. See his *The Amateur Democrat* (Chicago: University of Chicago Press, 1966).

9. Horace Cayton and St. Clair Drake, *Black Metropolis* (New York: Harper & Row, 1962), Vol. I, pp. 202–05; Vol. II, pp. 582–84, 600–10. "Bronzeville's people have never let poverty, disease, and discrimination 'get them down.' The vigor with which they enjoy life seems to belie the gloomy observations of the statisticians and civic leaders who know the facts about the Black Ghetto" (p. 386).

10. St. Clair Drake, "The Social and Economic Status of the Negro in the United States," *Daedalus*, Fall 1965, p. 778.

11. William F. Whyte, *Street Corner Society* (Chicago: University of Chicago Press, 1961); also "Social Organization in the Slums," *American Sociological Review*, 8, February 1943, pp. 34–39.

12. Elliot Liebow, *Tally's Corner: A Study of Negro Streetcorner Men* (Boston: Little, Brown, 1967).

13. Oscar Handlin, *The Newcomers: Negroes and Puerto Ricans in a Changing Metropolis* (Cambridge, Mass.: Harvard University Press, 1959), pp. 105–17.

14. Wilson, "The War on Cities," *op. cit.*, p. 32.

15. For a study of this problem in a Chicago community, see Peter H. Rossi and Robert A. Dentler, *The Politics of Urban Renewal—The Chicago Findings* (New York: The Free Press, 1961).

16. The Pruitt-Igoe project in St. Louis is a good, although probably atypical, example. See Lee Rainwater, "Fear and the

House-as-Haven in the Lower-Class," and Roger Montgomery's comments on Rainwater's article in *American Institute of Planners Journal*, January 1966, pp. 23–37.

17. Whyte, *Street Corner Society, op. cit.*, p. 132.

18. For a discussion of these problems in Los Angeles, see Paul Jacobs, "The Los Angeles Police: A Critique," *Atlantic Monthly*, December 1966, pp. 95–101.

19. Banfield and Wilson, *op. cit.*, pp. 329–46.

20. Edwin C. Banfield, *Political Influence* (New York: The Free Press, 1964), pp. 260–62.

21. Morris Janowitz, *Social Control of Escalated Riots* (The University of Chicago Center for Policy Study, 1967), p. 33.

CHAPTER 2

HOUSTON AND THE TSU RIOT

Bernard Friedberg

This is not a sociological study of the Negro in Houston, Texas, but primarily an account, based on fact but somewhat editorial in nature, of one event in the long history of a city. This event, however, is indicative of the reality of life for black people in the area and reflects the entire range of racial problems in Houston.

Houston was founded more than 130 years ago but its real development did not start until it became a port city in 1914, and its real population growth has been spread over the last twenty-five years. Its impressive skyline, looming over the plain, is only fifteen years old. Houston is a 132-year-old child and, at the same time, a case study in contradictions.

The city likes to be considered part of the Southwest, not the South, thus indicating a more liberal-western orientation. Yet more Negroes live in Houston (275,000) than in any city in the South, including Atlanta.

The citizens of Houston can appropriate, through a bond issue, $31,000,000 to construct an air-conditioned domed stadium, yet they seem unable to construct a zoning law that would aid in urban renewal and the elimination of some of the worst slum areas in the nation.

Houstonians elected a Negro woman to the school board in 1961, one of the most conservative groups in a conservative area, but defeated the same woman when she ran for re-election in 1967.

The same city that welcomed Harry Belafonte as an entertainer in 1964 greeted Belafonte and Dr. Martin Luther King, Jr., with stink bombs in 1967.

Houston, like the Texas of fact and legend, has more of many things than any other area. It has massive oil and space industrial complexes and high unemployment; it has more millionaires living in mansions and more poverty level families living in hovels. But primarily it is a twenty-first-century city with a nineteenth-century approach to the problems of society. For example, the school board sponsored a bond election in 1967 providing for the air conditioning of all new schools but ignored the fact that the new schools were being built in areas not accessible to Negro students.

It might be helpful to visualize what it is like to be a Negro in Houston. This description is not meant to indicate that all nonwhites in Houston are subject to the same continual discouragement and disillusionment, only that the following is somewhat typical for the majority.

A good composite example might be something like this. He is a high school graduate, the son of an unemployed former farmer. His house is not air conditioned, although Houston is the most air-conditioned city in the world. He has to draw water from the fire hydrant up the street for his morning shave although Houstonians use more water on their lawns than anywhere else in the country. He has to take the bus to work (not air conditioned, although suburban buses are). To get to the bus stop he has to walk on a dirt road although Houston has more miles of paved streets and freeways than any other city except Los Angeles. He rides the bus fifteen miles across town although Houston has more two-car families than any other American city. He works all day pumping gas although the city has a teacher shortage. He goes home at night and watches television, and the next morning repeats the same schedule.

Admittedly this is an extreme look at conditions for the Negro in Houston, but the civil rights movement flourished only briefly there and everyone, especially those benefiting from the status quo, has since gone back to the old homily, "We don't have any problems here."

On a relative scale, this homily has some truth to it. For example, the U.S. Department of Labor has reported that "a family of four could live more cheaply in Houston than in any of 20 other large cities in the country."[1] Further, unemployment does not scar the community quite as deeply as in Watts or in Oakland. In December 1966, for example, city officials estimated the unemployment rate at 1.7 per cent for Houston as a whole and at 7 per cent for the Negro population. It should also be noted that somewhat over half of Houston's Negroes were born in the Deep South (excluding Houston) or in some small Texas community. Not unnaturally, people who emerge from such an environment find Houston to be a comparatively open and comfortable place to live; indeed, some local Negro folk songs describe the city as "heavenly Houston."

Yet a closer look at some of the objective facts leads to a more somber portrayal of the Negro's situation in Houston:

Economically, the 1960 census reported that 22 per cent of Houston's population had an income under $3,000 a year. White families earned a median income of $5,902 while Negroes had an annual median of $3,426.[2] In a more recent study, done in 1965, the Houston antipoverty program sampled ten geographical areas which included 196,603 Negroes. The study indicated that 53 per cent of Negroes had family incomes of $4,000 a year or less, as compared to 36 per cent of whites and 11 per cent of Mexican-Americans who also lived in these "impoverished" sections.[3] Moreover, most objective observers agreed that the antipoverty program had come to a massive halt in Houston by 1968. Due to internal feuds, a significant proportion of the staff resigned. Following the lead of Earl Allen (former director of the Community Action Program), they founded HOPE—an activist group that sought to raise the ghetto by its economic bootstraps. The organization soon incurred the wrath of the white establishment.

Educationally, Negroes lagged drastically behind whites. White adults in Houston had completed a median of 11.3 years of schooling while Negroes had finished only 8.9 years.[4] A conservative majority of the school board, adhering to a notion of "neighborhood schools," managed to insure almost total racial segregation in the schools. The board even resorted to such measures as busing Negro children several miles past white schools to deposit them in ghetto schools. Whites, meanwhile, bussed in the opposite direction. At Texas Southern University, a predominantly Negro school, approximately 50 per cent of graduates failed to pass national achievement tests which would have allowed them to become teachers.

Housing in Houston presented an anomaly. A few high-income Negroes own homes costing from $40,000 to $125,000 in the gilded ghettos of "Sugar Hill" and Timbercrest. Nonetheless, most Negroes have to live in substandard housing, often without plumbing or water. In 1960 the census described 47.49 per cent of Houston housing as unsound, and Negroes occupied most of these premises.[5]

Unlike all other major cities in America, Houston has no zoning ordinance. This constitutes a bonanza for the financial community, since they can place a plant, supermarket, or night club anywhere they wish. For Negroes, the lack of zoning brings some benefits since a few people can, for example, commute more easily to their industrial jobs than in a city such as Chicago. Yet, the very lack of zoning carries with it major penalties for the poor. As one instance, Houston's haphazard planning disqualifies it from participating in the Model Cities program.

THE TSU INCIDENT

One could proceed at length with more statistics, but other chapters in this book present detailed accounts of the plight of

the Negro and the state of the human-rights movement. They
also give the reasons—poor housing, inferior education, lack of
employment opportunities, police insensitivity—and they quote
extensively from personal interviews indicating that the black
community is ready to explode and indeed has exploded in
most cities. Most of this material was prepared before the
report of the President's Commission on Civil Disorders was
written. The Commission's report makes even more abundantly
clear the accuracy of the assessment of black attitudes that have
reached a survival or genocide stalemate. This account of one
particular event in the broad spectrum of events daily crushing
the minorities in this country does not differ substantially from
accounts in other chapters in this volume.

However, it seems this account of a less than full-scale riot
illustrates a slightly different dimension of the problem—that
of public suppression of communication, elimination of Negro
leadership through subtle payoffs, and the lack of attention by
the national civil rights movement to an area crying for recognition and, in fact, no different from Oakland, Watts, and all the
other areas that have erupted. This particular event, like many
others, received national publicity and could have been the
motivating force behind a movement for reform. It was not and
could not be, for reasons that will be enumerated.

During the late evening hours of May 16 and the early morning hours of May 17, 1967 (the hot spring), the campus of
Texas Southern University, in the heart of Houston's Negro
ghetto, was the scene of a major racial incident that resulted in
the death of one police officer, the wounding of two other
officers and at least two students, minor injuries to several other
students, extensive damage to school and personal property, the
arrest of 488 persons, and the destruction of the already tenuous bridges between white and black people in Houston.

This incident was the culmination of (but not necessarily
caused by) six months of energetic organizational activity by a
number of individual students and nonstudents on the predominantly Negro campus and of two months of almost continuous
demonstrations on a variety of issues ranging from the location

of a garbage dump to a demand for the closing of a main street running through the university campus.

Mass-media coverage of the events of May 16–17 was extensive, as might be expected. Radio, television, and newspaper copy ran into tens of thousands of words and there were thousands of feet of news film. There was no doubt of the importance of this particular news on a local, regional, and national scale and it necessitated telling, indirectly, the Houston race-relations story. This story had never been told with veracity; therefore, the average citizen was unable to interpret these events except through the emotional outpouring of the moment, which tended to place the entire episode in the category of a national disaster.

As much as any other event in the history of Houston's race problems, the Texas Southern University incident is indicative of the total disregard, the denigration, the ignorance of the plight of the black man in the city. A summary of civil rights agitation in the city from September 1966 through May 17, 1967 will illustrate the atmosphere in which such events can take place.

At the beginning of the fall school term at TSU, a group known as the Friends of the Student Nonviolent Coordinating Committee, about twenty strong, began meeting on the school campus. For several months their activity consisted only of sporadic speechmaking and the distribution of handbills promoting the organization and attempting to recruit new members. These organizational efforts were only moderately successful and by March 1967 the movement was struggling to maintain its identity. However, at this point the university administration gave the SNCC group an unsuspected boost by denying them a meeting place on campus and simultaneously relieving the group's faculty advisor of his teaching duties, which brought immediate protests from the students still active in the organization. Campus meetings were held, speeches were made on the steps of the school auditorium, and demonstrations were staged in the school cafeteria. These events served to excite interest in heretofore uncommitted students and membership in SNCC began to rise rapidly. The administration soon granted official recognition to the group, but the banishment had nevertheless served as a springboard for rapid growth and produced areawide publicity.

On April 4 the situation on the campus reached a new climax. The administration, which had been acting cautiously, cracked down when three SNCC leaders allegedly threatened the lives of police officers during several campus rallies. The three were arrested and placed under $25,000 bond in the Harris County jail. The campus was aroused by this precipitous action and a protest march was immediately organized. Nearly 400 students marched peacefully from the campus to the courthouse, where a sidewalk vigil was maintained for nearly twenty-four hours. The three men were tried on April 7, pled guilty to a lesser charge, and were released when bail was lowered to $1,000.

Community attention remained focused on the university campus at this time, however, because of the appearance of Stokely Carmichael, then national chairman of SNCC. His arrival in Houston had not been planned to coincide with, or even closely follow, the courthouse demonstration, but this nevertheless appeared to be the reason for his visit. Carmichael spoke on April 13 and 14 at the University of Houston and TSU and drew large audiences at both schools. His presentations were moderate, and no incidents occurred during or immediately following his appearance.

Early in May TSU students began to congregate almost nightly on campus and on at least two occasions threw rocks and bottles at passing cars, causing some damage and injuring several persons. Thereupon the police closed the campus to all traffic and ringed the area with police emergency units.

The week of May 8 brought a series of daily demonstrations at two widely separated points in the city. One was held at a garbage dump in which a Negro child had recently drowned, and the other at a newly integrated junior high school in a blue-collar neighborhood. On May 17 approximately sixty arrests were made at these two sites; the demonstrators were jailed but released the same day.

At about 10:30 P.M. on the 16th, following a day of persistent rumors about the shooting of a Negro child by a white man, a student was arrested on the TSU campus. The arrest was made by two plainclothes policemen who were on campus as a general precautionary measure. Events developed swiftly. Students began throwing rocks and bottles, and a shot was fired, apparently from the men's dormitory, wounding one of the plainclothesmen and bringing a call for additional police assistance. Police reinforcements arrived and a period of general sniping followed, some of it between policemen themselves. Students in the dormitory rebuffed several attempts by recognized Negro leaders to negotiate a truce, and after a two-hour period when no shots were fired, a group of unidentified students rolled barrels into the main street on the campus and set them afire. This action seemed to tip the scale and the police began to advance on the dormitory with the intention of clearing it out.

Shots, again apparently from the dormitory, were answered by 3,000 rounds of pistol and automatic-rifle fire from the police. In the exchange one policeman was fatally wounded. The police then charged the building, forced their way in, and began removing students, 488 of whom were arrested, booked, and fingerprinted. Most were released the next day but five were held under $10,000 bond each on a charge of inciting to riot. The police subsequently searched the dormitory, destroying a great deal of personal property and ripping out ceilings and walls in a vain search for the weapons used to fire on them. This was Houston's riot, and thus far it was mostly a police affair.

The reason for this detailed account of a single incident, rather minor in the overall picture of the last three years, is its indication of the vast underlying problems facing the Negro community and the total attitude of whites toward blacks in Houston. This incident negates the necessity for a long history of the Negro in Houston, where he came from, his wants and desires, for, in actuality, Houston Negroes have no past—only a present and possibly a future.

The TSU affair revealed a total lack of public understanding of the state of race relations in the community (largely the fault of local media), the steps civil authority will take to preserve the status quo, the insensitivity of the police, and the lack of black leadership long ago bought off by the white establishment.

Let us take each of these charges and examine them.

THE ROLE OF THE NEWS MEDIA

That the TSU incident, and those preceding it, took the general public by such surprise is an indication of the dearth of news coverage in the area of race relations. There had simply been no in-depth coverage of racial stories or of the mass movements and organizations that had been prominent in most of the recent developments on the national scene. No attempt had been made to report the programs or purposes, when such have existed, of the established civil rights groups such as the NAACP and the Urban League, let alone the more militant SNCC, CORE, and Black Muslims. The ordinary newspaper-reading, television-watching citizen of Houston was, therefore, at a loss to interpret news of these organizations because he has been presented with only a palatable summary of their activities and has thus remained ill informed. The average Houstonian cannot recognize the names of leaders of these groups, cannot define any aspects of their programs, and has no knowledge of their methods (the term "black power" has never been adequately explained to him), and, in fact, the average Houston citizen, expressing a lack of understanding not necessarily of his own making, is perfectly willing to lump all civil rights organizations together under the general heading of "Communist agitation."

Also, little background information that might have provided citizens with a basis for interpreting the violence of recent years has been presented in the local media. Material on the general deprivation of a large portion of the country's population, the problem of poverty, job discrimination, housing bias, and the

denial of equal educational opportunities has been wholly lacking. Although such information was readily available to the
Houston media through national news services and the various
governmental agencies concerned with these problems, it was
either not sought or not used.

On the other hand, the media have focused on press releases
from the office of the mayor of Houston that describe the progress being made through the city's efforts, citing apparently successful programs in almost all areas of the city dealing with
problems affecting intergroup relations in the community. This
emphasis has created a smoke screen behind which the public
has settled into a false sense of security, not realizing the depth
of the problems or the shallowness of the stop-gap solutions
being fostered by the city. Further, this overemphasis on positive programing has created a widening gap between the expectations of the minority community and its hope for more
effective measures in solving problems, and the realities of the
situation, which indicate painfully slow progress.

The creation of this euphoria resulted in the disproportionately shocking impact of a single event on the citizenry. People
reacted uniformly, decrying the situation and expressing total
dismay that it could happen in their community.

The reporting of incidents which occurred prior to the major
disturbance at TSU was not only sketchy but also unbalanced,
and served mainly to implant the false idea in the public mind
that the problems being protested were new (created by agitators) and of little significance. The realistic and symbolic
importance of these protests was not explained or even commented on in the local media, and again background coverage
was absent. For example, the demonstrations at the junior high
school received some notice in the media but at no time was
mention made of the repeated fights between white and black
residents and their children or the seemingly arbitrary discipli-
nary measures meted out to Negro students involved in a disturbance at the school and the absence of equally harsh discipline for white students embroiled in the same disturbance.
Similarly, little notice was given to the precipitating factor in
the demonstrations at the dump site, namely, the drowning of

a Negro child in one of the water-filled holes in the dump. Neither was any conclusion drawn from the fact that a remarkably similar demonstration by whites at a compost-plant site in a fashionable section of the city resulted in no arrests and the closing of the plant.

There was no advance notice of Stokely Carmichael's visit to the local campus and the rock-throwing incidents were shoved under the rug because apparently, in the judgment of the media, the citizens of Houston were not capable of understanding the situation. It is no wonder then that Houstonians were caught by surprise by the violent events at TSU. They had falsely been led to believe that good race relations existed in their city.

The first reporting of the TSU events, recognizing the fluidity of the situation, was as accurate as could be expected and responsible to a fair degree. The stories used the following day were a good deal less objective. Radio, television, and newspaper coverage was radically unbalanced in that it failed to recognize the possibility of other than student guilt for the incident or that a large percentage of the student body was not involved in any way. Outside agitators and nonstudents were attacked by the press, whose anger showed in an overreaction to the disturbance (showing a lack of knowledge of basic causes) and an immediate attempt to place blame on someone. Sharp focus was placed on the death of the police officer, including stories about his wife and family, but little mention was made of the injured students or of the fact that one wounded student received no medical attention for twelve hours.

The mayor and the police chief became the only spokesmen to whom the media listened. The mayor's words tended to be defensive and self-justifying, producing the unmistakable impression of student and TSU administrative guilt brightly contrasted with police and city government innocence. Student activists and spokesmen, school administrators, and persons simply caught up in the general disorder were not approached for comment by local media, and it was left for the national networks to follow this aspect of the story.

These shortcomings in the Houston media are possibly peculiar to the area but more likely are expressions of the faults of the communications media in general. There is an obvious need for skilled reporting, complete candor, and careful objectivity in reporting racial stories. Room for error is great because of the extremely emotional subject matter; therefore, editing and headline writing must be done with unusual care. More high-management supervision at the news-desk level is needed. However, the overriding need is for an educational program aimed directly at the media to sensitize them to the problems of the minority communities, a kind of human-relations education, to provide them with the insight and knowledge necessary to make intelligent and perceptive news reporting possible in the race-relations field. Obviously, no amount of information would have totally prepared the public for the TSU problems, but total surprise could have been avoided by an objective and informative appraisal, months or years ago, of the underlying causes of the complex social problems of our times. The mass media must take the responsibility for informing the citizens of the community.

Perhaps too much emphasis is placed here on the media; however, the importance of establishing the climate in a community cannot be overemphasized. Community opinion, both positive and negative, has been a major contributing factor in the creation of riot situations and their prevention.

REACTIONS OF WHITE HOUSTONIANS

The white climate of opinion in Houston has been clearly outlined in a public-opinion poll conducted by political scientist Victor Emmanuel.[6] In 1967 Emmanuel selected a probability sample (accurately reflecting geographical and income groups in the city) from the voting-registration list of Houston. Considering only the 320 "Anglos" in the study, one finds that, on the basis of their reported voting behavior, about 74 per cent could be classified as "conservative," 13 per cent as "independent," and 13 per cent as "liberal." Thus, despite the influx of northerners into such operations as the Manned Space Craft Center, Houston has remained an essentially conservative city.

This basic conservatism naturally reflected itself in attitudes toward Negroes and rioting. Only 22 per cent of white Houstonians believed that poverty contributed to rioting (in direct contrast, as a later chapter shows, to the beliefs of Negro Houstonians). Twenty per cent believed that Communists were the basic cause of riots, when, in fact, it would be extremely difficult to find a single Communist of any variety in Houston's civil rights movement.

When asked what steps should be taken in response to riots, white Houstonians flatly affirmed their belief in violent repression: 77 per cent wanted to "call in the army," "shoot the rioters," or use some other kind of force. Only 16 per cent could think of other measures, and the remaining 7 per cent just did not know what to do.

Most white Houstonians (47 per cent) had either hazy notions or no ideas at all about what long-range solutions might alleviate the conditions underlying riots. The elimination of slums, for example, occurred to only 7 per cent as a possible solution. A much higher proportion (25 per cent) preferred to enhance the authority, power, and numbers of the police as the solution.

REACTIONS OF CIVIL AUTHORITIES

In such an atmosphere, one could hardly expect civil authorities, particularly those who held elective office, to respond in an enlightened manner to civic disturbances.

The insensitivity of civil authority—in Houston, the mayor's office—has long contributed to the establishment and maintenance of the status quo and has in essence prevented the development of local Negro leadership that would better serve the interests of the general community. Speaking more specifically, the mayor of Houston has long maintained that his communications with Negro leaders was all that was necessary to prevent civil disorders; he could always call on his friends to get the facts and to set the black community straight. This may have been true five years ago but the mayor has failed to keep himself abreast of events in the civil rights field and, blinded by the lack of general civil rights agitation in Houston, has assumed his theory to be correct. In fact, no one person or group can today speak for the black citizens of Houston or any other city. All the communication in the world will not prevent an explosion, and communication with the traditional Negro leadership can only anger the more militant younger generation and precipitate the incendiary actions that traditional leaders are trying desperately to avoid.

Only recently has Houston, under the direction of the mayor, taken any action to convince black people that the city cares about them. A department of city government has been established, staffed by two men, which serves as a complaint-processing mechanism to placate the militant blacks. This office also serves as a hedge for the mayor when someone asks what he is doing about community tensions, the problems of the slums, police brutality, or any other problem that concerns race relations. This smoke screen has been effective thus far but very real actions must be taken by the city before tensions will be eased, and they will only be taken when city government, including the Houston school board, which wields tremendous power, becomes truly sensitive to minority-group problems, especially poverty and education. Many private citizens and special-interest groups are attempting to educate city government, but the road is difficult and the conservative attitude in Texas will not be breached easily.

Houston is not unique in that accredited and potential Negro leadership is eventually bought off by subtle or overt means. Students leading demonstrations suddenly appear as highly paid members of the poverty program. Ministers influencing large congregations to more militancy are soon seen heading federally financed education projects. The Negro middle class in Houston looks on, sometimes in dismay but more often as if these problems were not their concern. This lack of developed, trusted leadership has resulted in an ineffec-

tive poverty program when the program could have been a
step toward effective community action, the bettering of life for
a large number of minority citizens, and a portion of credibility
to Houston's claim of progressive activity. This long-standing
system of paying off minority leadership has resulted in a
vacuum easily filled by "outside agitators" and extremists, who
are more likely to destroy the status quo than any other element of society.

THE ROLE OF THE POLICE

Another major factor in racial unrest in Houston is the attitude
and makeup of the police force and the image projected by the
chief of police, who was especially appointed by the present
mayor. Unlike Atlanta, Houston's major competitor for leadership in the South, the Houston police had adopted none of
the recommendations of the Kerner Commission report and
had often made apparent their disdain for the advancements
being made elsewhere in police-community relations. The chief,
Herman Short, a good, hard-headed policeman, has no room in
his department for a study of the underlying causes of racial
unrest, and he makes no secret of this attitude. His desire to
keep order transcends the equal enforcement of the law and
even the normal measures used to quell civil disturbances. For
instance, during the TSU incident his order to charge and clean
out the dormitory was given without any regard for those students who were not taking part in the disturbance. No bull
horns were used to inform the dormitory residents of the
impending attack and no tear gas was used at any time. Instead,
there was a barrage of rifle and pistol fire that could have killed
scores of students.

As in most other major cities, Houston needs policemen who
are thoroughly trained in human relations as well as combat
techniques. The department is underpaid and understaffed, but
this is no excuse for being undertrained.*

*Belatedly, in 1968, Houston police officers were given a short course in
human relations.

It is doubtful that conditions in Houston are any more or less degrading for the Negro than they are in other areas, but the contrast between what can be accomplished by the community will in Houston and what is being accomplished in the elimination of the causes of riots and disturbances is truly frightening. The gap between the haves and have-nots is widening almost as fast as the population and skyline are growing. The problem is that Negroes and other minorities in Houston have begun to see the gap. They are beginning to want what white Houston has now. They will develop their own leadership, and that new leadership will find it easy to point out these discrepancies. There is still time in Houston to prevent the serious rioting that has occurred in most American cities, but it is the eleventh hour.

REFERENCES

1. *Houston Post*, February 19, 1967.

2. "Nowhere to Go," Episcopal Society for Cultural and Racial Unity, Houston, p. 3.

3. "Dimensions of Poverty," Houston-Harris County Economic Opportunity Organization, Houston, 1965, p. 13.

4. "Nowhere to Go," *op. cit.*, p. 2.

5. Derived from 1960 census data for the City of Houston.

6. Victor Emmanuel, "Houston Citizens' Survey," unpublished study, University of Houston, 1967.

CHAPTER 3

WATTS: THE REVOLT AND AFTER

John Howard & William McCord

Sometimes in history an event which seems awesome and terrifying in its dimensions is dwarfed by subsequent occurrences of even more immense dimensions.

The Watts riot of the fall of 1965 appeared at the time to be a climactic event in American history. By 1968, however, it seemed that it was merely a curtain raiser of modest dimensions. It will be instructive, nevertheless, to discuss Watts in terms of some of the causes of its riot. It was the beginning, and no one knows where the end will be. We can, however, at least gain some understanding of the beginning.

Many people expressed astonishment immediately following the Watts riot that it could happen there. After all, the Negro in Los Angeles had for decades enjoyed the kinds of rights that were denied southern Negroes well into the 1960's. Watts, it was pointed out, was not as squalid as Harlem, not as decayed as Boston's Roxbury section. How then could it happen in Los Angeles? Two years later the same kind of question was asked about Detroit and Hartford.

In this chapter we shall attempt to answer why a city like Los Angeles exploded in a state like California.

Fifty years ago Watts was an orchard of orange trees tended by a handful of "Anglo," Negro, and Mexican-American farmers.* As people moved outward from the city center, small suburban houses in the 1930 Spanish style sprouted among the farms, and Mexican-Americans came to dominate the region. But with the unprecedented influx of Negroes in the late 1930's, the whites and most of the Mexican-Americans departed, and Watts became the "port of entry" for hundreds of thousands of Negroes who gradually moved north toward the civic center and south toward the ocean. As the census maps of 1950 and 1960 show, Watts became a solidly black ghetto in the heart of Los Angeles.

Housing: Today at least 94 per cent of Los Angeles' Negroes live in the central section of the city. Between 1950 and 1960, 151,410 Negroes moved into this zone—and 206,509 whites moved out of it to the suburbs. Similarly, many of the communities directly adjacent or near to the Watts area increased in population dramatically between 1950 and 1960 but managed to remain almost entirely white.† Thus the population of Torrance, a community southwest of Watts, increased over 350 per cent in a decade but remained virtually free of nonwhites. Fullerton increased by over 300 per cent, Newport Beach by over 100 per cent, and Culver City by over 60 per cent, but only 2 per cent of their populations was nonwhite in 1960.

Discrimination, then, created a black island in the city, a region which few whites ever saw except for fleeting glimpses as they sped to the beach along the Harbor Freeway.

*Technically, the term "Watts" applies to a small area inhabited by some 34,000 people, only eighty-five of whom were classified as whites by the 1960 census. More generally, the word symbolically encompasses the forty-six-square-mile "curfew area" of central Los Angeles where the great majority of Negroes live. Some writers refer to Watts as equivalent to the 77th Street Police District. Using this definition, the assessed value of all property in the area as of 1965 was $201,338,258. Thus, the riot wiped out a good part of Watts' entire economy.

†In these comparisons, we are defining Watts as equivalent to the 77th Street Police District.

Some 25 per cent of the homes in Watts are considered deteriorated and dilapidated, as opposed to 7 per cent for the county as a whole. About twice as many people crowd into homes in Watts than into homes located in other sections of Los Angeles. And, as a recent UCLA study has shown, minority-group families not only live in less desirable quarters than other families with the same income, but they pay more.[1]

Employment: The employment and income facts on Negroes in Los Angeles are stark and simple. Between 1959 and 1965, at a time of growing prosperity in the nation, the median income of Los Angeles Negroes *dropped* 8 per cent. At a time when the economic sluggishness of the Eisenhower years was being overcome, the unemployment rate among Negroes *rose* from 12.6 to 19.7 per cent, and for males in Watts in 1965 it stood at 30 per cent. A review of union-apprenticeship programs suggests something of the employment status of Negroes; in 1965 they made up 1.69 per cent of the total in the electrical trades in Los Angeles; 2.92 per cent in carpentry; 4.28 per cent in auto repair; 3.24 per cent in bricklaying; 1.87 per cent in painting and glazing; 3.05 per cent in printing; 6.48 per cent in roofing; 1.16 per cent in sheetmetal working; and none in ironworking, boilermaking, and telephone installation.

Even Manpower Development Training Programs were inadequate to meet the overwhelming catastrophe of the unemployment rate among Los Angeles' blacks. For example, training for service-station work required a seventh-grade reading level whereas most of the youth who applied read at the sixth-grade level or below.[2]

Thus, the employment situation in Watts is bad because of discrimination and also because a substantial proportion of the population is not employable in terms of conventional criteria, *i.e.*, they do not have the required amount of education, they cannot pass written tests, and so forth.

Education: An evaluation of the Los Angeles school system made by the McCone Commission, which investigated the Watts riots, showed that children in slum schools consistently fell behind citywide and national norms of achievement and that there were systematic differences between slum and nonslum schools, with slum schools being inferior in a number of areas, including more double sessions, fewer libraries, and less-experienced teachers, among others.

This means that in Watts, as in other urban ghettos, even those children who remain in school (and, as elsewhere, the slum school dropout rate is higher than in nonghetto schools) receive substantially less education during the years they attend school than do middle-class students.

Welfare: The predominant welfare program in the riot area was Aid to Families with Dependent Children (AFDC); about two-thirds of the people receiving public assistance are on it.

Strangely enough, some members of the McCone Commission concluded that poor people move to California for the purpose of getting on welfare, a conclusion that reflects a widespread public belief that is catered to by Governor Reagan's state administration, which has promised a crackdown on "welfare chiselers."

The astonishing nature of these allegations becomes clearer if we view welfare as an exchange relationship. The mother on AFDC surrenders her status as an adult (the case worker can make inquiries as to how she is spending her money, the implication being that she is not mature and responsible enough to spend it properly), her status as a woman (any relationship with a male is suspect; she is expected to lead a celibate life), and her control over her own home (the case worker can come in and inspect it for any signs that she is not taking proper care of her children), in return for which she receives a stipend that only with extreme care can be stretched to support a family. In terms of the standards of the Office of Economic Opportunity, and often those of Bureaus of Public Assistance, this stipend is below subsistence.

Popular belief also has it that the average female head of the household will have an extra child or two in order to get more of the tax payers' money. The fact is, however, that a mother on welfare receives $1.00 per month for transportation for each child; $1.35 for his personal needs, and fifty cents for recreation. A family of ten receives $4.00 per month for "education and incidentals." The monthly food allowance for a woman is

$27.00, and for each growing child she has she receives $4.00 more.[3]

You will have heard people say that if welfare recipients had any self-respect and initiative they would go out and get a job. But that isn't as easy as it sounds—and there may even be penalties for working. Robert Conot has discussed this:

> One case was that of a woman with nine children living in a public housing project. She had been receiving $371 per month, the maximum possible amount, even though her needs, according to the schedule, were almost $100 greater. When this woman had gone to work at $333 per month as an aide in the Anti-Poverty War Neighborhood Adult Participation Project, her salary—except for a $25 allowance for on-the-job expenses, and an additional small work-incentive allowance—had been deducted from the check. The public housing authority had promptly raised the rent from $56 to $114, absorbing all the additional money, and, in effect, punishing her for going to work.[4]

Most women want to go off welfare, and getting married is one way of doing so. But even here the system throws up a roadblock. This was discussed by Mrs. Johnnie Lee Tillman, a member of one of the welfare-rights organizations in Los Angeles:

> Yes, a lot of the girls would like to be married and through with welfare. But they make it hard for you even to do that. You don't just meet a man one day and ask him to marry you the next. You got to get to know him and he wants to get to know you and your kids. You got to go around with him for a while. But both of you have to look out for welfare regulations about what they call "a spouse-like relationship." If they accuse your boyfriend of contributing to your support while you are still on welfare then both of you may be accused of welfare fraud. Yet when you're going around with a man and building up to getting married, naturally he is going to buy food for the family sometime and maybe clothes for the kids when school starts.
>
> I had a boyfriend a couple of years back and we was just about at that point of talking about marriage when my case

worker came in here and found him having dinner with us. She began to ask him a lot of questions and talk about welfare fraud and his going to jail. He got scared and that messed it up between us. I haven't seen him in two or three years.

WATTS: ORIGINS OF REVOLT

Watts was the prelude to Newark and Detroit, and within Watts there were preludes to the riot of August 1965. Let us review the gradual buildup.

Since 1961 there have been ugly clashes between the police and Negroes that should have been recognized by the white citizens of Los Angeles as symptoms of the anger festering in the ghetto. On Memorial Day in 1961 there was a racial incident in Griffith Park that caused resentment in the black community, and in April 1962 a group of Black Muslims exchanged gunfire with the police when a burglary suspect was searched outside a Muslim temple.

The incidents became more intense. In 1964 alone there were small-scale riots at Jefferson High School, at the Central Receiving Hospital, and on Avalon Boulevard (later a scene of mass destruction). In 1964, after having issued an earlier prediction, the Los Angeles County Human Relations Commission stated:

> About two years ago, this Commission stated that a situation was developing in the community in which police-minority group conflicts were becoming almost a "self-fulfilling prophecy." We feel that the same situation again exists. A significant and ever-growing number of minority-group persons are being led to feel that in any contact they have with the police officers, they are going to be treated roughly. On the other hand, a growing number of law-enforcement officers feel that in any contact they have with members of minority groups they are likely to meet with resistance. These "expectations" on the part of both groups are likely to produce what each expects.... We believe that the climate has deteriorated in the past several weeks between law-enforcement agencies and minority-group communities.[5]

Again, in May 1964, Assistant Attorney General Howard H. Jewel explicitly warned that demonstrations in Los Angeles could well be joined by the entire Negro community. Jewel wrote:

> In Los Angeles if demonstrators are joined by the Negro community at large the policing will no longer be done by the Los Angeles Police Department, but by the State Militia. If violence erupts millions in property damage may ensue, untold lives may be lost and California will have received an unsurpassed injury to her reputation.[6]

Mayor Sam Yorty, Chief of Police William Parker, and Governor Edmund Brown ignored these repeated predictions. When the riots broke out in 1965, Yorty flew to San Francisco, apparently believing that police could handle the situation. And Governor Brown expressed both his shock and his naïveté when, after viewing the effects of the Watts riot, he commented, "Here in California, we have a wonderful working relationship between whites and Negroes. We got along fine until this happened...."

Later almost all responsible officials recognized that they had failed to understand the scope of the problem. "We just did not communicate with the right people," said Mrs. Ethel Bryan, a Negro executive assistant to Mayor Yorty. "We only talked to middle-class 'leaders' when, really, Watts had no leaders at all." Similarly, in 1967, a police inspector admitted the same problem: "Soon, I hope, we will have a conference between officers and the true leaders down there ... but we will all check our guns outside."

For anyone who talked with the people of Watts during the tragic days of August 1965 the true feelings of the Negro community soon became apparent. However inchoately expressed, the rioters again and again said that they had rebelled for three reasons: to protest against "police brutality," to get all the material goods that "whitey" had, and to demonstrate their manhood and dignity. To understand this reasoning is a first step in comprehending why Watts exploded.

"Police Brutality": "Never again," said Marquette Frye,

whose arrest triggered the riot, "never again in this neighborhood will any young man, like my brother and me, stand by
and take abuse from an officer."[7] Rightly or wrongly, almost
every Negro who participated in the riot echoed this sentiment.
"Police brutality is like when they arrest you where it can't be
seen and whip you," a twenty-two-year-old Negro explained to
reporters Jerry Cohen and William Murphey. "They grab you
when you walk down the street. They pull you over and beat
on you. That ain't right. Man, I was born in California—in
Long Beach. But I'm a Negro, so I been arrested."[8]

I[*] found no evidence of the kind of true brutality I saw in
Mississippi where, at first hand, I witnessed police terrorism,[9]
but my evaluation must be tempered by two qualifications.

First, the Los Angeles police admittedly participated in
sweeps of "duck ponds"—areas of high criminality—before the
riots of 1965. During these raids, police randomly selected
people on the street, interrogated them, and checked, for example, to see if they had failed to pay a traffic penalty. These
"field investigations" were conducted regularly in Watts but
never in the rich suburbs of Los Angeles. At the minimum,
therefore, the Los Angeles police submitted the people of
Watts to a continuing surveillance which most Negro citizens
considered an insult to their dignity.

Second, during the riot itself, individual policemen may well
have acted in a brutal fashion. There is conflicting testimony
on this issue, so no final conclusion may be drawn. In the midst
of flames and snipers, however, it is certain that some officers
reacted with a fear and hatred that normally they would have
controlled.

The story of Laurence Jacques, which was contradicted by
the testimony of the police officers involved, typifies what many
Negroes—with or without valid reason—believed happened
during the riots.[10]

Jacques witnessed the shooting of one looter and the arrest of
another. He, too, was then arrested, although he claimed he
had done nothing, and was forced to lie on the ground with

*The "I" in this case is William McCord.

another Negro. Jacques said later that one policeman had asked another, "How many did you kill?"

The second man, supposedly answered, "I killed two niggers. Why don't you kill those two lying on the ground?"

According to Jacques, the first man replied, "They won't run."

"One officer came up to me and put a shotgun at the back of my head," said Jacques. " 'Nigger, how fast can you run the fifty-yard dash?' "

"I said, 'I can't run it at all.' He kicked me in the side two times, and the other officer put his foot on the back of my head."

No officers were convicted for their behavior during the riot. Yet stories such as Jacques's—even if they might have been complete fabrications—undeniably added fuel to the riot's flames.

"Get What Whitey Has": Looting of liquor, appliance, grocery, and furniture stores cost their owners millions of dollars. Most of the looters had never before been known as criminals (75 per cent of the adult rioters did have criminal records, but the typical adolescent looter had never been arrested before).

One unemployed man on welfare explained the motivation of some of the rioters: "They wanted everything the whites had, including color TV. They saw the stores were open. If you are hungry and don't have no money, you want anything and everything. Having no job isn't no fun. With store windows broken and the police doin' other things, what would you do?"

Objective social conditions prompted this desire to "get what whitey has." Not only did Watts have a generally high rate of unemployment, but joblessness was especially acute among young males. In the age group of seventeen to twenty-five—the element most likely to riot—about 41 per cent had not been able to find jobs.

Repeated promises in 1964 and 1965 that War on Poverty funds would soon be forthcoming were not fulfilled. The federal Office of Economic Opportunity stipulated that representatives from poor areas should participate in handling poverty funds, but city officials refused to change the composition of the responsible boards.

The looters, in other words, saw tempting items spread before them along 103rd Street, but they had no money to purchase them. Not unnaturally in a climate of anarchy, they took what they wanted.*

The Search for Dignity: An intangible but pervasive impulse guided many of the rioters: a simple desire to prove their manhood. Many men viewed the riot as an insurrection against the white establishment, as a way of bringing attention to them and to their area, which had been neglected for so long.

Joe, a jobless young Negro interviewed by reporters after the riot, articulated this sentiment.[11] He believed that white policemen were always stopping him during the so-called field investigations:

> It seemed like they always were trying to see if they could make me break, make me do something that would save them time. It seemed like they figured they'd eventually have me in jail and they wanted to save time.

He recalled an incident that had happened long before the riot:

> One night . . . a cop stopped me and said: "I've seen you before. You've been in jail. I'm gonna check on you, punk."
> That night I really wanted to do something—something to that white face. But I kept thinking about my mother, how she always had told me to stay out of trouble. I figured I'd gone this far without trouble, so I held back.

When the riot began, Joe interpreted the looting in this fashion:

> I didn't realize what they were doing when the looting began. I didn't understand the object of the looting. At first it just began with people breaking windows and taking nothing. Then I realized the object of the looting: it was to move all

*Thousands of guns were stolen during the riot. Of these, only some 700 have been recovered by the police—a bad omen for Watts, if rioting occurs again.

the whites out of Watts. We don't want white people in Watts.

Asked if another explosion might occur in Watts, Joe replied:

> Would I riot again? I just don't know. But I know the slightest thing could touch me off.
>
> If it comes again? I guess I will be there. Everybody has to be willing to sacrifice something for what he believes in. I'd be out of place, wouldn't I, if my race was out there fighting and I wasn't?
>
> We really don't live alike, the whites and the Negroes. As long as the whites keep trying to brutalize my people, I'll have to be out there trying to stop them.

Another Negro, a college graduate, summarized the search for dignity in this way:

> You can stand on 103rd Street, on the edge of Will Rogers Park, and look up and see the big silver and gray jetliners pass overhead. Watts is on one of the approach routes to Los Angeles International Airport. If you fly over and look down you cannot tell Watts is there. It does not look any different from any other part of the city. The things that make it Watts are invisible.
>
> Watts is a state of mind as well as a place. Part of what it is is symbolized by the low, sweeping passage of planes overhead. Standing in the heart of Watts, you can look up and see the big world, the expensive and expansive world, but the people in that world cannot see you. Your existence is not visible to them. You can see them but they cannot see you. You can never reach them. You can shout but they won't hear you. Waving or running or jumping will not make them see you.
>
> There was only one time when the people up in the sky saw the people down on the ground. . . .
>
> That was when the flames of Watts riots leaped and spiraled into the air, lighting up the approach route to Los Angeles International Airport.

The importance of these motives as instigating elements in the riot can be illustrated by a comparision between Watts and

Compton. The city of Compton directly borders on the riot area and 50 per cent of its population is Negro, yet it largely escaped the Watts conflagration. There were attempts to spread the riot to Compton, and over 150 people were arrested there, but about half of them came from outside the city. Nonetheless, the "fire next time" did not really ignite the Compton area.

Many explanations can be offered for this anomaly. In 1965 Compton was still an integrated area. While the Negro proportion of the population rose rapidly from 4 per cent in 1950 to 50 per cent in 1960, the persuasive work of Compton's Human Relations Commission had largely stemmed the outflow of whites by the time of the riot. Even in the most densely concentrated Negro census tract in Compton, living conditions were better than those in Watts: median income ($5,523) was higher, people had achieved more education (a median of 10.2 years), and fewer houses were considered to be "deteriorated and dilapidated" (about 8 per cent).

Compton had developed a Negro middle class, a group with deep economic stakes in the community that was on relatively amicable terms with the white "establishment" and with the police. Clearly, a different spirit prevailed in Compton: a feeling of close cooperation between Negroes and police, a sense of integration, and a belief that the economic gains achieved by Negroes should be defended by Negroes themselves against "hoodlums."

"I think it would be naïve to say that problems are all solved—they're not all solved," a white Compton policeman, Captain Harold Lindemulder, commented after the riot.

> People still have prejudices—they're not wiped out overnight, and it will take a long time before all of people's prejudices are gone. We have problems in Compton but I think the community as a whole is trying to face up to them and solve them. I'm sure that with everyone working together and continuing as they have been, in the years ahead we'll see an easing of these problems.[12]

THE AFTERMATH

Since 1965 many agencies have launched serious efforts to transform Watts into a community like Compton.* Federal aid, in the form of antipoverty funds, has poured into the area. New programs—credit unions, "Head Start" training, even an art festival—have been created. Proposition 14, the measure designed to imbed segregation legally in California, has been declared unconstitutional. The mayor has appointed a city Human Relations Commission and ordered fuller integration among City Hall employees. And the American Civil Liberties Union has established complaint bureaus where citizens may voice their grievances and receive legal counsel.

Within Watts itself, numerous indigenous organizations have sprung up. Groups such as "SLANT" and "US" adhere to a black-power ideology or emphasize the African cultural heritage of American Negroes.

"The Sons of Watts," composed in part of former rioters, attempts to build community spirit by, among other things, distributing litter cans to help clean up the debris of Watts. And, in 1966, during the "Watts Festival," this group policed a large parade (regular officers stayed out of the area) so effectively that Mayor Sam Yorty rode in an open car and the parade was unmarred by any incidents.

Another group, the "Citizen's Alert Patrol" armed itself with tape recorders and cameras and followed police to the scene of every arrest as a guard against "police brutality."

Still another organization, which cannot be named, claims to

---

*Some of these attempts have been well-meaning but naïve. The Los Angeles County Commission on Human Relations, for example, issued a series of recommendations in 1965, one of which was to establish an "Adult Advisor Corps" to act as "big brothers" to deprived children: "The youngsters to be served come from homes and environments that often prevent their being exposed to such cultural, educational pursuits as attendance at enriching exposures to Music Center offerings, trips to the Art Museum, associations with persons from communities other than their own—*i.e.*, Thanksgiving meals with the aforementioned."[13] Thanksgiving meals will hardly cure such problems as the extraordinarily high rate of unemployment.

have infiltrated all of the others in the hope of guiding black-power energies into constructive channels. Its young leader believes that the proliferating organizations in Watts can be brought together in a union which will become a base for Negro economic independence and Negro political power.

All these movements may have wrought a psychological change in Watts. Indeed, former rioters themselves make up a majority of their membership. In 1967 one detected more hope, more dignity, and a greater sense of importance in Watts than before the riot.

But, without denigrating this possible change in spiritual climate of the central district, it must be recognized that the basic problems of Watts remain unsolved.*

One barometer of potential trouble is the attitude of the younger, unskilled males. The 120 men interviewed in 1967 as part of our random sample of the Watts population voiced considerable anger about their situation. Fifty per cent believed that the riot had helped Watts; only 20 per cent believed that it had hurt. Eighty-one per cent favored the use of violence in defense of civil rights; only 19 per cent definitely opposed it. Fifty per cent said the police were abusive toward them; only 3 per cent thought the police adhered to "fair" standards of treatment. A very high proportion (78 per cent) admired the concept of black power; only 6 per cent opposed it.

Objective measures of the socioeconomic situation in Watts confirmed that little has changed since 1965:

Unemployment apparently has not been reduced. While conflicting reports exist, the weight of evidence indicates that joblessness has stayed at about the same level as before the 1965 riot. The Chamber of Commerce attempted a crash program to produce more jobs but, according to the County Human Relations Commission, came up with perhaps 200 to 300 jobs and

---

*The abortive riot of March 1966 indicates that there is still a potential for violence. Triggered by conflict between Negro and Mexican-American gangs, mobs once again took to the streets of Watts. This time the rioters were well armed. Two men, both innocent bystanders, were killed. Police mobilized quickly and a sobered adult Negro community cooperated in quieting the youths. Nevertheless, East 103rd Street, the heart of the Watts business community, was a scene of destruction and looted stores.

job-training opportunities when at least 5,000 were needed to make a serious impact upon the Watts problem.[14]

Further, a phenomenal high of $5,500,000 in welfare aid went into the riot area each month in 1966—a rather sure indication that the conditions of unemployment had not been alleviated. Roughly 60 per cent of Watts residents were on relief that year.

Despite these disillusioning facts, some 2,000 Negroes continue to arrive in Los Angeles each month, still lured by the promise of a better life. Almost all of them settle in the central district, and few have the technical qualifications demanded by Los Angeles industry.

The face of Watts has changed little since 1965. The rubble has been cleared and littered parking lots have replaced the burned-out stores. Few businessmen have re-established their enterprises, often because they are unable to secure insurance for their premises. The businesses which have been rebuilt resemble fortresses: massive, windowless, concrete structures.

There are no signs in most of the central district, as there are in Compton, of the emergence of a Negro business class to replace whites. Some groups, such as Westminster House (a Presbyterian organization), encourage Negro "industry," but the products produced by untrained handicraft workers—ashtrays made from discarded Coke bottles, papier-mâché bracelets—could hardly bring prosperity to the region.

Despite the repeal of Proposition 14, the housing pattern of Los Angeles has showed no evidence of greater integration. The Negro population has been growing at a rate about four times that of the white, and, as we have noted, almost all Negro families are congregated in the central district.

The ultimate effect of this trend has been prophesized for Los Angeles by urban expert Victor Palmieri: "This . . . is the city of the future—the very near future. A black island spreading like a giant ink blot over the heart of a metropolis which is bankrupt financially and paralyzed politically."[15]

Palmieri reasons that three established factors—the rate of population growth of Negroes, the increasing mobility of whites, and the resulting "domino effect" upon schools—

guarantees that the core of Los Angeles will be all black by 1980.

He points out that Los Angeles in 1967 can hardly handle her financial problems, since the property tax rate approaches $10 per $100, a level regarded as one of "negative return" by most economists because of its hindrance to local economic growth.

Beyond this, Palmieri argues that Los Angeles County will not manage her political problems. The region is split into more than seventy autonomous cities (and even more independent school districts) which cannot reach a consensus on such issues as urban renewal, open-housing laws, or police-review boards.

Although more optimistic in its conclusions, the McCone Commission considered a similar possibility: a complete breach between whites and blacks which could result only in further violence. The Commission concluded: "So serious and so explosive is the situation that, unless it is checked, the August [1965] riots may seem by comparison to be only a curtain raiser for what could blow up one day in the future."

Yet Los Angeles has still not looked deeply into its future. Although the McCone Commission put forward some constructive ideas, it failed to recommend drastic changes in existing white institutions or to suggest ways of linking the values of the Negro subculture with those of the larger society.

Unless there are radical changes, such objective observers as sociologists Robert Blauner and Victor Palmieri foresee a crippled, festering Los Angeles, increasingly populated with frustrated Negroes. The rioters expressed their unwillingness to continue to accept indignities; until the white community realizes this, Los Angeles can look forward to more holocausts.

REFERENCES

1. Associated Press report, March 17, 1966.
2. Robert Conot, *Rivers of Blood, Years of Darkness* (New York: Bantam Books, 1967), p. 101.

3. *Ibid.*, p. 126.

4. *Ibid.*, p. 127.

5. "Report and Recommendations Concerning Incidents Involving Police and Minority Groups," Los Angeles Commission on Human Relations.

6. Letter from Howard H. Jewel to Attorney General Stanley Mosk, May 25, 1964.

7. Jerry Cohen and William Murphy, *Burn, Baby, Burn* (New York: E. P. Dutton, 1966), p. 47.

8. *Ibid.*, p. 204.

9. William McCord, *Mississippi: The Long Hot Summer* (New York: W. W. Norton, 1965).

10. Cohen and Murphy, *op. cit.*, p. 179.

11. *Ibid.*, p. 208–9.

12. Captain Howard Lindemuller, *Why No Fire Next Time?*, a broadcast by Pacifica Foundation radio station KPFK, Los Angeles, May 30, 1966.

13. "Proposals for the Improvement of Human Relations in Los Angeles Metropolitan Area," Los Angeles County Commission on Human Relations, November 1965, p. 13.

14. *Ibid.*, p. 27.

15. Victor H. Palmieri, "Hard Facts About the Future of Our Cities," Los Angeles County Commission on Human Relations, 1967, p. 3.

PART II

INDIVIDUAL
LIFE STYLES

How does the individual Negro respond to life in Houston, Watts, Oakland, or any large city? This is the central issue which we face in the next chapters.

Some men become "cool cats"; others are criminals, skid-row bums, civil rights militants, rioters, or simply hard-working laborers and professionals. Some women follow the path of a "white folks' Negro," while others seek salvation in an other-worldly church, or in their children's future, or in hard work— and a few bravely lead their children for the first time to the doors of an all-white school.

Why do they choose different alternatives? What happens to them after they have committed themselves to a particular style of life? Why do they change their strategies by, say, joining the Black Muslims and then defecting?

We have attempted to answer these questions by intensive interviews with over 600 people who represent extreme examples of different ways of life. These individuals were identified either by their actual *behavior* (*e.g.*, residence on skid row) or by their *reputation* in the community (*e.g.*, being labeled as a "civil rights leader" by their fellow citizens).

We make no pretense that this group represents a random sample and we certainly do not wish to imply that these "ideal types" are immutable or mutually exclusive. Obviously, any per-son—such as Sonny Wells, who describes himself in Chapter 6—may start life as a juvenile delinquent (our "rebel without a cause"), have a bout with alcoholism (our "defeated"), and emerge later as a talented journalist (our "achiever").

We hope to illustrate exactly this great diversity in ghetto life styles. Too often the public has viewed the ghetto in a monolithic fashion. As Robert Blauner has noted:

Three positions on Negro cultural orientations can be distinguished. The most popular approach was given sociological legitimacy by Myrdal, who characterized the black man as "an exaggerated American." In this view Negro values and interests are carbon copies of the patterns prevailing in the dominant white society. A second view sees Negro culture and community as deviant because of a history of forced adaptation to an environment weighted with the exigencies of the color line. From this approach, the patterns of Negro life are essentially reactive. The third position argues that segregation and special circumstances over time have provided the insulation necessary for autonomous cultural values to develop indigenously in the Negro community that are neither copies nor caricatures of white dispositions nor simple responses to exclusion and deprivation.[1]

We follow Blauner in believing that there is some truth in each viewpoint and that these three "cultural vectors" are reflected in various behavioral reactions.

In the opening chapter we discuss the methods used in conducting our research and define the seven life styles studied. In the next chapter we first examine the overall views of more than a thousand randomly selected Negroes concerning the conditions of their lives, their opinions about civil rights, and their attitudes toward society and the future. We are also concerned with how broad social factors—education, occupation, age, etc.—correlate with the verbal opinions expressed by urban Negroes. In the succeeding chapters, we then analyze specific life styles.

Our concern in this part of the book is to ascertain not only the verbal opinions of the urban Negro, but also to probe a little more deeply into his "strategy of survival," his actual behavior, and the "escape routes" people have often followed in the American Negro ghetto.

REFERENCE

1. Robert Blauner, "The Unique Americans," mimeographed, Berkeley, Calif., p. 10.

CHAPTER 4

TAKING THE PULSE
OF THE GHETTO:
A NOTE ON METHODS

William McCord

In the 1960's we have witnessed a new phenomenon in the black world: the emergence of the previously inarticulate Negro poor into public prominence. We believe that it is of the utmost importance for the survival of the American polity to understand the problems, attitudes, and actions of this formerly submissive group. This submerged Negro population has too often been ignored. An unfortunate number of public-opinion polls, for example, have used white interviewers to seek information from Negroes. Why should an unemployed Negro laborer tell the truth to a well-dressed white man who has knocked at his tenement door? For that matter, could the two even "speak the same language"?

Our first goal, then, in conducting the research reported in this book was to reach the Negro poor, those previously invisible men who today are most likely to join the ranks of rioters and revolutionaries, and thus, in the great majority of cases, the interviewers themselves were low-income Negroes unfettered by the biases that afflict white, or even middle-class Negro, interviewers. (White interviewers, however, talked with officials and policemen in the various cities.)

It seemed important, too, to compare the black ghettos in cities in which violence had erupted (Watts) and in which apparent calm prevailed at the time of the majority of interviews (Houston); which had intense residential segregation (Houston) and which were *relatively* open (Oakland); which were characterized by a southern traditon (Houston) and which were, supposedly, free of traditional discrimination (Oakland, Watts); and which were noted for high employment (Houston) and which were truly depressed (Watts).

Since the usual methods of social research hardly seemed appropriate, we used an admittedly eclectic mixture of methods in attempting to understand the ghetto Negro. Our opinions were derived from the following sources:

1. Formal interviews with 572 randomly selected Houston Negroes, gathered in the summer of 1966 (before the violence that characterized the spring and summer of 1967).*

2. Formal interviews with 187 randomly selected Oakland Negroes, gathered in the winter of 1967 (during the Hunters Point riot and a minor disturbance over school integration in Oakland).

3. "Natural dialogue" interviews with 426 randomly selected Negroes in Watts, gathered during the first six months of 1967. In the "natural dialogue situation," which was developed by Dr. Blair Justice, the interviewers held conversations with fellow Negroes in bars, barber shops, pool halls, hospital waiting rooms, etc., without saying that they were conducting interviews. The opinions were recorded immediately afterward on cards. Naturally, less information can be secured in this manner, but—at least in some cases—the interviewee is presumably more open and honest.

4. Formal interviews with 620 people who, by their behavior or reputation, exhibited a particular style of ghetto life.

*Respondents were chosen on this basis: every middle house on the right-hand side of the street in every predominantly Negro precinct was contacted. In only six cases did the head of the household refuse to be interviewed. The questionnaires are described in the appendix; in some cases, different questions were asked in different samples. Consequently, we are not always in a position to make direct comparisons. Nonetheless, the surveys in Houston, Watts, and Oakland all touched on the same basic issues.

5. Interviews with approximately 75 white leaders and policemen in Houston, Watts, and Oakland.

In addition, a handful of brief, harried, and necessarily informal interviews were gathered by the authors in Houston, Watts, San Francisco, Detroit, Newark, Oakland, and Orangeburg, South Carolina, when these cities exploded in riots.

Our broadest goal was to examine not only the individual responses of particular Negroes but the entire social context of the ghetto and the new social outlets provided by urbanization. The urban milieu has created a greater potential for mass retaliatory violence, allowed the Negro to exert more political influence, and led to attempts at "collective bargaining" between residents of the black ghetto and the white world.

The information we have gathered, we believe, has unusual significance since the interviews reflect the authentic views of thousands of urban Negroes as revealed in conversations with fellow Negroes—before, during, and after the riots of 1965 to 1968. Nonetheless, our discussion must be tempered by several disclaimers.

Only future research will tell whether our conclusions can be extended to other urban centers, particularly in the North. We fully recognize that no one can generalize about *the* Negro. Indeed, our book is intended only to give some idea of the great variety of ways in which people respond to the ghetto. And we certainly do not want to create the racist impression that we are discussing only American Negroes. Quite the contrary: our thesis is that rapid urbanization, human degradation, and "colonialism" produce similar reactions throughout the world.

Nor does concentration on Negro opinions deny the white man's guilt and responsibility. White prejudice and white discrimination and white indifference have created the black ghetto. The so-called "Negro problem" is, as the Kermer Commission report has made explicit, the problem of white racism. To admit this guilt, however, will not in itself solve the problems of Negroes.

One further qualification is in order: we cannot possibly

differentiate the effects of urbanization itself versus the unique position of Negro Americans in ascertaining their opinions or response to life. I know, for example, a number of Negroes in the most rural sections of Mississippi who might well be called "revolutionary." Since we talked only with urban Negroes in this present study, however, we cannot say, for example, whether Mississippi Negroes in the Delta area would be more or less "militant" than Negroes in Houston, Watts, or Oakland.

Interviews are, of course, merely verbal responses to questioning. In an effort to get a clearer picture of the actual life styles of people in urban areas, we have looked more closely at individuals whose behavior is representative of certain key groups in the ghetto, and this is the core of the material presented in Part II.

In his classic study, *The Nature of Prejudice*, Gordon Allport delineated some of the traits that can result from victimization. Following his lead, we too have attempted to examine some of the possible responses to oppression. We assume that beneath the diversity of ghetto life each person has consciously or unconsciously made one of three basic choices in orienting his life:*

1. He can seemingly accept his role as a victim of the ghetto or he can, with switchblade or protest sign, rebel against his status.

2. He can channel his response through organized groups—gangs, churches, lodges—or he can go it alone on an individualistic path.

3. He can react to his situation in an overtly aggressive, violent manner or he can suppress whatever rage he feels and, perhaps, direct it against himself.

We have devoted much of our work to exploring how and why an individual makes these choices, as well as to the result-

*These are not, of course, absolute or mutually exclusive choices. They should rather be viewed as "dimensions": a person may range from apparently total acceptance of his role, through apathy, up to open revolt. And, naturally, any individual may change his responses as his life progresses.

ing consequences. Specifically, we have examined seven life styles—or, rather, seven types of people—which seem to represent the most common reactions to "internal colonialism":

1. The *"stoic,"* who is outwardly apathetic and accepting and finds some happiness in joining a traditional Negro church or simply by resigning himself to being an "invisible man."

2. The *"defeated,"* who has been crushed by life and escapes from a reality which he can no longer tolerate into a world of drugs, alcohol, or psychotic hallucination.

3. The *"exploiter"*—the blockbuster, numbers man, mortician—who has a stake in maintaining the status quo in the ghetto.

4. The *"achiever,"* who seeks to better his own lot in life but may have little concern for the collective condition of American Negroes.

5. The *"rebel without a cause,"* who rejects existing society and expresses his rebellion through, say, delinquency, but who is not working toward any long-term social reform.

6. The *"activist,"* who hopes to change society by reform measures.

7. The *"revolutionary,"* who has rebelled militantly against American society and hopes to effect a total change in the Negro way of life.

CHAPTER 5

NEGRO OPINIONS

William McCord & John Howard

As a prelude to describing specific responses to ghetto life, we would like to present in broad perspective some Negro opinions concerning certain of the central issues which urban Negroes confront.

METHODOLOGY

The limitations of any opinion or attitude survey must be recognized, particularly when the subject being studied is as volatile as issues in the Negro community. It would be wise, first of all, to make a distinction between attitudes and opinions. As S. S. Sargent and R. C. Williamson have commented: "Attitudes are treated as fairly consistent and lasting tendencies to behave in certain ways—towards persons, activities, events, and objects. Some would say they reflect the deeper, inner core of personality. Opinions are considered closer to the conscious level, more transient, and more likely to be verbalized than attitudes."[1] In this chapter, we have clearly dealt only with opinions. Further, Negro concern about protests, housing, education, employment, and the other matters we have touched are undoubtedly subject to rapid change. A deep core of discontent probably exists in the heart of every American Negro simply because of the nature of our society. Whether he is willing to *say* this to some interviewer or, even more importantly, to take action to alleviate his discontent cannot be determined by a traditional survey of opinions.

Any investigator must face another problem: the sheer difficulty of reaching the "grass-roots" Negro. Thomas Pettigrew has enumerated a disquieting list of problems relevant to Negro personality research and public-opinion surveys.[2] We have attempted to minimize some of these difficulties by calling upon "grass-roots" people to do the actual interviewing and, in Watts, by using the "natural dialogue" approach. Nonetheless, whatever the method used, it is abundantly clear that economically and educationally deprived people have difficulty in verbalizing their opinions—and, indeed, are more suspicious of being interviewed at all than are "higher strata" groups.

Finally, we must recognize that it is impossible to extrapolate from opinion data to actual behavior. In a critical situation—where, say, a white policeman has shot a pregnant Negro woman—apparently law-abiding, highly religious people can easily be drawn into a brawling crowd. With all of these qualifications in mind, we can still regard our 1,185 interviews as a tentative "sounding" of urban Negro opinion in the 1960's.

A COMPARISON OF AMERICAN CITIES

In order to put Houston, Watts, and Oakland in some national perspective, we have relied on three publications which have outlined Negro opinions in a number of other cities. One is the John F. Kraft report;[3] the second is the research done by Gary Marx;[4] and the third is a set of *Newsweek* polls conducted by William Brink and Louis Harris.[5] Some of the questions asked in these studies were practically the same as the questions used in our research, so that a direct comparison was possible.

First, it is clear that Negroes in the Far West and North are most disturbed by the slow pace of desegregation, while, expectedly, a Deep South city such as Birmingham appears most satisfied.

SPEED OF INTEGRATION

	OAKLAND (N:187)*	NEW YORK (N:190)	WATTS (N:426)	HOUSTON (N:572)	CHICAGO (N:133)	ATLANTA (N:192)	BIRMINGHAM (N:200)
Too slow	68%	51%	48%	44%	38%	31%	24%
About right	23	39	50	51	55	63	72
Too fast	4	2	—	4	3	2	1
No opinion	5	8	2	1	4	4	4

The striking features of these findings are that the Negro residents of Houston, a presumably southern city, were about as concerned with the speed of integration as citizens of northern cities. Indeed, the level of discontent was higher in Houston than in Chicago. The extraordinary degree of dissatisfaction in Oakland may be due to the fact that the interviews were done just after a crisis about school integration.

When questioned about the main problems facing them, Negroes in the different cities predictably disagreed about their specific grievances:

MAIN PROBLEM FACING NEGROES

	HOUSTON (N:572)	WATTS (N:426)	OAKLAND (N:187)
Jobs	55%	20%	62%
Education*	14	—	18
Housing	11	15	7
Police, discrimination, other problems with "power structure"	10	23	7
"Troublemakers"	—	10	—
No opinion/No problem	10	32	6

*N=number of respondents.

In Houston, jobs seemed a paramount concern (although public disputes in recent years have centered on school integration). In Watts, the relatively greater concern with the police (*cum* "power structure") seems a natural outcome of the 1965 riot. Oakland's overwhelming concern with jobs again reflects an objective situation where unemployment and underemployment of Negroes characterizes the city. Perhaps the most curious figure is the large number of Watts residents who did not specify any particular grievance. Conceivably this indicates some degree of success of antipoverty programs or of the indigenous movements that have emerged since the riot. One finds it difficult to accept this interpretation, however, since, as we will note later, most Watts Negroes do not believe that such programs have been particularly successful. It seems more probable that the people in Watts have learned not to express grievances openly, even to a casual acquaintance (one of our interviewers) whom they have just met in a bar.

Despite the fact that residents of Watts never mentioned integrated schooling as *the* primary issue, and the citizens of Oakland seldom cited bad schooling, it is quite clear that they disapprove of their "neighborhood" schools to an even higher degree than Houstonians.

OPINION OF SCHOOLS

	HOUSTON (N:572)	WATTS (N:426)	OAKLAND (N:187)
Disapprove of current system	42%	53%	73%
Approve of or neutral about current system	55	47	20
No opinion	3	—	7

Specific questions about the quality of housing were not asked in Houston, but comparable opinions from Watts and Oakland were derived. On the whole, Watts residents disliked their housing conditions more than Oakland Negroes, yet few in either group rated their living conditions as excellent or good.

OPINION OF HOUSING

	WATTS (N:426)	OAKLAND (N:187)
Excellent/Good	8%	29%
Fair	32	45
Poor	40	21
No opinion	20	5

On some grievances, the citizens of the three cities disagreed strikingly. When asked, "What do you think about the police in your neighborhood?" only a minority in each community expressed approval (or even "neutrality"), but more Houstonians said that they liked the police or were neutral toward them than in other cities.*

OPINION OF POLICE

	HOUSTON (N:572)	WATTS (N:426)	OAKLAND (N:187)
Favorable	46%	16%	14%
Unfavorable	31	36	56
Mixed reaction**	—	45	26
No contact	15	—	—

The higher degree of resentment found in Oakland is difficult to interpret. Perhaps the reforms initiated in Watts after the 1965 riot have, comparatively, lowered active hostility toward the police. The complacency of Houston Negroes regarding the police cannot be attributed to the greater tolerance, restraint, or training of the Houston police; the most reasonable interpretation is that Houstonians are overwhelmingly of southern birth: 98 per cent of the Houston sample was born in Texas or elsewhere in the South, as compared to 51 per cent

---

*Polls taken by Dr. Blair Justice after rioting took place on the Texas Southern University campus in Houston suggest that approval of the police dropped sharply.

**Once again, where a blank occurs, it does not necessarily indicate a total absence of opinion in that category, but rather that the question was stated in a slightly different fashion and thus could elicit different responses.

of the Oakland group, and only 21 per cent of the Watts sample. In other words, the great majority of Houston Negroes have experienced only the behavior of southern policemen; perhaps, then, their expectations about "fair" treatment from the police are much lower than that of the other groups.

In spite of their condemnation of ghetto conditions, very few Negroes in any of the urban areas have actively participated in trying to change their cities. When asked if they had taken part in the civil rights movement—by protesting, picketing, boycotting stores, etc.—only 18 per cent of Houstonians and 26 per cent of Oakland citizens claimed to have engaged in civil rights activity. Indeed, even in Watts, only 32 per cent said that they had protested and 25 per cent responded that they were simply not interested. Thus, while many expressed discontent, it appears that the massive apathy and hopelessness of the slums prevents most people from trying to alter their situation in life through collective action. This conclusion was reflected in the fact that a high degree of political ignorance was found in urban ghettos. In Houston, only 16 per cent of the respondents could correctly identify the mayor and even in Oakland, a presumably more sophisticated city, only a minority (43 per cent) correctly recalled the name of the mayor.

When questioned about the usefulness of riots in aiding the Negro cause, no systematic differences appeared among American cities—although New York, surprisingly, condemned rioting more than other areas. Fifty-seven per cent of New Yorkers (in the Marx research) said that "no good can ever come from riots"; 38 per cent in Chicago agreed, as did 26 per cent in Atlanta, 39 per cent in Birmingham, 37 per cent in Houston, and 27 per cent in Oakland.

From our own data, it was possible to probe more deeply into opinions concerning urban disturbances during 1966–67. Formal questionnaires utilizing the same questions were administered in Oakland *after* it had experienced a minor riot and in Houston *before* the violent incidents of 1967. As the following figures indicate, Oakland clearly emerged as a more militant city than Houston.

OPINION OF RIOTS IN WATTS AND OTHER CITIES

	HOUSTON (N:572)	OAKLAND (N:187)
Helped	30%	51%
Hurt	37	27
Both	10	2
Neither	3	12
No opinion	20	8

When asked specifically, "in what situations, if any, do you think violence on the part of Negroes is justified?" both Watts and Oakland appeared to be more militant cities than Houston. It should be noted, however, that even in a southern city such as Houston only a minority of people responded that they were *always* opposed to violence.

USE OF VIOLENCE

	HOUSTON (N:572)	OAKLAND (N:187)	WATTS (N:426)
Never justified	45%	20%	23%
Justified in self-defense	24	44	47
Justified for other reasons ("only way," "to gain attention," etc.)	26	13	29
No opinion	5	23	1

Expectedly, Watts residents appeared most willing to use violence and, also, the great majority had made up their mind on the issue, while in Houston almost half the respondents said they would never use violence and a quarter of the Oakland sample appeared undecided on the issue.

The reactions of the Watts residents to the 1965 riots were strangely mixed. Although apparently willing to resort to violence, only 10 per cent of the Watts sample thought that still another riot would aid them. At the same time, very few people (11 per cent) believed that conditions had improved in Watts since the riot. And, despite the massive funds which have been poured in Watts since 1965, only a minority (31 per cent) believed that the War on Poverty was doing a "good job" in their neighborhood. Thus more people in Houston and Oakland—areas which had not experienced a full-scale riot—believed that the Watts riot had been beneficial than did the residents of Watts themselves. This finding may indicate that after there has been a full-scale riot there is a decreased possibility that another violent confrontation will occur again in that area.

THE INFLUENCE OF OTHER FACTORS

In addition to our concern with differences among the cities, we were also interested in the relationship of occupation, education, age, sex, and intensity of religious faith to a person's expressed opinions. In this section we will concentrate upon Houston and Watts because of the sheer size of the two samples and because even though the interviews were based on different approaches they generally produced similar results. In other words, when there are hundreds of interviews to work with, it is sometimes possible to match subgroups of the same occupation, age, sex, and education and analyze whether religious attitudes as such, for example, have any discernible influence on opinions about community issues. At first it might appear that highly religious people are most likely to condemn the use of violence and yet this could easily be a spurious finding if highly religious people were also predominantly old and it developed that, when all other factors were held constant, age seemed the best predictive factor concerning opinions about violence. Therefore our strategy was to locate the level of unrest or concern in these cities and then specifically pinpoint those who were the most concerned.

THE YOUNG VERSUS THE OLD

In many respects the young and the old in both Houston and Watts held similar views. They agreed about the main problems facing them; they had the same opinion about the schools; and they had participated in the civil rights movement to about the same degree. On the surface, however, the young seemed more militant. To take Houston as an example, twice as many young people (defined as under thirty) disliked the police than did the older people, and a majority of the young were willing to use violence.

OPINION OF POLICE
(*Houston*)

	YOUNG (N:277)	OLD (N:288)
Favorable	43%	50%
Unfavorable	42	19
No contact	11	21
No opinion	7	4

USE OF VIOLENCE
(*Houston*)

	YOUNG	OLD
Never justified	31%	58%
Justified in self-defense	27	22
Justified for other reasons	35	16
No opinion	7	4

However, when the young and the old are compared within the same occupational and educational subgroups, the apparent greater militancy of the young is less pronounced. In order to make a more refined comparison of the effect of age on opinions, we selected one group of men under thirty in Houston and another in Watts, matched for education (some high school) and occupation (unskilled worker), and compared

them with groups of older men in each city from the same educational and occupational subgroups. We felt that the younger
group had unusual significance, since the 1965 Watts rioters
came largely from their ranks.

As the following tables show, the young men were *not* generally more dissatisfied with their life and they were *not* generally
more militant, but, as one would predict, the Watts group as a
whole was more angry and frustrated. First, let us present the
comparison by cities.

OPINION OF PRESENT JOB
(*Matched Groups: Men Under* 30)

	WATTS (N:36)	HOUSTON (N:57)
Satisfied	19%	23%
Not satisfied	36	5
Mixed reaction	42	60
No opinion	3	12

In terms of specific opinions about the police, the Watts
group was again more militant.

OPINION OF POLICE
(*Matched Groups: Men Under* 30)

	WATTS (N:36)	HOUSTON (N:57)
Favorable	3%	3%
Unfavorable	50	43
Mixed reaction	44	39
No contact/No opinion	3	15

These examples could be multiplied: Houston Negroes
believed that jobs were usually easy to find while only 16 per
cent of the Watts group agreed. Forty per cent of the Watts
sample thought that their salaries *never* provided a decent
living, as opposed to 21 per cent of the Houstonians, almost
twice as many young men in Watts as in Houston regarded

their schools as substandard; and many more Watts residents approved the use of violence.

USE OF VIOLENCE
(*Matched Groups: Men Under* 30)

	WATTS (N:36)	HOUSTON (N:57)
Never justified	19%	27%
Justified in self-defense	39	10
Justified for other reasons	33	29
No opinion	0	34

While there was an apparent difference between the two cities, there was *not* a great gap between the young and the old, either in Houston or in Watts. The supposed generational difference—at least among unskilled, relatively uneducated men—did not exist. To cite a few examples:

In Watts, 47 per cent of the young men believed that the schools were not being integrated effectively; 57 per cent of the older men agreed with them. Nineteen per cent of the young men were "always opposed to violence," and an almost equal proportion of older men (17 per cent) shared the same opinion; 79 per cent of the young men favored "black power" but so did 60 per cent of the older men. Exactly the same pattern held true in Houston. Indeed, the older men sometimes expressed slightly more militant opinions than the younger: 43 per cent of the young men regarded the police with antagonism, for example, as opposed to 53 per cent of the older group.

It appears, then, that the Negro revolution is by no means confined to younger people. The young may be "where the action is" but they apparently have the tacit support of many gray-haired men who do not directly protest or riot.

RELIGIOUS VERSUS NONRELIGIOUS

Many writers, when viewing the Negro community, have agreed with Marx that "religion is the opium of the masses." They have contended that religion has served to deflect Negro concerns from this world to the "next world," to instill an ethic of humility, and to divert potential revolutionary urges into harmless religious channels. To attempt to evaluate this view, we examined religion in relation to various Negro opinions.

In Houston we asked, "How religious are you?" Twenty-two per cent answered "very," 49 per cent "some," and 26 per cent "little or no." In Watts it was not possible to ask such a direct question in a presumably casual conversation, so the respondents were asked, "How important do you think religion is to people today?" Thirty per cent answered "very," 48 per cent "not so important," and 20 per cent "not at all." Despite the extreme differences in wording and meaning, the responses were strikingly similar. Whether asked directly or indirectly, people had approximately the same response.

First, viewing Houston alone, it does indeed seem that the intensity of one's religious commitment correlates with one's attitude toward civil rights. For example, the less religious Negro was more concerned about stepping up the pace of the civil rights movement. He was also slightly more inclined to believe that the Watts riot had aided the Negro cause. And he was definitely less condemnatory about the use of violence.

SPEED OF INTEGRATION
(Houston/N:572)

	VERY RELIGIOUS	SOMEWHAT RELIGIOUS	MILDLY OR NOT AT ALL RELIGIOUS
Too slow	39%	39%	56%
About right	51	55	42
Too fast	8	5	2
No opinion	2	1	—

OPINION OF WATTS RIOT
(Houston)

	VERY RELIGIOUS	SOMEWHAT RELIGIOUS	MILDLY OR NOT AT ALL RELIGIOUS
Helped	29%	34%	34%
Hurt	44	42	33
Both	10	14	7
Neither	3	2	5
No opinion	14	7	24

USE OF VIOLENCE
(*Houston*)

	VERY RELIGIOUS	SOMEWHAT RELIGIOUS	MILDLY OR NOT AT ALL RELIGIOUS
Never justified	61%	48%	25%
Justified in self-defense	19	26	27
Justified for other reasons	0.8	1.5	3
No opinion	19.2	24.5	45

While the question asked in Watts was much more indirect, an apparent lack of religious faith was also positively correlated with opinions about the speed of integration and about the use of violence. Less religious people were more distressed about the slow speed of integration and more often supported the use of violence.

On the surface, at least, it would appear that religion either exerts a "cooling" effect on people's opposition to the status quo or that persons who already hold "moderate" opinions tend to join churches more often.

The relation of religious orientation and attitudes toward violence is perhaps most pronounced in that group which has, apparently, most often behaved in a violent fashion. Specifically, from the Houston sample, we selected young males who had at least some high school education and examined the correlation of their reported attitudes toward religion with their attitudes toward violence. As the following table shows, opposition to violence was prominent only among young, relatively uneducated men who claimed to be highly religious.

It is also worthy of note—and perhaps an ominous sign for the future of our society—that a very high proportion of nonreligious young men are willing to turn to violence for "other" reasons, such as the only way to achieve their goal, protect their property, or get back at "whitey."

USE OF VIOLENCE
(*Houston/Matched Groups: Men Under 30*)

	VERY RELIGIOUS (N:19)	SOMEWHAT RELIGIOUS (N:57)	MILDLY OR NOT AT ALL RELIGIOUS (N:46)
Never justified	58%	26%	20%
Justified in self-defense	32	32	26
Justified for other reasons	10	34	43
No opinon	0	9	11

MALE VERSUS FEMALE

What do the women believe? Are they pushing their men toward revolt? Or, on the contrary, are they attempting to exert a calming effect? Our results are confusing but lead, generally, to the conclusion that males and females in the Negro urban ghetto had about the same feelings.

In Watts, for example, we could not discover any significant differences between the sexes on the major issues facing them or even on the means that should be used to fight the "white establishment."

In Houston few differences emerged, and often these contradicted "common sense." In general, males and females had the same opinion about the speed of integration; they were equally optimistic about their children's future (84 percent of males and 86 per cent of females believed that their children's life would be better); they participated in direct civil rights activity with the same frequency; and they disapproved the use of violence at about the same degree.

The slight disagreements between males and females in Houston occurred in only one area, their attitude toward the police.

OPINION OF POLICE
(*Houston*)

	MALES (N:274)	FEMALES (N:296)
Favorable	52%	42%
Unfavorable	23	35
No contact	18	16
No opinion	8	7.

Unexpectedly, females more often condemned police behavior. When, however, other variables—age, education, and occupation—were controlled, the few differences in opinion between males and females disappeared. In comparing a group of young unskilled people who had some high school education, for example, the females disapproved of the police to a slightly greater extent but the differences were not significant.

OPINION OF POLICE
(*Houston/Matched Groups: Under* 30)

	MALES (N:74)	FEMALES (N:70)
Favorable	39%	37%
Unfavorable	45	50
No contact	13	10
No opinion	3	3

Similarly, the matched groups of males and females held similar views about the main problems facing Negroes, the speed of integration, the quality of their jobs, etc. They claimed participation in the civil rights movement at an equal level. The one area of disagreement in these samples was that males more often approved of the use of violence.

USE OF VIOLENCE
(*Houston/Matched Groups: Under* 30)

	MALES (N:74)	FEMALES (N:70)
Never justified	28%	40%
Justified in self-defense	27	16
Justified for other reasons	36	36
No opinion	9	9

It appears, then, that women in Negro society are not exerting the "pacifying" influence that one might expect. They do not differ strikingly from their male counterparts except in one area: the use of violence; but even here, most of the women interviewed agreed with the men that violence is justified either in self-defense or for other reasons.

OCCUPATIONAL DIFFERENCES

One would naturally expect that unemployed people or those scraping along in ill-paid, semiskilled jobs would be most antagonistic toward the status quo. However, we found only slight evidence to support this view and, indeed, some information which would lead to the view that the more a person participates in the middle-class world the more he fights against white society.*

In Oakland we could not note any difference between occupational groups in their opinions about existing society or in their beliefs about how society should be changed. In Watts, with a few exceptions, a similar pattern emerged. Houston exhibited greater disagreements among people of different incomes than the other cities.

*This seems particularly true in terms of educational advancement, a topic which we will discuss in the next section.

Taking Houston as an example, we divided people into four groups: unemployed, unskilled (including domestics), skilled (e.g., plumbers, carpenters, masons), and white-collar (ranging from well-paid business employees through professional groups). There was no significant variation among the various occupational groups about the general state of American society, the speed of integration, the quality of schools, etc. To cite one typical illustration of this virtual unanimity, the population of each occupational group divided almost equally on the question, "In the attempts of Negroes to gain their civil rights, have things been going too slowly, about right, or too fast?"

SPEED OF INTEGRATION
(Houston)

	UNEMPLOYED (N:43)	UNSKILLED (N:360)	SKILLED (N:110)	WHITE-COLLAR (N:35)
Too slow	44%	42%	45%	51%
About right	51	52	50	46
Too fast	5	5	5	3
No opinion	0	1	0	0

In two areas—the major problems facing Negroes and opinions of the police—the occupational groups predictably differed. Quite naturally, the unemployed and the unskilled were more concerned about jobs and more condemnatory of police than the higher-income groups.

MAIN PROBLEMS FACING NEGROES
(Houston)

	UNEMPLOYED (N:43)	UNSKILLED (N:360)	SKILLED (N:110)	WHITE-COLLAR (N:35)
Jobs	66%	58%	48%	46%
Education	8	12	16	26
Housing	11	12	8	6
Police, discrimination, other problems with "power structure"	8	9	18	11
No opinion	7	9	10	11

OPINION OF POLICE
(*Houston*)

	UNEMPLOYED (N:43)	UNSKILLED (N:360)	SKILLED (N:110)	WHITE-COLLAR (N:35)
Favorable	49%	44%	57%	34%
Unfavorable	44	31	23	17
No contact	2	18	13	26
No opinion	5	7	7	23

While middle-class people more often claimed to have protested against existing society through such semilegal means as
boycotts, the unemployed expressed the greatest willingness to
use violence in defense of the Negro cause.

PARTICIPATION IN PROTESTS, BOYCOTTS, ETC.
(*Houston*)

	UNEMPLOYED (N:43)	UNSKILLED (N:360)	SKILLED (N:110)	WHITE-COLLAR (N:35)
Never	84%	83%	83%	69%
Once	16	14	15	17
Twice	0	1	2	11
Three or more times	0	2	1	3

USE OF VIOLENCE
(*Houston*)

	UNEMPLOYED (N:43)	UNSKILLED (N:360)	SKILLED (N:110)	WHITE-COLLAR (N:35)
Never justified	26%	46%	48%	51%
Justified in self-defense	23	23	31	29
Justified for other reasons	47	25	19	14
No opinion	4	6	2	6

When other variables—age, sex, and education—were held
constant the pattern did not change. Thus, it would seem that
the lowest occupational groups are, quite naturally, most wor-
ried about employment and most hostile toward the police.
They are also most willing to use violence to achieve their

goals.* On other issues, however, occupational status does not seem to affect people's opinions.

EDUCATIONAL DIFFERENCES

Naturally, education correlates highly with the other factors we have examined. Older Negroes, for example, tend to have less education while the white-collar classes generally have more. Nonetheless, when other factors were held constant, education in itself seemed to have a decided effect on Negro opinions.

In Houston we divided the sample into three groups: those who had an eighth-grade education or less, those who had some high school, and those who had attended at least one year of college.

The major correlations of Negro opinions and education were these:

• The higher his education, the more a person said he approved of the *immediate* conditions of his life. As might be expected, college-educated Negroes expressed more satisfaction with their jobs and with housing conditions, and were more optimistic about their children's future.

• In viewing the *general* condition of the Negro community, however, the college-educated group differed in several ways from the less educated. They more often cited bad schooling as the major problem of Negroes (26 per cent of college-educated, 13 per cent of high school-educated, and only 8 per cent of elementary-school group). Predictably, too, they more often condemned the general conditions of Houston's schools.

In relation to the police, relatively few of the college-educated group expressed approval of police behavior—but then a high proportion claimed (perhaps truthfully) that they had no contact with the police.

*Only the white-collar group emphatically denied that the Watts riot might have helped the Negro cause: 8 per cent of white-collar people (as opposed to 24 per cent of the skilled workers, 33 per cent of the unskilled, and 25 per cent of the unemployed) believed that the riot might have aided Negroes.

OPINION OF POLICE
(*Houston*)

	8TH GRADE OR LESS (N:86)	SOME HIGH SCHOOL (N:417)	SOME COLLEGE (N:55)
Favorable	53%	47%	29%
Unfavorable	21	34	24
No contact	16	13	35
No opinion	18	6	12

Concerning integration itself, a majority of the college-educated group expressed discontent with the speed of integration.

SPEED OF INTEGRATION
(*Houston*)

	8TH GRADE OR LESS	SOME HIGH SCHOOL	SOME COLLEGE
Too slow	28%	46%	53%
About right	59	50	45
Too fast	11	4	2
No opinion	2	0	0

Further, the college-educated claimed participation in civil rights activities with greater frequency than the other groups, even though the number who had taken part was still a minority.

PARTICIPATION IN PROTESTS, BOYCOTTS, ETC.
(*Houston*)

	8TH GRADE OR LESS	SOME HIGH SCHOOL	SOME COLLEGE
Never	76%	88%	53%
Once	21	10	35
Twice	1	1	7
Three or more times	2	1	5

The well educated and the least educated in Houston expressed an equal abhorrence of violence, even in self-defense.

USE OF VIOLENCE
(*Houston*)

	8TH GRADE OR LESS	SOME HIGH SCHOOL	SOME COLLEGE
Never Justified	56%	41%	60%
Justified in self-defense	22	25	25
Justified for other reasons	17	28	11
No opinion	5	6	4

While education correlated with Negro opinions in Oakland in about the same proportion, Watts presented a more complicated picture. While the same correlations held in Watts as in Houston on such issues as the speed of integration and attitudes toward immediate conditions, there were two significant reversals in Watts. First, education had no relation to claimed participation in civil rights activity. Second, college-educated people were *least* opposed to the use of violence: 28 per cent of the elementary-school group, 49 per cent of the high school group, and only 21 per cent of college-educated group felt that violence was never justified. In Watts, therefore, we may have witnessed a unification of highly different educational groups in favor of violence, while in Houston the opposite has occurred. This in itself may be one effect of a major riot upon the urban Negro.

NEGRO PERCEPTION OF WHITE OPINION

One canon of social science is that people come to believe what others think of them. As we have already indicated, many Negroes have absorbed an image of themselves as "inferior" by a very early age. We were, therefore, interested to see if this unfortunate heritage from white society continued into adulthood. Consequently, in Houston, we asked, "What do you think the average white person thinks about Negroes?" As one would predict, only a handful of Negroes in our sample (proba-

bly quite realistically) thought that whites had a high opinion
of them.

OVER-ALL NEGRO OPINION OF HOW WHITES JUDGE THEM
(*Houston/N:572*)

Ignorant and inferior	49%
Aggressive	4
Bad in general/"Crazy"	9
Good in general	10
Mixed (good and bad)	1
No opinion	27

Distinct differences appeared when the responses were analyzed by occupational strata.

NEGRO OPINION OF HOW WHITES JUDGE THEM: BY OCCUPATION
(*Houston*)

	UNEMPLOYED (N:42)	UNSKILLED BLUE-COLLAR (N:352)	SKILLED BLUE-COLLAR (N:107)	WHITE-COLLAR (N:32)
Ignorant and inferior	61%	50%	37%	31%
Aggressive against whites	0	2	9	9
Bad in general/ "Crazy"	9	9	11	9
Good in general	2	11	9	9
Mixed (good and bad)	0	1	1	6
No opinion	26	24	30	34

The lower the occupational level the more the Negro evaluates
the white opinion of him as being ignorant and inferior. The
figures are small, but it is interesting to note the higher percentages that are attributed to "aggressive against whites" by the
higher occupations.

Although there is absolutely no difference between sexes
about the Negro estimate of white opinions about them, the
younger group leans more to the idea that whites think they are
ignorant and inferior.

NEGRO OPINION OF HOW WHITES JUDGE THEM: BY SEX AND AGE
(*Houston*)

Males	(N:255)	47%
Females	(N:278)	48
Under 30	(N:254)	53
Over 30	(N:279)	42

CONCLUSIONS

It would be pointless to recapitulate those of our findings that simply confirm what common sense tells us or other studies have amply demonstrated. The banal observation that unemployed people are dissatisfied with their position in life, their housing, and their community conditions hardly needs reiteration.

Yet some of our results contradict the usual impressions and indeed should lead to some disquiet, particularly among American whites. All the opinions we solicited indicated a high degree of discontent in Houston, Oakland, and Watts and suggested that the rash of civil disorders that has spread in American cities during the last few years will not soon abate, at least not without fundamental changes in the urban American social structure:

• Despite differences in geographical areas, dissatisfaction about the speed of integration is stirring a supposedly southern city like Houston at about the same level as it is a northern city like Chicago. While the specific grievances differ among cities, it is an ominous sign for the health of the American society that only a minority of urban Negroes in any area felt that violence was never justified. (Of course, a sample of whites—a cross section of our gun-happy society—might well have demonstrated the same fact.)

• While relatively high percentages of Houston and Oakland Negroes believed that riots might help their situation, it is—perhaps—a hopeful sign that only a tiny minority in Watts

believed that another riot of the 1965 variety would significantly help them.

• Both in Watts and in Houston (holding other factors constant) people who claimed to be "very religious" were the least
dissatisfied with ghetto conditions and the least likely to protest
in any way against the status quo. For example, in Houston, 58
per cent of people who said they were very religious opposed
the use of violence, as opposed to 26 per cent who claimed they
were "somewhat" religious and 20 per cent of those who were
not religious at all. Our evidence, therefore, tends to support
those writers who have contended that religion has served to
deflect Negro concerns from the present to the "next world."
Religion, however, may be losing its influence in the Negro
community. In Houston only 22 per cent of our respondents
said they were "very religious" and in Watts (using a more
indirect question) only 30 per cent said they thought religion
was "very important" to other people in their neighborhood.

• When we compared matched groups in Houston and in
Watts, it became clear that men and women held similar views
about the main problems which face Negroes. In fact, in only
one area was there significant disagreement between them: the
utility of violence. Twenty-eight per cent of male respondents
condemned the use of violence under any circumstances as
compared to 40 per cent of a matched group of women.
Nonetheless, a majority of both groups believed that violence is
justified at certain times.

• When other variables—age, sex, and education—were held
constant, we did not discover any major differences among
occupational groups in Watts. Whether in a white-collar
profession or unemployed, the Watts sample seemed equally
militant. In Houston, however, a more complicated pattern
emerged. As might be predicted, the unemployed in Houston
regarded jobs as their major problem more often than other
occupational groups did. Again, also predictably, the unemployed evinced greater hostility toward the police. Forty-four
per cent of the unemployed as opposed to 17 per cent of the
white-collar group regarded the police as abusive. Further, only
2 per cent of the unemployed versus 26 per cent of the white-

collar group claimed never to have had contact with the police. A majority of the white-collar group (51 per cent) believed that violence was never justified while only a quarter of the unemployed (26 per cent) always condemned violence. In Watts, therefore, we may have witnessed a unification of occupational groups on basic issues but in Houston predictable differences in opinion among the various economic strata continue to exist.

• While education is, of course, highly correlated with such other factors as occupation, educational attainment was, in itself, deeply related to other opinions. In general, the higher the individual's education, the more often he expressed satisfaction with the immediate conditions of his own life, such as his job or housing conditions. Nevertheless, in appraising the condition of the Negro community in its entirety, the most well-educated group expressed greater concern about the speed of integration, claimed to have participated in civil rights activities more often, and condemned police behavior with greater vehemence than the less educated. Only two differences separated Houston from Watts. First, in Watts educational level had no relation to the amount of participation in civil rights activity. Second, in Watts college-educated people were least opposed to the use of violence, while in Houston there were no consistent differences among the various educational groups. In Watts, 21 per cent of the college-educated group and 28 per cent of the elementary-school group felt that violence was never justified, while 49 per cent of the high school group completely eschewed the use of violence. Perhaps, again, another effect of the 1965 violence was to form an alliance of opinion between the least- and the best-educated urban Negroes.

• As could be predicted, most Negroes believe that whites regard them as ignorant, inferior, "crazy," etc. It should come as no surprise, then, that movements emphasizing Negro dignity and even superiority are able to win over many ghetto residents. For example, in Watts 58 per cent of the respondents favored the concept of "black power," 24 per cent opposed it, and the remainder were "neutral" or had never heard the term.*

• The young were *not* generally more dissatisfied with their life and they were not more militant than older people. It appears that the "Negro revolution" is by no means confined to younger people, but that they may only be willing to express more openly the feelings of malaise that still plague the older generation as well.

As we have noted, behavior may be predicted from opinions, but it cannot be done with certainty unless expressed opinions are correlated with real actions. In the following chapters, therefore, we attempt to assess the relation of opinion to actual behavior. Specifically, we chose several life-styles that seem to be characteristic of the urban ghetto and interviewed not only persons whose behavior, by definition, placed them in a particular group (*e.g.*, an admitted drug addict) but those whose reputation in the Negro community assigned them a particular "label" (*e.g.*, individuals regarded as civil rights leaders or "Uncle Toms").

Many urban Negroes, as our various tables show, say that they have "no opinion" on various issues or are disinterested in civil rights matters. These are people who are simply concerned with their everyday life, with trying to survive in the city. It is this group—"the stoics"—whom we will first examine.

*This question was only asked in Watts, because of the timing of the questionnaire.

REFERENCES

1. S. S. Sargent and R. C. Williamson, *Social Psychology* (New York: Ronald Press, 1958), p. 407.

2. Thomas F. Pettigrew, "Negro American Personality: Why Isn't More Known?", *Journal of Social Issues*, XX, No. 2, 1964.

3. "A Report of Attitudes of Negroes in Various Cities," prepared for the Senate Subcommittee on Executive Reorganization by John K. Kraft, privately circulated, 1966.

4. Gary Marx, *Protest and Prejudice* (New York: Harper & Row, 1967).

5. William Brink and Louis Harris, *Black and White: A Study of U.S. Racial Attitudes Today* (New York: Simon & Schuster, 1967).

CHAPTER 6

THE STOIC

William McCord & John Howard

Mrs. Madison* is an old woman (she doesn't know her exact age) living alone in the most desolate section of Houston's Fifth Ward. She belongs to the "Heavenly Baptist Church" and adheres strictly to the teachings of her minister, Reverend Stanton.* The minister has consistently told his congregation to bear the sufferings of this life with fortitude, since the next life will bring salvation. He admonishes church members to "keep out of trouble" and, specifically, "don't go around getting 'The Man' riled up."

Mrs. Madison follows this advice. She believes that "the world is in too much of a hurry" and that the civil rights movement is going "too fast." "We should wait on the Lord," she says. "If a thing is right it will come to be; we should wait for it. You've got to wait. The devil is around too, you know. He'll use you if he can."

Mrs. Madison exhibits in her personal life her belief that "we should take it easy and let the Lord do it." Several years ago her doctor told her that she needed a cancer operation immedi-

*Fictitious name.

ately. She then consulted Reverend Stanton, who advised her not to go to the hospital, but rather to pray. She waited, despite the doctor's repeated warnings that it might be too late if she continued to hesitate. After some weeks Reverend Stanton visited her. He noticed her deteriorated condition and said, "It's all right, you can go now. It is the Lord's will." Fortunately, the operation was a success.

Mrs. Madison believes that we live in an evil world and that the next generation will have a "worse time" than her own, explaining that "each generation is both weaker and wiser." She has little faith in formal education: "Mother wit will survive when education alone won't."

Although Mrs. Madison has undoubtedly never heard of the philosopher Zeno or of the Stoa in Athens from which he preached, she could easily be considered a stoic. She believes, like Zeno, that man should strive to be free from passion and unmoved by the vicissitudes of life, and that he must submit without complaint to the unavoidable necessity by which all things are governed.

She has many companions in the black ghetto. A random sample of 572 Negroes in Houston indicated that 31 per cent could justly be called stoics. Similar random samples suggested that 27 per cent of the 426 Negroes in Watts and 22 per cent of 178 Negroes in Oakland follow the same teachings.*

Stoicism, of course, has many colloquial meanings: apathy, indifference to pleasure and pain, the ability to repress feelings, endurance, insensibility.† Using the word in all its varied shadings, we believe that four rather distinct types of stoics exist in the Negro population.

The Religious Stoic, who, like Mrs. Madison, says he finds

---

*In the random sampling, Stoics were defined as people who 1) believed that fate rather than planning determined one's lot in life, 2) did not participate in any type of civil rights activities, and 3) believed that improvements in the Negro situation in America were either coming "too fast" or "just about right."

†After much debate, we settled on the term stoic as an admittedly vague label for a large group. Other terms—the "uninvolved," the "resigned," the "passive"—could also be applied. Obviously, we are not using the term stoic in its literal, classical sense.

the strength to endure life by belonging to a conventionally oriented church.

The Cultist Stoic, who, like some members of the Black Muslims, strives to maintain his dignity by membership in a deviant, ascetic religious group.

The Cool Stoic, who apparently does not care for religion but tries to maintain a "cool" front (an apparent indifference to pain) and pursues some kind of illegitimate but nonviolent "hustle" (racket).

The Passive Stoic, who says he finds little consolation either in religion, a cult, or in a "hippie" life but simply accepts the humiliations of being a Negro in a white society, without overtly rebelling.

Despite their differences, these four types of people share certain characteristics: a relative indifference toward politics or participation in the civil rights movement; a belief that certain feelings must be repressed or controlled; and a conviction that their destiny is largely controlled either by "higher forces" or, at least, by circumstances beyond their control.

THE RELIGIOUS STOIC

"The strongest Negro institutions have centered in the churches," Talcott Parsons has observed, "a vital complex which must be preserved carefully against some of the disintegrating tendencies of urban life."[1] And, as St. Clair Drake and Horace Cayton noted in *Black Metropolis,* "It has become customary in America to refer to Negroes as a 'religious people.' ... A walk through Bronzeville lends confirmation to this belief, for the evidences of an interest in 'praising the Lord' are everywhere—churches are omnipresent."[2]

Our data indicates that Negro churches (still largely segregated) continue to have an influence in the urban ghetto. In two of the cities we investigated, many people claim that religion is important to them and say that they belong to a church. In Houston 71 per cent said that religion had either great or "some" importance to them; 65 per cent responded similarly in Oakland.*

Naturally, one should view these responses with some caution. If, for example, a church member is asked how religion has influenced his life, only a tiny minority can mention any *specific* impact. This may be due to sheer inarticulateness or, equally, it may be evidence that the contemporary urban Negro simply gives lip service to a traditional institution.

As usual in American history, most Negroes follow the Baptist faith. In Houston, 64 per cent call themselves Baptists. The Baptist churches—as well as many of the other faiths—offer a variety of benefits to American Negroes. Most importantly, of course, they give spiritual solace to an underprivileged group. But, as St. Clair Drake has written, the church has still other attractions:

> Young people with talent find wide scope for expressing it in choirs, quartets, and sextets which travel from church to church (often bearing colorful names like The Four Heavenly Trumpets or The Six Singing Stars of Zion) . . . Such groups channel their aggressions in widely advertised "Battles of Song." . . .
>
> Adults as well as young people find satisfaction and prestige in serving as ushers and deacons, "mothers," and deaconesses, Sunday School teachers and choir leaders. . . .
>
> The "organized" lower-class is oriented primarily around churches whose preachers, often semi-literate, exhort them to "be in the world" but not of it.[3]

Black Metropolis well describes what might be termed the typical Negro church. But Joseph Fichter has pointed out an additional role for the church as an institution for Negro protest. Fichter believes that Negro churches have historically functioned to sustain or lead Negro revolts:

> The organized church . . . has provided continued protest against all forms of racial injustice and discrimination. The most famous slave insurrections were lead by Negro preachers, Gabriel Prosser in 1800, Denmark Vessy in 1822, Nat Turner

*The question was not asked directly in Watts.

in 1831. . . . Anyone who has been observing developments on the racial front since the 1955 Montgomery bus boycott need not be reminded that "Negro ministers constitute the largest segment of the leadership class."[4]

We should, then, distinguish two varieties of Negro churches: the "other-worldly" institution, which emphasizes salvation in the next world and appeals to the religious stoic, and the "this-worldly" church, which stresses reform of the status quo. Other-worldly churches distribute "opium to the masses"; this-worldly churches seek to better the Negro's condition before he reaches heaven.

In Houston we attempted to determine the attitudes of these contrasting orientations by sampling fifty members of other-worldly churches and fifty-one adherents of this-worldly churches.

AN OTHER-WORLDLY CHURCH

The "Heavenly Baptist Church," headed by Reverend Stanton, claims 1,500 members. About 500 attend the usual Sunday service. The church is a large red-brick structure with a Sunday school, cafeteria, and meeting rooms, next door to Reverend Stanton's home. He personally holds deed to the property as well as to other land in Houston.

Reverend Stanton teaches middle-class morality, while admitting that the "flesh may be weak." Although an octogenarian, he was recently married to a woman in her twenties. At the eleven o'clock Sunday service he thunders damnation from the pulpit and exhorts his flock to abandon the ways of the devil.

Sunday school classes for children and adults meet throughout the day. On Wednesday nights Reverend Stanton leads a "prayer rally" and conducts numerous special services for "Women's Day," "Youth Day," "Father's Day," etc. Lodges meet in the church and Reverend Stanton often presents musical extravaganzas, dramas, or other social events.

As an individual, Reverend Stanton is definitely engaged in "this world." He is a shrewd businessman and does not hesitate to advise his congregation about how to vote. Nonetheless, his preaching centers largely on heaven and hell. He admonishes his congregation to avoid drinking, smoking, cursing, and women. He promises them, in return, the rewards of a delightful heaven—a paradise delectably pictured in the church's stained-glass window.

A recent survey indicates that Reverend Stanton is typical of Negro ministers. "As a leadership group, Negro clergymen scored well behind other elite groups in advocating militant policies. It was only after other people had endorsed demonstrations and assumed militant roles that the clergy as a group took up the cry."[5]

Mrs. Madison and many others in the church describe it as the center of their existence. "Babylon" does not tempt them, for they know that God has ordained a happier place for them after death.

A THIS-WORLDLY CHURCH

The "Pemberton Avenue Church" would have little appeal for a religious stoic such as Mrs. Madison. Its preacher, Reverend Layman,* does not promise immortality, but rather encourages his congregation to protest, to agitate, to seek "freedom now." Reverend Layman himself has led various protests, headed "radical" movements, and participated actively in helping groups ranging from NAACP to SNCC.

The church is an unimpressive wooden structure furnished with hard benches and a small speaker's stand. But Reverend Layman's message is a clear one: stand up for your rights in this world. To join, a member must swear to spend six hours a week in social service to the Negro community.

Mr. Chandler* is a typical member of the congregation. He is thirty-five years old, a graduate of the University of Texas, and a chartered accountant. In 1964 he participated in some of the original sit-ins. He is angry about white discrimination and has even contemplated suicide, "in the past, when I was younger and had less faith in religion." The Pemberton Church

*Fictitious name.

provided him with a reason for living: "Religion is very important for me. It is the foundation on which I live. After I die, however, I have no idea what will happen. Probably it will be an eternal sleep." He went on to say, "Religion is essential for this life—for the sanity and well-being of the individual. It is, too, a path of progress for the entire race. It is a functional way of relating to this life, not a retreat from reality."

Thus, while Mrs. Madison is a resigned, religious stoic, Mr. Chandler is a militant who wishes to alter the universe as much as any individual can. In both background and attitude, these two represent in microcosm the differing nature of their two churches.

BACKGROUNDS OF "RELIGIOUS STOICS"

As one would expect, such churches attract very different congregations.* This-worldly churches have more males (60 per cent) than the other-worldly (40 per cent). The occupational and educational level of this-worldly churches are also considerably higher.

OCCUPATION

	OTHER-WORLDLY CHURCHES (N:50)†	THIS-WORLDLY CHURCHES (N:51)
Unskilled, skilled, and housewife	70%	25%
Student	0	15
White-collar	10	40
Professional	10	15
Retired	10	5

*This-worldly church members were defined as people who believed they could influence their own fate but adhered to religion. Twenty-four members of the "Pemberton Avenue Church" are included, as well as members of other similar congregations. Conversely, other-worldly church adherents put their faith totally in the hands of fate or God. Seventeen members of the "Heavenly Baptist Church" fell in this category, in addition to people from other churches.

†N = number of respondents.

EDUCATION

	OTHER-WORLDLY CHURCHES (N:50)	THIS-WORLDLY CHURCHES (N:51)
8th grade or less	40%	5%
Some high school	60	30
Some college	0	40
Post-graduate college	0	25

Age seems to be one of the most important differentiating factors, since this-worldly churches disproportionately attract young people:

AGE

	OTHER-WORLDLY CHURCHES (N:50)	THIS-WORLDLY CHURCHES (N:51)
15–25	10%	15%
25–35	10	15
35–45	10	30
45–55	30	20
Over 55	40	20

Obviously, the two congregations differ in their social make-up. These factors alone, as Chapter 5 has shown, may well explain the contrasts in their attitudes about life, society and themselves. From our data, it is impossible to say whether a particular church simply attracts a congregation amenable to its teachings or whether the church exerts some influence in altering the beliefs of its members. For whatever reason, however, it is eminently clear that the congregations of the two churches disagree on many issues.

ATTITUDES OF "RELIGIOUS STOICS"

Although the two church groups responded similarly on several topics (such as the main problems facing Negroes), they differed dramatically in four areas: the civil rights movement; political orientation; general attitudes toward life; and the degree to which they reported psychosomatic ailments.

As could be predicted, the other-worldly church members were relatively inactive in the civil rights movements and condemned the use of violence. When asked, for example, "How have you participated in the civil rights movement?", the two groups reported:

PARTICIPATION IN PROTESTS, BOYCOTTS, ETC.

	OTHER-WORLDLY CHURCHES (N:50)	THIS-WORLDLY CHURCHES (N:51)
Protest march	10%	80%
Picketing	10	40
Boycott	10	70
Voting	20	90
None	30	10

When asked, "If you were asked by people whom you respected, would you participate in the civil rights movement?", other-worldly church members still exhibited great reluctance to become involved; 30 per cent would still refuse to do anything at all, even vote.

Expectedly, the other-worldly church members generally abhorred violence in the civil rights movement and did not anticipate that racial violence would come in their city, as the following tables show.

USE OF VIOLENCE

	OTHER-WORLDLY CHURCHES (N:50)	THIS-WORLDLY CHURCHES (N:51)
Never justified	60%	20%
Justified in self-defense	30	80
Generally justified	10	0

Opinion of the Watts Riot

	OTHER-WORLDLY CHURCHES (N:50)	THIS-WORLDLY CHURCHES (N:51)
Helped	20%	50%
Hurt	50	20
Both	10	30
No opinion	20	0

Could a Major Riot Occur in Houston?

	OTHER-WORLDLY CHURCHES (N:50)	THIS-WORLDLY CHURCHES (N:51)
Yes	20%	50%
No	40	40
No opinion	40	10

When, on April 22, 1967, students at the predominately Negro Texas Southern University threw bricks and bottles at passing cars of white men, Mrs. Madison and Mr. Chandler responded typically to this minor riot. Mrs. Madison: "It was the devil's work." Mr. Chandler: "It was long overdue. The students are sick and tired of being kicked around. This is the only way they can express their discontent."

The other-worldly church members exhibited distinct conservative qualities and general political ignorance. Fifty per cent of Mrs. Madison's fellow believers had no opinion about the Governor of Texas, and 60 per cent felt neutral about the Mayor of Houston (as opposed, respectively, to 20 per cent and 15 per cent of this-worldly church adherents). Astoundingly, 70 per cent of the other-worldly respondents had no opinion about State Senator Barbara Jordan, even though she was the first woman Negro ever elected from their own district or, for that matter, in Texas, and the poll was taken in the midst of her campaign. Five per cent of the this-worldly church members had no opinion.

The other-worldly respondents tended to support the status quo. Generally, they approved of the police force in Houston (but wanted more police protection); they selected white politicians (Lyndon Johnson, John F. Kennedy, etc.) as their "most admired" figures; and they endorsed NAACP policies, as the following tables indicate.

MOST-ADMIRED PERSON

	OTHER-WORLDLY CHURCHES (N:50)	THIS-WORLDLY CHURCHES (N:51)
White personality (*e.g.*, Johnson)	70%	30%
Negro personality (*e.g.*, M. L. King)	2	60
Gandhi	0	5
No opinion	28	5

OPINION OF POLICE

	OTHER-WORLDLY CHURCHES (N:50)	THIS-WORLDLY CHURCHES (N:51)
Generally good	10%	5%
Generally good/ Need more	70	5
Generally bad	10	40
Bad/Racial discrimination	10	40
No contact	0	10

MOST EFFECTIVE CIVIL RIGHTS GROUPS

	OTHER-WORLDLY CHURCHES (N:50)	THIS-WORLDLY CHURCHES (N:51)
NAACP	80%	40%
"Militant" groups (*e.g.*, PUSH*)	0	60
No opinion/None	20	0

*PUSH was a local organization that conducted protests and a march in the hopes of gaining more school integration.

The two church groups also contrasted in their opinions about the efficacy of science and how much influence a person had over his own life. When asked what determined "success" in life, 40 per cent of the other-worldly people believed that luck or fate was the deciding factor; only 10 per cent of the this-worldly church shared that opinion. Fifty per cent of the other-worldly churchgoers (as opposed to 10 per cent of the this-worldly group) believed that "human nature" could not be changed. Seventy per cent of the other-worldly sample believed that science would never solve all of the riddles of life; fully 80 per cent of the this-worldy group expressed greater faith in science.

Despite their presumed acceptance of destiny, the other-worldly church members tended to distrust other persons. When asked, "When you meet someone for the first time, what should you do?" the response was as follows:

OPINION OF OTHERS' TRUSTWORTHINESS

	OTHER-WORLDLY CHURCHES (N:50)	THIS-WORLDLY CHURCHES (N:51)
Trust him until he proves untrustworthy	20%	50%
Be cautious until you know him better	60	30
Don't trust him because he may take advantage of you	20	20

One other difference should be mentioned: the this-worldly group suffered more often from various psychosomatic complaints than the other-worldly group; twice as many admitted to "feeling nervous" and three times as many said they had considered taking their own lives.*

Religious Stoics, then, may find some sort of peace in their church. Religion, for the other-worldly people, is apparently a

*However, the higher educational and occupational level of the this-worldly church members may account for the difference.

way of escaping the pains of existence and of avoiding involvement in the volatile movements of our day. The fact that the
other-worldly churches attract less educated and older people
may mean that their days are numbered. As education
increases, the more activist churches could well draw greater
numbers of people into their ranks.

THE CULTIST STOIC

Another outlet for the religiously oriented stoic class does, of
course, exist. He can join a deviant cult that rejects many of
the usual teachings of American Negro churches. At the moment, the Black Muslims apparently have the greatest appeal of
the various cults that flourish in the ghetto.

The Lost-Found Nation of Islam in the Wilderness of North
America, commonly known as the Black Muslim movement,
claims a small but fanatically devoted membership among the
Negroes of our major cities. The way of the "Messenger" is
rigorous for those who follow it. The man or woman who
becomes a Muslim accepts not only an ideology but an all-
encompassing code that amounts to a way of life.

A good Muslim does a full day's work on an empty stomach.
When he finally has his one meal of the day in the evening, it
can include no pork, nor can he have a drink before it or a ciga-
rette after; strict dietary rules are standard procedure, and
liquor and smoking are forbidden under any circumstances. His
recreation is likely to consist of reading the Koran or participating in a demanding round of temple-centered activities, running
public meetings, or aggressively proselytizing on the streets by
selling the Muslim newspaper, *Muhammad Speaks*.

Despite allegations of Muslim violence (adverse publicity
arising from the slaying of Malcolm X supports the erroneous
notion that Muslims preach violence), the member's life is basically ascetic. Why, then, in a nonascetic, hedonistically
oriented society, do people become Muslims? What is the life
of Muslims like? These are questions I* asked in research
among West Coast members. Specifically, I wanted to know:

*The "I" in this case is John Howard.

• What perspective on life makes membership in such an organization attractive?

• Under what conditions does the potential recruit develop those perspectives?

• How does he happen to come to the door of the temple for his first meeting?

• The Black Muslims are a deviant organization even within the Negro community; the parents or friends of many members strongly objected to their joining. So how does the recruit handle pressures that might erode his allegiance to the organization and its beliefs?

Presenting my questions as an attempt to "learn the truth" about the organization, I was able to conduct in-depth interviews with nineteen West Coast recruits, following them through the process of their commitment to the Nation of Islam.

Two main points of appeal emerged—some recruits were attracted primarily by black nationalism, others by the emphasis on self-help. Those who joined the organization for its aggressive black nationalism, the "Muslim militants," will be discussed in Chapter 12. Those who were attracted more by the Muslims' emphasis on hard work and rigid personal morality may be aptly termed Protestant-Ethic Muslims."

PROTESTANT-ETHIC MUSLIMS

The "Protestant" Muslims all came from backgrounds with a strong tradition of Negro self-help. In two cases, the recruit's parents had been followers of Marcus Garvey; another recruit explicitly endorsed the beliefs of Booker T. Washington; and the remaining two, from upwardly mobile families, were firm in the belief that Negroes could achieve higher status if they were willing to work for it.

When asked what had appealed to him about the Muslims, Norman X* replied:

*Fictitious name.

They thought that black people should do something for themselves. I was running this small place [a photography shop] and trying to get by. I've stuck with this place when it was paying me barely enough to eat. Things always improve and I don't have to go to the white man for anything.

Ernestine X* stressed similar reasons for joining the Muslims:

You learn to stand up straight and do something for yourself. You learn to be a lady at all times—to keep your house clean—to teach your children good manners. There is not a girl in the group who does not know how to cook and sew. The children are very respectful; they speak only when they are spoken to. There is no such thing as letting your children talk back to you the way some people believe.

Despite their middle-class attitudes in many areas, Protestant-Ethic Muslims denounced moderate, traditional civil rights organizations such as the NAACP just as vigorously as militant Muslims do. Norman X said that he had once belonged to the NAACP but had dropped out:

They spent most of their time planning the annual brotherhood dinner. Besides, it was mostly whites—whites and colored doctors and lawyers who wanted to be white. As far as most Negroes were concerned they might as well not have existed.

Lindsey X*, who had owned and run his own upholstery shop for more than thirty years, viewed the conventional black bourgeoisie with equal resentment.

I never belonged to the NAACP. What they wanted never seemed real to me. I think Negroes should create jobs for themselves rather than going begging for them. That's why I never supported CORE.

In this respect Norman and Lindsey were in full accord with the more militant Amos X, who asserted:

They [the NAACP and CORE] help just one class of people. . . . Let something happen to a doctor and they are

*Fictitious name.

right there; but if something happens to Old Mose on the corner, you can't find them.

The interviews made it clear that most of the Protestant-Ethic Muslims had joined the Nation because, at some point, they began to feel the need for organizational support for their personal systems of value. For Norman and Lindsey it was an attempt to stop what they considered their own backsliding after coming to California. Both mentioned that they had drunk to excess and indulged in what they regarded as a profligate way of life. Guilt feelings apparently led them to seek Muslim support in returning to more enterprising habits.

Muhammad Ali (Cassius Clay) is the most famous convert to the Muslims. Despite his reputation for belligerency, Ali more closely resembles the Protestant-Ethic Muslim than the militant. During informal talks in various boxing gymnasiums and at Rice University in 1967 he rejected the belief that all white men are devils:[6]

> It would not be right to hate a man simply because he is white. If I did, people would have every right to hate me for my blackness. No, I don't hate, I just know. Why, if a wild tiger were to jump right here in the middle of this room, I'd be the first one out of here. I don't have time to *hate* the tiger. I just *know*. So just like the tiger, I *know*.

When asked about how the Negro cause could best be helped, Ali replied:

> We Africans and Arabs must do it ourselves. If you don't clean up your own neighborhood, if you don't make any attempt to clean it up, if you don't want to clean it up, why expect anyone to help you? No, I am against government aid. We Africans and Arabs, the so-called Negroes, are able to help ourselves and must help ourselves before we can make the rest of the world respect us.

Clearly, Muhammad Ali emphasizes the self-help aspect of his religion. He has also made statements that directly oppose the militant wing of the Negro movement. When questioned about his attitude toward Stokely Carmichael and black power, Ali answered:

> Because Stokely is a friend of mine, I let it go with saying, "I don't think some of the things he says are too wise. You are not going to get freedom for the black man if you get it by taking away the white man's freedom." Besides, Stokley has no guns and no planes. He is not going to fight a war.

When asked why he sometimes preaches sermons that sound full of bitterness and hatred, Ali explained it as a form of catharsis:

> Well, some of Elijah's higher-ups say it is a good way to drain off Muslim hatred. I mean by preaching that way we get rid of all that stuff without it hurting our efforts to improve ourselves. You know we are the only ones that hear it mostly so nobody hates us for it. Also Elijah says it helps to get people who want to hear that stuff.

Why does he remain a Muslim? One may hypothesize three reasons. First, he is truly absorbed in the Islamic teachings of the Koran. Second, he says that he does not wish to sacrifice his position of leadership. And third, there may possibly be an element of fear, even in a man who has so thoroughly proven his bravery. "Some of my Muslim friends got some funny strong ideas," he once remarked. "Some of them even kill people. I do not want to go the way of Malcolm."

COMMITMENT TO DEVIANCE

The Nation of Islam is a deviant organization and as such it is subject to public scorn and ridicule. Thus it faces the problem of consolidating the recruit's allegiance in an environment where substantial pressures operate to erode this allegiance. How does it deal with this problem?

The structural characteristics of the Nation tend to insulate the member from the hostility of the larger society and thus contribute to the organization's survival. To begin with, the ritual of joining the organization itself stresses commitment without question.

At the end of the general address at a temple meeting, the minister asks those nonmembers present who are "interested in learning more about Islam" to step to the back of the temple. There they are given three blank sheets of ordinary stationery and a form letter addressed to Elijah Muhammad in Chicago:

Dear Savior Allah, Our Deliverer:

I have attended the Teachings of Islam, two or three times, as taught by one of your ministers. I believe in it. I bear witness that there is no God but Thee. And, that Muhammad is Thy servant and apostle. I desire to reclaim my Own. Please give me my original name. My slave name is as follows . . .

The applicant is instructed to copy this letter verbatim on each of the three sheets of paper, giving his own name and address unabbreviated at the bottom. If he fails to copy the letter perfectly, he must repeat the whole task. No explanation is given for any of these requirements.

Formal acceptance of his letter makes the new member a Muslim, but in name only. Real commitment to the Nation of Islam comes gradually—for example, the personal commitment expressed when a chain smoker gives up cigarettes in accordance with the Muslim rules even though he knows that he could smoke unobserved. "It's not that easy to do these things," Stanley X* said of the various forms of abstinence practiced by Muslims. "It takes will and discipline and time . . . but you're a much better person after you do." Calvin X told of periodic backsliding in the beginning, but added, "Once I got into the thing deep, then I stuck with it."

This commitment and the new regimen that goes with it have been credited with effecting dramatic personality changes in many members, freeing alcoholics from the bottle and drug addicts from the needle. It can be argued, however, that the organization does not change the member's fundamental orientation. To put it somewhat differently, given needs and impulses can be expressed in a variety of ways. Thus a man may give vent to his sadism by beating up strangers in an alley or by

*Fictitious name.

joining the police force and beating them up in the back room of the station.

"Getting into the thing deep" for a Muslim usually comes in three stages:

1. Participation in organizational activities—selling the Muslim newspaper, eating at a Muslim restaurant, attending and helping run Muslim meetings.

2. Isolation from non-Muslim social contacts—drifting away from former friends and associates because of divergent attitudes or simply because of the time consumed in Muslim activities.

3. Assimilation of the ideology—marking full commitment, when a Muslim has so absorbed the organization's doctrines that he automatically uses them to guide his own behavior and to interpret what happens in the world around him.

The fact that the organization can provide members with a full social life furthers isolates them from non-Muslims. Participation is not wholly a matter of drudgery, of tramping the streets to sell the paper and studying the ideology; the organization also presents programs of entertainment for its members and the public. For example, in two West Coast cities a Negro theatrical troupe called the Touring Artists put on two plays, *Jubilee Day* and *Don't You Want to Be Free?* Although there was a high element of humor in both plays, the basic themes—white brutality and hypocrisy and the necessity of developing Negro self-respect and courage—were consonant with the organization's perspective. Thus the organization makes it possible for a member to satisfy his need for diversion without going elsewhere to do so. At the same time, it continually reaches him with its message through the didactic element in such entertainment.

Carl X's* experiences were typical of the recruit's growing commitment to the Nation. When asked what his friends thought when he first joined, he replied: "They thought I was crazy. They said, 'Man, how can you believe all that stuff?'"

*Fictitious name.

He then commented that he no longer saw much of them, and added:

> When you start going to the temple four or five times a week and selling the newspaper you do not have time for people who are not doing these things. We drifted—the friends I had—we drifted apart.... All the friends I have now are in the Nation. Another brother and I get together regularly and read the Koran and other books, then ask each other questions like, "What is Allah's greatest weapon? The truth. What is the devil's greatest weapon? The truth. The devil keeps it hidden from men. Allah reveals it to men." We read and talk about the things we read and try to sharpen our thinking. I couldn't do that with my old friends.

THE PROBLEM OF DEFECTION

Commitment to the Nation can diminish as well as grow. Four of the members I interviewed later defected. Why?

These four cases can be explained in terms of a weak point in the structure of the Nation. The organization has no effective mechanisms for handling grievances among the rank and file. Its logic accounts for this. Muslim doctrine assumes that there is a single, ultimate system of truth. Elijah Muhammad and, by delegation, his ministers are in possession of this truth. Thus only Elijah Muhammad himself can say whether a minister is doing an adequate job. The result is the implicit view that there is nothing to be adjudicated between the hierarchy and its rank and file.

Grievances nevertheless do arise, however. The four defectors were, for various reasons, all dissatisfied with Minister Gerard X.* Since there were no formal mechanisms within the organization for expressing their dissatisfaction, the only solution was to withdraw.

For most members, however, the pattern is one of steadily growing involvement, and once the ideology is fully absorbed, there is virtually no such thing as dispute or counterevidence. If a civil rights bill is not passed, this proves the viciousness of

*Fictitious name.

whites in refusing to recognize Negro rights. If the same bill *is* passed, it merely proves the duplicity of whites in trying to hide their viciousness.

The ideology also provides a coherent theory of causation, provided one is willing to accept its basic assumptions. Norman X interpreted his victory over his wife in a court case as a sign of Allah's favor. Morris X* used it to account for the day-to-day fortunes of his associates:

> Minister X had some trouble. He was sick for a long time. He almost died. I think Allah was punishing him. He didn't run the temple right. Now, the brothers make mistakes. Everyone does—but Minister X used to abuse them at the meetings. It was more a personal thing. He had a little power and it went to his head. Allah struck him down and I think he has learned a little humility.

When a man reasons in this fashion, he has become a fully committed member of the Nation of Islam. His life revolves around temple-centered activities, his friends are all fellow Muslims, and he sees his own world—usually the world of an urban slum dweller—through the framework of a very powerful myth. He is still doing penance for the sign of Yakub, but the millennium is at hand. He has only to prepare.

The Nation of Islam does not in any real sense convert members. Rather, it attracts Negroes who have already, through their own experiences in white America, developed a perspective congruent with that of the Muslim movement. The recruit comes to the door of the temple with the essence of his ideas already formed. The Black Muslims only give this disaffection a voice.

THE COOL STOIC

Far removed (in appearance) from the ascetic cultists are the "cool cats"—the "dukes," "hustlers," "giggers"—the young men who spend their time on street corners, in pool halls, or in run-

*Fictitious name.

ning some type of racket.* In Los Angeles they are known as "street people"; in Houston, they call themselves "conkies" (people with processed hair). They have their own distinctive way of life, speech, and earning a living.

In common with other stoics, however, they have "opted out" of the usual American system; they have little interest in the civil rights movement and they have withdrawn from the political and economic struggles which characterize American life. They attempt to live a "cool" life, insensitive to the pains and troubles that come their way.

In their autobiographies, Claude Brown and Malcolm X present the best subjective portraits of the life of cool people.[7] Both men, of course, eventually left the world of hustling. Brown went on to become a college student and Malcolm X, a deviationist from the Muslims, died at the hands of assassins. Nonetheless, the descriptions of their early lives provide some of the best raw material for understanding the "cool cat."

INITIATION AND WAY OF LIFE

Malcolm X, for example, tells of how he drew his own brother into hustling (a process which seems to be quite common):

> After awhile, my brother Reginald had to have a hustle, and I gave much thought to what would be, for him, a good, safe hustle. After he'd learned his own way around, it would be up to him to take risks for himself—if he wanted to make more and quicker money.
>
> The hustle I got Reginald into was very simple. It utilized the psychology of the ghetto jungle. Downtown, he paid the two dollars, or whatever it was, for a regular city peddler's license. Then I took him to a manufacturer's outlet where we bought underwear, cheap rings, watches, all kinds of quick-sale items.

*It is impossible to draw fine distinctions between the "cool" people and others. Some of them, for example, drift into cultist movements such as the Black Muslims. Some respond to life in a violent fashion, as described in Chapter 9. Here we are concerned only with those individuals who spend most of their time simply "hanging out" on the corner, trying one hustle or another.

Watching me work this hustle back in Harlem, Reginald quickly caught on how to go into barbershops, beauty parlors, and bars acting very nervous as he let the customers peep into his small valise of "loot." With so many thieves around anxious to get rid of stolen good-quality merchandise cheaply, many Harlemites, purely because of this conditioning, jumped to pay hot prices for inferior goods. It was perfectly legitimate. It never took long to get rid of a valiseful for at least twice what it had cost.[8]

The authors agree on the process of initiation into the cool life. At an extremely early age (no later than six), friends or even relatives taught them the various "hustles" by which one could earn an easy but illegitimate living.

After his initiation, the cool person graduates into more sophisticated hustles—conning, pimping, thievery, or selling drugs. As John Horton, in his excellent study, *Time and Cool People*, observed: "The woman game was common. As one dude put it, 'If I have a good lady and she's on County, there's always some money to get.' In fact, there is a local expression for getting county money. When the checks come in for child support it's 'mother's day.' So the hustler 'burns' people for money."[9]

Horton intensively studied twenty-five cool people in the Negro area of Venice, California. His research presents the most systematic evidence we have on their style of life. Horton's sample ranged in age from eighteen to twenty-five. In addition to hustling, they held irregular, unskilled jobs. Most had dropped out of school and spent their lives in apparent nonactivity, hanging around on the street. Although the cool people maintained a posture of indifference to pain, they almost continually found themselves in trouble with the police, with their women, or with their employers. As Horton observed:

> The intensity of street life could be gauged in part by the intensity of the "heat" (police trouble). The hotter the street, the fewer the people visible on the street. On some days the set was empty. One would soon learn that there had been a "bust." Freddy had run amok and thrown rocks at a police

car. There had been a leadership struggle; "Big Moe" had been cut up, and the "fuzz" had descended.[10]

For cool people, Horton commented, time has a quite different meaning than for the ordinary resident of the ghetto. Typically, the cool person gets up in the late morning or early afternoon. He drifts down to "the set," talks, gambles, drinks, and looks for "action." "Time is 'dead' when money is tight," Horton noted; "time is alive when and where there is action. It picks up in the evening when everyone moves on the street.... Time is high on Friday nights when the 'eagle flies' and the 'gig' [party] begins."[11]

Being "on time" has no meaning for cool people. In contrast, middle-class Negroes have a great consciousness of the standard time sense. Indeed, the middle-class person often talks jokingly of CPT (Colored People's Time), referring disparagingly to a presumed Negro tendency to be late for appointments. In contrast, Horton found, the cool people had not even heard of CPT.

"Style" and "soul," however, have immense significance for cool people. Style means dressing well, looking tough, understanding other people, appearing inviolate, fearless—and stoical. A cool person has soul when he acts sincerely, warmly, and avoids deceit or hypocrisy.

Horton concluded that cool people were political outsiders: they had little knowledge of political affairs; they did not participate in civil rights activity; they did not vote.

This inactivity, however, hid a great deal of anger. Typically, they approved of the Watts riot, held Malcolm X as their hero, and advocated revolutionary changes in the country.

THE BACKGROUND OF COOL PEOPLE

We know little about why a person chooses this style of life. The evidence is meager: autobiographies, Horton's study, and our own survey of eleven cool people in Houston offer about the only clues. If one puts these sources together, however, a portrait of the cool person emerges. He is young and usually abandons street life before he reaches thirty, by which time he is either in prison or has entered some legitimate occupation. He is from the lower socioeconomic depths of the ghetto, comes from the most disorganized family backgrounds, fails in school, and doesn't find (or, perhaps, want) a job.*

One former member of the Houston cool set, J. D. Sonny Wells, has told in his own words of the environment which produces this response to life.[12] Wells was raised by a prostitute mother and an alcoholic father. He lived in the "red-light" district:

> As a small boy of seven, I knew the taste of cheap bootleg corn liquor and liked it. I knew the district's gamblers, pimps, bootleggers, and other would-be hustlers. I knew the ministers, teachers and deacons of the church who came to the district to do no preaching or teaching. I knew the city and county officials who, in secret, slipped me quarters whenever they came for their share of the "dirty money" or just seeking the favors of the ladies. . . .
>
> I remember the sharp gamblers who spent their spare time hanging around my beautiful mother. They played with me and taught me the tricks of the trade. At nine, I knew how to ink and crimp the other guy's cards and how to carry from three to five dice concealed between my fingers. I remember the flashy clothes of the gamblers and pimps and the sharp automobiles. I recall that I had been very anxious to grow up so that I could be one of them.

Children at school called Wells a "white nigger" because of his skin color and because no one really knew who his father was. At thirteen he was expelled from school because the leader of the crap game in the boy's restroom was from a "good family" and only "*that* woman's boy" could have been responsible. At fifteen he was seduced by a prostitute on the back seat of a car. He soon came to believe that "life is meaningless, that my name was a zero, that whites—a majority, insensitive, brutal, gloating—controlled everything, mostly my destiny."

Predictably, Wells became a member of the cool group in Dallas and Houston. He was an excellent gambler, until liquor

*Clearly, this pattern does not differ significantly from that of the usual juvenile delinquent, except that the "cool" people are normally nonviolent.

deprived his fingers of their dexterity, and then he turned to burglary, theft, and forgery. He avoided violence, except for one incident during an alcoholic "blackout" when he attacked a policeman.

Wells spent many years in prisons. (Once, while he was serving as secretary of the prison A.A. group, guards caught him making home brew—that cost him twenty-one days in solitary on bread and water.) Intermittent confinements did little to change him, for he could always find some new hustle on the outside.

He began his last stretch in prison in 1963:

> I was living with a working girl in Dallas. She was working in a private home and wore her boss lady's jewelry. She would wear a piece of the jewelry and carry it back. One day a ten-carat diamond ring, which costed $3,000, was missing and the boss lady reported the missing ring to the police.
>
> The police came to where we were living and she denied having the ring. After the officers left, I talked to her. . . . "You give me this thing and I'll go and hide it."
>
> When the police returned to look for the ring the second time, they found it in my pocket. I was given four years for receiving and concealing stolen goods.

This escapade ended Wells's career in the cool set. For intangible reasons (Wells gives credit to Dr. George Beto, Director of Corrections in Texas), Wells gave up his old life. Today he is a respected journalist in Houston.

Throughout Wells's unpublished autobiography, *Descent Into Darkness*, a single theme recurs. His life as a cool person was an attempt to achieve "identity," dignity, and a reputation for himself as a man. In this orientation, he is not atypical. As Robert Blauner has written, "the hustler is the relevant manhood model for many ghetto youth."[13] Blauner proceeds to observe, "Despite their differences in class, life style, and political goals, the 'cool cats' in the ghettos, the Black Muslims, the youthful rioters in Watts and other cities, and the civil rights activists are all oriented toward demanding dignity as they see it."[14]

Usually, as in Wells's case, the life of cool people offers only a fleeting sense of dignity. Almost inevitably the police arrest them and they suffer the humiliations of trial and imprisonment. Another strategy of survival, that of the "passive stoic," offers a viable and certainly less dangerous way of responding to ghetto existence.

THE PASSIVE STOIC

"Apathy (with the self-hatred that produces it) is the worst disease of the Negro slum," Charles Silberman has observed.[15] Indeed, as we have noted, about one-third of the Negroes in our sample could be labeled as passive stoics: apathetic, uninvolved, uninformed—committed, if at all, simply to making a living. They find little or no consolation in religion; they eschew the civil rights movement; they do not even bother to lead a "cool" life. They have resigned themselves to fate and accept their destiny without trying to influence their lot in life.

The prevalence of apathy and passivity in the Negro slum should not be surprising. The entire system of American slavery was designed to reduce men to a state of complete dependence. Slave masters did not reward their victims for ambition or initiative, and certainly not for rebelliousness.

Stanley Elkins, in his probing book on the history of slavery, has drawn an illuminating parallel between the American slave system and Nazi concentration camps.[16] In both cases, systematic oppression turned mature adults into passive, servile children. For camp inmates as well as slaves, food became the primary interest in life. For some victims, the authority figure—whether SS guard or slave owner—became somehow really "good." The concentration camps transformed men into passive stoics in a short period of time.

In our random sampling of Houston, we found 179 people (out of 572) who could be considered as passive stoics. They did not participate in the civil rights movement and believed that the movement was going either "too fast" or "about right"; they felt religion had little importance to them; and they believed that human nature and man's fate generally could not be changed.

Mrs. Reagon,* thirty-eight, typified this group. Even though she has a high school education, she has found work only as a servant. She has been married twice; her current husband serves as a janitor in a large store. She adheres to the Baptist religion but seldom attends the church. "That minister," she says, "couldn't influence a flea. He doesn't preach good."

Mrs. Reagon claims to contribute money to the NAACP but, like most of the Houston sample, has never boycotted a store, attended a civil rights rally, or marched in a protest. She disapproves of violence and riots. She places her hope for Negro improvement in education. "George Washington Carver is my hero," she said. In her opinion, human nature will never change; man will not be able to control such phenomena as floods (because "the Bible says these things will come to pass"), and she believes that "life is just a gamble—there is no point in planning ahead since you don't know what can happen."

Mrs. Reagon cannot identify local political leaders, and said, "I'm a Democrat but it doesn't really matter who gets in. They are all lousy."

Despite this presumed lack of concern, Mrs. Reagon's passivity covered a deep sense of outrage. "The thing that makes me maddest," she said, "is when white folks call me a girl when really I am a woman. Sometimes they look at you as if you were dirt, instead of being a real human being." This apparent strange combination of apathy and indignation appeared repeatedly among the outwardly passive group. Indeed, when we compared the passive stoics to "activists"—forty-eight people drawn from the random sample who claimed to have participated often in protests, boycotts, and other demonstrations—few differences in basic attitudes appeared. The apathetic as well as the activist expressed equal distress about the Negro's situation in America, about joblessness, about the need for improvement. Indeed, in some cases, the passive person expressed *more* verbal indignation than did the activist. The

*Fictitious name.

passive stoic, however, confined his grievances within a shell of apathy. The reasons for their inactivity can, in part, be traced to their social background.

BACKGROUNDS OF PASSIVE STOICS

Historically, the activist—or revolutionary—has seldom been drawn from the ranks of aged, uneducated, and unskilled people. This generalization still seems to hold true in Houston:

AGE

	PASSIVES (N:179)	ACTIVISTS (N:48)
15–30	30%	50%
31–40	28	23
Over 40	42	27

EDUCATION

	PASSIVES (N:179)	ACTIVISTS (N:48)
8th grade or less	58%	29%
Some high school	38	37
Some college or more	4	34

OCCUPATION

	PASSIVES (N:179)	ACTIVISTS (N:48)
Unemployed	7%	2%
Unskilled/Semi-skilled	58	48
Skilled	18	19
Housewife	13	17
White-collar/Professional	4	14

One might also predict that women exhibit greater passivity than men, but actually the opposite seems true: 46 per cent of the passive people were women versus 58 per cent of the activists. Perhaps this is one more reflection of the Negro slum's matriarchy; perhaps, also, Negro men experience discrimination more directly than women and surrender more easily in what seems to them a hopeless situation.

Thus, passive people—in Houston, at least—are usually older, less educated, and less skilled men. In certain salient respects, their attitudes distinguish them from the smaller group that actively participates in politics and the civil rights movement.

THE ATTITUDES OF PASSIVE STOICS

Politically, the passive people adhered to a strange admixture of apathy and resentment. They seldom voted. Yet when compared with the activists, they more strongly disapproved of the existing political structure. For example, in describing their attitudes toward the Governor of Texas and the Mayor of Houston, the passives more often condemned these officials specifically for their racial policies than did the activists.

OPINION OF GOVERNOR

	PASSIVES (N:179)	ACTIVISTS (N:48)
General approval	16%	37%
General disapproval	13	14
Disapproval because of racial policies	54	37
Neutral/No opinion	17	12

OPINION OF MAYOR

	PASSIVES (N:179)	ACTIVISTS (N:48)
General approval	14%	23%
General disapproval	18	19
Disapproval because of racial policies	48	29
Neutral/No opinion	20	19

When questioned specifically about Barbara Jordan, the Negro State Senator, the passives gave her surprisingly little support:

OPINION OF NEGRO STATE SENATOR

	PASSIVES (N:179)	ACTIVISTS (N:48)
General approval	39%	64%
General disapproval	18	12
Neutral/No opinion	43	24

In the actual elections, both the mayor and the state senator overwhelmingly carried the Negro precincts. Politically, then, the passives lacked sophistication or simply avoided voting. Beyond this, the passives apparently did not like *anyone* in the power structure, regardless of the color of his skin or the policies he advocated.

Expectedly, the passive people *said* that they were more contented with local conditions in Houston than did the activists. Fifty-two per cent of the passives generally approved of the Houston police force; only 29 per cent of the activists shared this opinion. Sixty-four per cent of the passives but only 35 per cent of the activists approved of the local school system.

Since Houston was in the throes of school desegregation, we asked both groups where they would prefer to send their children: an integrated school or an all-Negro school. The passives seemed relatively less enthusiastic about the prospects of integration:

PREFERENCE IN SCHOOLS

	PASSIVES (N:179)	ACTIVISTS (N:48)
Integrated school	55%	78%
Negro school	21	10
No opinion	24	12

Despite their seeming contentment, the passives (like other-worldly church members) had little trust of other people and little faith that the universe would treat them fairly. Forty-eight per cent of the passives, for example, believed that luck alone determined one's destiny; only 19 per cent of the activists agreed. The passives' opinion about the honesty of other human beings was revealed in their response to a hypothetical situation: "You buy something in a large department store, and discover after leaving you have been shortchanged seventy-five cents. You go back to the sales clerk and you ask for your money. Do you think you will get it back?"

OPINION OF OTHERS' HONESTY

	PASSIVES (N:179)	ACTIVISTS (N:48)
Clerk would refund	42%	63%
Clerk would not refund	42	25
Clerk might refund	16	12

The passive stoics, then, are apathetic in at least several senses of the word. They do not participate in politics; they say they are contented with their position in life; and they put their trust in luck rather than planning. Underneath this façade, however, they apparently feel deeply resentful about the world and tend to distrust other people. For such people, it is but a short step to enter the world of the utterly defeated and to seek escape in such palliatives as alcohol or drugs.

REFERENCES

1. Talcott Parsons, "Full Citizenship for the Negro American?" in *The Negro American*, Talcott Parsons and Kenneth Clark, eds. (Boston: Houghton Mifflin, 1966), p. 738.

2. St. Clair Drake and Horace Clayton, *Black Metropolis* (New York: Harper & Row, 1962), Vol. II, p. 388.

3. St. Clair Drake, "The Social and Economic Status of the Negro in the United States" in *The Negro American, op. cit.*, p. 12.

4. Joseph Fichter, "American Religion and the Negro" in *The Negro American, op. cit.*, p. 412.

5. Stephanie Reuter, "The Long Range Influence of 'Slave' Christianity on Negro Militancy," unpublished paper, Rice University, p. 20.

6. The interviews with Muhammad Ali were not conducted by John Howard.

7. See Claude Brown, *Manchild in the Promised Land* (New York: New American Library, 1965); and Malcolm X, *The Autobiography of Malcolm X* (New York: Grove Press, 1966).

8. Malcolm X, *ibid.*, p. 112.

9. John Horton, "Time and Cool People," *Trans-Action*, Vol. 4, No. 5, April 1967, p. 7.

10. *Ibid.*, p. 7.

11. *Ibid.*, p. 8.

12. J. D. Sonny Wells, *Descent Into Darkness*, unpublished manuscript.

13. Robert Blauner, "The Unique Americans," mimeographed, Berkeley, Calif., p. 12.

14. *Ibid.*, p. 12.

15. Charles Silberman, *Crisis in Black and White* (New York: Random House, 1964), p. 74.

16. Stanley Elkins, *Slavery: A Problem in American Institutional and Intellectual Life* (Chicago: University of Chicago Press, 1959).

CHAPTER 7

THE DEFEATED

William McCord

"I was just born black, poor, and uneducated," a Harlem drug addict told Kenneth Clark, "and you only need three strikes all over the world to be out.... I have nothing to live for but this shot of dope."[1] This man, aged twenty-six, had given up all hope for a "normal" life, a regular job, or a decent marriage with a woman who did not "turn tricks." "Your environment, I read somewhere, is just a mirror of yourself," he said. "So what can I do?... I don't think I could be rehabilitated, you know, not now, in this society."[2] He counted himself as enlisted for life in the ranks of defeated men: those who have fled the harsh realities of life to seek solace in dreams, hallucinations, or the total extinction of feeling.

Surely escapism or complete withdrawal are attractive alternatives for those who must endure the humiliations and brutalities of the ghetto. It is not surprising, therefore, that a relatively high proportion of American Negroes find an outlet for their miseries in drugs, alcohol, or psychotic delusions.

While national statistics seldom reveal a true picture of the situation, almost all studies indicate an uncommon tendency

purpotal

for urban Negroes to seek release in ways disapproved by our society:

• Urban Negro alcoholism rates are two to four times higher than white rates.[*3]

• Urban Negroes account for approximately 60 per cent of identified drug addicts.[4]

• The incidence of Negro psychoses, particularly schizophrenia, exceeds white rates by about 200 per cent.[5]

Whatever the many differences in causation, these three life styles have several characteristics in common. They all represent ways of withdrawing from reality; they are—at least in the eyes of an outside observer—self-destructive; and they are, in one fashion or another, an admission of defeat, a confession that one no longer wishes to confront every-day life. One would expect, then, that American Negroes would also choose the ultimate escape of suicide more frequently than American whites. The opposite is true; Negroes commit suicide about half as often as whites.[6]

To understand why Negroes choose certain solutions to their dilemmas—and avoid a seemingly logical escape route, such as suicide—one must, then, ask three central questions:

1. What causes these particular phenomena *sui generis*?

2. Why do so many Negroes—but still a minority—resort to alcohol or drugs, or suffer psychotic withdrawal, in their attempts to solve their problems? What differentiates them from white Americans who, proportionately, commit suicide more often?

3. What distinguishes the utterly defeated Negroes from the Negro stoics, achievers, and militants who somehow cope with life in the ghetto?

No one can hope to provide answers to these complex questions, without resort to a massive, cradle-to-grave study of thou-

---

*In Houston, although the statistics are far from accurate since police do not record all offenses, the Negro incidence of arrests for drunkenness exceeds the white rate by 50 per cent. Los Angeles and the Bay Area approximate the national rate. Conceivably, since more Houstonians have arrived from rural areas, this difference may reflect a true rural-urban differential.

sands of Americans. For the moment, we can only offer some suggestions based partially on interviews with seventy-five "defeated" people: residents of skid row who seek happiness in a bottle of wine or a shot of heroin. We have also examined the records of Negro suicides and psychotics to see how they differ from the usual ghetto resident.

THE ALCOHOLIC*

"I don't know why I drink," John, a Negro alcoholic, told me, "If you can get me in a hospital, maybe I can quit." Actually, John had been in and out of hospitals and prisons. At times he could stop drinking for as long as six months. Then, a single beer would trigger a year's binge.

John had started drinking at fourteen and, by eighteen, had what he called "drunk complaints." Born on a plantation in Louisiana, he had quit school after the third grade to start picking cotton. He moved to Beaumont, Texas, and then to Houston, working at unskilled jobs in shipyards, iron works, and cafes. He started gambling and learned how to use loaded dice.

John married twice and had five children. One wife left in 1945 because of his drinking and the other deserted him for another man in 1954.

Now, at the age of forty-three, he finds himself alone in life. His mother occasionally takes him off the streets and even gives him money for liquor. He drinks anything he can find. He prefers whiskey, but usually settles for a cheap wine.

He lives under a bridge or, in the colder seasons, in jail. "These cops, they aren't really so bad. Sometimes I'm freezing,

---

*Definitions of what constitutes "alcoholism" are notoriously vague. We define as alcoholic a person who has been publicly labeled as such (by arrest, incarceration, or hospitalization) or who defines himself as alcoholic by, say, membership in A.A.). This definition leaves out "secret drinkers" and others who might be considered as excessive drinkers by one standard or another. The ghetto is very tolerant of heavy drinking—consequently, many Negroes who might be called alcoholic in white society are considered "normal" in the ghetto. On the other hand, middle-class whites, particularly women, are better able economically to hide the effects of excessive drinking.

eating dog food, and I'm so drunk I can't see straight—then the cops bring me in. Sometimes, if I'm really down, I just take myself to jail." Jail has indeed become a haven for him. He has 300 arrests on his record. The police have made him a trusty and, whenever he re-enters jail, he goes back to a relatively plush job as a cook. In jail he does not drink, even though home brew is readily available. "I just don't know why I get rid of the habit here. I feel I don't need it." This pattern has often been noted. In the sheltered, supervised, dependent environment of the jail, the "revolving door" drunk loses his desire for liquor. As soon as he works off his fine and leaves jail he returns to drinking.

Why did he become a drunk? John himself doesn't know. "I used to blame everybody—particularly you whites," he said, "but now I know it's just in my own heart. I like to get away from it all. I guess I drink to forget the mess of my life." His father drank heavily, his mother nips about a half pint of whiskey a day, and his four brothers also drink. John does not, however, regard them as alcoholic.

John has gradually disengaged himself from ordinary society. He passed through the stages typical of the Negro alcoholics whom we interviewed. In his very early youth he engaged in heavy social drinking (usually Saturday-night binges); by his late adolescence he had begun drinking more steadily, more heavily, earlier in the day, and by himself; by his late twenties he had lost his job and his family, and had started living on skid row.

Skid row itself provides a total way of life for the committed habitué: a new language, status distinctions, and new means of earning a living—from being a "mission stiff" to John's pattern of depending on police largesse. Samuel Wallace, in his definitive study, *Skid Row As a Way of Life*, has aptly summarized this segment of American society:

> As the only fully acculturated member of skid row subculture, the drunk—including the various sub-types such as the wino, the lush, and the rubbydub—lives his life totally within the deviant community. He sacrifices everything to the drinking practices and needs of the group. The push of community con-

demnation and the pull of drinking companions, plus a habitual desire for drinking have combined to structure his life around alcohol. . . . In his own eyes as well as in the eyes of others, skid-rowers and non-skid-rowers alike, he has become a totally committed member of a deviant group.[7]

For the Negro, skid-row life offers a unique attraction: an experience of true companionship between black and white. The great majority of drunks eat, sleep, and drink together; they are comrades, even though they find their companionship in misery. "We all help each other out," John observed. "It don't matter whether you are colored or white. If anyone has got a bottle he shares it with the other men—no matter who they are." It is an ironic commentary on America that the bleary drunks of skid row achieve a degree of brotherhood which the rest of our polite society cannot tolerate.

What draws one man rather than another to this milieu? Some answers can be proposed that seem to apply to any American, regardless of skin color. In a prior study it was possible to trace both Negro and white alcoholics from childhood, *before* they became alcoholic, into adulthood.[8] We were also able to compare the alcoholic to another group of "normal" people and criminals who had been similarly observed in childhood. The major characteristics differentiating the alcoholic, black or white, from others were these:

1. *Family Background—General Stress:* The potential alcoholic typically underwent a variety of frustrating experiences. He was more likely, for example, to have been raised in a family disrupted by a high degree of conflict, basic disagreement, incest, or illegitimacy.

2. *Family Background—Erratic Satisfaction of Dependency Needs:* One of the major forces that seemed to lead a person under high stress to express his anxiety in alcoholism was erratic frustration of his dependency needs. Typically, the prealcoholic had been raised by a mother who alternated between loving indulgence and overt rejection, who was likely to see herself as a "martyr," and who tended to react to crises in an escapist manner.

3. *Family Background—Inadequate Male Model:* The

potential alcoholic's father tended to be antagonistic to his child and to escape—through alcohol or other means—from the pressures of critical situations.

4. *Childhood Personality:* In childhood and adolescence the prealcoholic seemed to be supermasculine, aggressive, outwardly self-confident, and highly independent. One can reasonably assume, however, that this façade of self-reliant manhood masked conflict and anxiety.

5. *Adult Personality:* For a person who outwardly appears independent but inwardly craves warmth and security alcohol provides an attractive outlet. When intoxicated he feels secure and omnipotent. His strong desire to be dependent is satisfied. At the same time, he can maintain his image of independence and self-reliance. The hard drinker in American society is pictured as tough, extroverted, and manly—exactly the masculine virtues the alcoholic strives to incorporate into his own self-image.

6. *The Drift Into Alcoholism:* The alcoholic's almost continuous state of intoxication naturally interferes with many other aspects of his life. His occupational efficiency falters, he loses his role as the "rock" of the family, and his image of himself as an independent male is undermined in various ways. He eventually becomes a social outcast, and repressed traits of dependency, inferiority, and passivity become manifest; his attempt to maintain a façade of independent manliness collapses.

Clearly, Negro ghetto life strongly reinforces exactly those factors which lead to alcoholism in the general population. As we have previously contended, Negroes in our culture experience an unusually high degree of stress; they are often raised in families where the father neither exemplifies nor enforces the responsibilities of the male role; Negro boys often react to their confusion by creating an independent façade; and, in adulthood, white society continually undermines the Negro's tenuous concept of manhood.

Undoubtedly, other specific elements of the American Negro role contribute to the high incidence of drunkenness. The few studies in which drinking patterns in the Negro ghetto have been examined indicate that the tavern, as much as the church, serves as an important community institution. As Muriel Sterne has commented: "Although church and tavern represent the extremes of respectable and nonrespectable behavior, they serve analogous functions: each is an accepted area for seeking individual recognition and for relatively uncircumscribed behavior, provides a mode of relief from problems, attracts a regular clientele to customary, ritual-like attendance, and is run by and for Negroes."[9]

Although middle-class Negroes and some religiously oriented women may disapprove of this saloon tradition, lower-class men find release, companionship, and tolerance at the tavern. Consequently, heavy drinking, particularly on weekends, has become a generally accepted part of ghetto life.

Further, it appears that American Negroes tend more often to use alcohol for utilitarian reasons—to relieve anxiety, to ease fatigue, to get away from life. In a study of drinking among urban Negro youth, Lee Rainwater found that the straightforward purpose of drinking was to become "high."[10] Similarly, a TAT (Thematic Apperception Test) analysis showed that Negro students (as opposed to white students) regarded alcohol primarily as a tool for "modifying reality" rather than as a way of promoting conviviality.[11] This orientation, as well as the greater tolerance in slums for intoxication, explains some of the patterns of Negro drinking.

Other differences between white and Negro drinking may well have significance. Negroes tend to begin drinking earlier in life. In one sample of urban teenagers, almost everyone drank (94 per cent of boys and 91 per cent of girls).[12] And, as might be expected, teenage Negro drinking is much more prevalent in cities than in rural areas.

Proportionately, many more Negro women become alcoholics than white women,[13] and this is particularly true for the more highly educated groups. Such a discrepancy should be expected: since more Negro women bear the burdens of a "man's role," their vulnerability to alcoholism is greater.

One other difference in Negro and white drinking patterns

deserves attention. A major study of 588 cases of homicide revealed that alcohol played some part in 70 per cent of Negro murders as opposed to 49 per cent of white murders.[14] It may well be that alcohol permits the expression of the rage that so many Negroes feel, while the causes for white homicide go far below the level of the inhibitions released by alcohol.

Our small survey of Negro alcoholics in Houston revealed a few more clues concerning background and attitudes of skid-row residents and, in addition, confirmed some prior impressions:

• About 60 per cent of the group were under age thirty, a rather strikingly low age for confirmed skid-row people. As in John's case, they had "become men" early in life and manifested this, partially, by hard drinking.

• Predictably, skid-rowers expressed a deep fatalism about life. Sixty-five per cent, for example, said that "luck" determined success in life.

• Skid-rowers reported an unusually high rate of family disorganization in childhood. Only 39 per cent claimed that their parents had lived together. Also, 96 per cent reported that they had been punitively treated as children.

• As could be expected, the alcoholics had no contact with the usual institutions of American society. Only one man claimed that religion was important to him; only four said that they had been associated in any way with the civil rights movement.

• Although skid-row people are stereotyped as passive and nonviolent, the interviewees often openly expressed their rage against the white world. About 50 per cent believed that the Watts riot had "helped the Negro cause"; 88 per cent said that violence is justified in defending Negro rights; 100 per cent believed that whites looked down on Negroes.

One function of alcohol, then, may be to appease the great anger that Negro skid-rowers apparently feel toward white society. It may be that those Negroes who experience the greatest feelings of injustice are most likely to seek escape from their sense of powerlessness by taking to alcohol.

THE DRUG ADDICT

In some urban ghettos, particularly Harlem, narcotics addiction has become a major pathway of escape for young Negro men. Kenneth Clark has reliably estimated that some 25,000 to 36,000 addicts live in Harlem. And Claude Brown, a most perceptive writer who was reared there, believes that narcotics addiction has reached epidemic proportions. By 1957, Brown writes, "The only thing that seemed to matter, to my generation in Harlem, was drugs. Everybody looked at it as if it were inevitable. If you asked about somebody, a cat would say, 'Oh, man, he's still all right. He's goin' pretty good. He's not strung out yet.' "*14

This drift of some Negroes into addiction represents a distinctive historical change. At the turn of the century only one minority group, the Chinese, used drugs heavily. Moreover, the incidence among white females was extraordinarily high: women addicts used to outnumber men.

Today addiction has become indelibly merged with the ghetto subculture,† and yet even in the most deprived areas, the extent of the addiction has undoubtedly been overestimated. As with so many American social problems, a variety of myths have sprung up concerning this one. Any reasonable discussion of Negro drug addiction should start by clearing up several prevalent misconceptions.

*Recent reports from the Federal Narcotics Bureau indicate a 15 per cent decrease in Negro drug addiction—a hopeful sign that perhaps the newest generation has learned something of the ravages of drug addiction since Claude Brown's time.

†Since the urban Negro subculture is one that discourages a strong drive for achievement or intense, competitive striving, one reason for the high rate of Negro drug addiction may, perhaps, be traced to the culture itself. Abraham Wikler has convincingly demonstrated that civilizations such as the Chinese and East Indian, with their passive, accepting, fatalistic ideals, have traditionally been tolerant of drug use, but not of alcohol.[16] Conversely, civilizations that have aggressive, competitive, striving goals generally have disapproved of narcotics but tolerated alcohol. If one thinks of the Negro subculture in America as resembling in some respects the East Indian, Wikler's thesis may help explain the relatively high incidence of drug use by Negroes. Yet the Negro subculture is also tolerant of the use of alcohol. This contradiction, however, can possibly be explained by the ambiguity of the Negro subculture, with its mixture of different life styles.

First, for America as a whole, drug addiction is *not* increasing; in all probability it has declined since the turn of the century (except in urban Negro ghettos). In 1915, the year after the Harrison Act declared opiate addiction illegal, responsible scientists estimated that 215,000 Americans were addicts; by 1922 the number had dropped to 110,000 (undoubtedly most of those who gave up the habit were not true addicts); by 1964 the Federal Bureau of Narcotics reported only 55,899 known addicts in the United States—a figure that, however open to criticism, is the best available and shows a declining rate of addiction.

Second, drug addiction does *not* cause crime; it may, in fact, decrease it. Many addicts—about two-thirds—are, of course, criminals. The "junkie" is likely to rob or shoplift or burglarize or turn to prostitution. But the best studies of the subject show that drug addiction tends to redirect the delinquent from more serious crimes toward those that will bring him the money to buy drugs. In all probability drug addicts are less likely to commit really violent crimes such as rape, assault, or murder. The "flattening" effect of heroin often causes sexual desire to disappear and also reduces aggressiveness. In some recorded cases, addiction has actually eliminated vicious criminal tendencies.

Third, drug addiction *per se* does not seriously injure either the mind or the body, as do barbiturates, alcohol, or tobacco. Even after fifty years of addiction, in some cases, no discernible physical or mental harm has been traced to the use of narcotics. Further, the habit can be cured. Although hospital treatment has been discouraging (about a 90 per cent rate of failure among adult addicts), Synanon, a group similar to Alcoholics Anonymous, has reported a high degree of success. Studies of teen-age addicts show that about 26 per cent spontaneously cure themselves. Cured or not, however, many addicts continue to work—indeed, some deteriorate only when taken off drugs.

The average drug addict is an unhappy person plagued by a sense of futility and aimlessness. Typically, he comes from a highly deprived background (about 97 per cent of youthful addicts come from families affected by divorce, desertion, or open hostility among their members). He tries narcotics at an early age, usually by sixteen. Normally he takes his first dose at the encouragement of a friend rather than as the result of a "pusher's" influence. For such young people—passive, dependent, loveless—the drug serves to reduce intolerable anxiety.

The way of life of the Negro addict can be illustrated in the case of a man I shall call Otis. When I first met Otis, he had voluntarily committed himself to a hospital in the hope of breaking his heroin habit. He was suffering withdrawal pains—intense cramps, chills, and fainting spells—since he had been in the hospital for only two days. Although only twenty-eight, he had been jailed many times for theft, armed robbery, burglary, and selling drugs. This time, he hoped, life would change for him.

He had started using heroin, almost by chance, six years earlier. He had been on a drinking spree with two companions. They took him to their apartment and had already made a "fix" for him. "I didn't want to be no chicken, so I tried the 'shit,' " he said, "Anyway, I thought one time couldn't hurt you." He enjoyed getting high so much that he immediately began to seek his own supply of drugs. "It's hard to describe what it's like. At first, you go way up, everything is lovely. Then you get numb and rosy. The world stops still. Man, you think you can do anything in the world—like climbing Mt. Everest." He treated his wife to the narcotic and soon she too shared his obsession.

At first Otis could afford to purchase his supply. Although he came from the most deprived section of Houston, he had finished high school, received technical training, and was earning a good salary as a fiberglass journeyman. "The junk didn't bother me when I worked. I did everything as it should be." By the time I met him, however, he needed a cap of heroin a day, costing some $250 a month. He had lost his job primarily because he had to spend so much time searching for drug pushers. "I just had to keep moving to find them. If the police cracked down, it took me eight or ten hours to find my man. When I didn't have the junk, I didn't care about nothing else but getting him. Some days I wouldn't eat nothing." (His weight dropped from 210 to 150.)

Although he already had a record as a juvenile delinquent, Otis began stealing more to pay for his habit. His wife became angry with him. "You know, when you got the hunk in you, you just don't want no women, no nothing," he said; "that made her mad." His wife dropped the drug habit and, together with Otis' mother and his three children, pleaded with him to stop. He had reached the point where heroin no longer made him high; it simply kept him feeling "normal."

When he finally brought himself to the hospital for treatment, Otis attributed his "cure" both to his wife's influence and to a chance encounter with a sixty-two-year-old addict. "When I saw that bum," he recalled, "I just suddenly didn't want to be like him. He was dirty all over. But I knew I was really just the same." Whether Otis can, in fact, cure himself cannot be predicted—but the discouraging national figures on hospitalization make one pessimistic.

Otis could give few reasons for his addiction. Like most addicts, he blamed the drug itself: "Once you taste it, you can't quit." He had a vague awareness that the simple fact of being Negro might have contributed to his problem. "You know," he said, "colored men feel sort of empty, sort of useless. The junk makes you feel important." Claude Brown has recorded the same feeling with an ex-addict who joined the Black Muslims:

> "The junkies have to use drugs, man, to stand this life. I couldn't do it myself, man, without using drugs. I don't see how you do it. Everybody with a little bit of sensitivity would have to use something or else kill himself. . . . They ain't got nobody to look up to but that white god. That's hard to accept, man. Can you imagine being a Negro in a place where the only Supreme Being is a white god, and he's in the white people's corner, and the white people are fucking over you? . . . You might as well kill yourself."[17]

The theme of death recurs often in discussions with Negro addicts, for in fact going on a "nod" is a way of completely extinguishing feeling. This feeling is aptly described in James

Mills's sympathetic report, "The World of Needle Park," in which are recorded the interminable conversations of addicts concerning what produces the "best high":

> Do you know what the best high *really* is? The voice was serious. Everyone turned and stayed very quiet to hear, maybe, of a new kind of high that was better than heroin, better than anything else. The best high—the voice was low and somber— is death. Silence, man, that's outta sight, that's somethin' else. Yeah, no feelin' at all. Everyone agreed. The best high of all was death.[18]

Certainly addicts seek an elusive Nirvana. And Negro addicts in particular have every reason to escape into a world without feeling.

Many Negroes, if not a majority, have a chance at least to try drugs, since in certain sections of the ghetto exposure to drug use is almost inevitable. In his comprehensive study of Harlem, Isidor Chein found that 45 per cent of *eighth-grade* boys indicated they personally knew a heroin user, about 40 per cent claimed to have seen a person shooting heroin, and 10 per cent said that they had already tried the drug themselves.[19] Despite the opportunity, the fact remains that only a minority of Negroes use drugs and only a tiny portion have become addicted. Since the majority of urban Negroes are exposed to drug use, the most pertinent issue, then, is what differentiates the Negro drug addict from the Negro nonaddict.

Two important studies offer some answers to this question. Isidor Chein and his colleagues have done a massive investigation of 1,844 juvenile addicts in New York and compared them to nonaddicts.[20] John Fort intensively examined a different sample, 100 young male heroin addicts at the Public Health Service Hospital in Lexington, Kentucky.[21] In spite of some contradictions between their studies, Chein and Fort arrived at strikingly similar conclusions.

Most generally, Chein found that Negro users (both delinquent and nondelinquent) came from more economically deprived areas than Negro nonusers. Their homes were typically located in the most crowded and dilapidated section of the city. Fort, on the other hand, found that his Negro patients had not generally suffered from real poverty, although most came from slum areas. Chein's findings may come closer to the truth, since his sample represented a cross section of the entire population of young drug addicts in New York.

Although a relatively higher level of socioeconomic deprivation may be associated with Negro drug addiction, neither researcher was satisfied with explaining the problem on this gross level. In probing the familial environments of addicts, both studies indicated that Negro addicts came from pathological backgrounds. Almost invariably the addicts' parents were divorced, separated, or openly hostile toward each other. Usually the father was absent or, if present, rejected his son. "The mothers of these patients," Fort observed, "were as significant by their ubiquitous and all-embracing presence as the fathers were by their absence."[22] The mothers either overindulged their sons or were highly overprotective. Usually the mothers had vague or contradictory standards for disciplining their children and, according to Fort, if they did set goals for their sons, their aspirations far exceeded what the child could be expected to accomplish.

These studies suggest that the typical Negro addict has enormous difficulty in "becoming a man" and that it is this confusion about his sexual role that lies at the heart of the problem. Fort, discussing Negro patients, puts it this way:

> Many of them had been reared in an atmosphere in which they constantly heard from their mothers or mother surrogates (frequently grandmothers) violent recriminations against men, especially against their fathers, who had in most cases more or less deserted them. The resulting engram of masculinity in their minds was usually one of hostile, evil identification. The mothers often fostered a considerable sort of dependency which later on increased the young man's guilt over being a man.[23]

Fort believes that many Negro addicts hide their confusion by becoming aggressive members of street gangs and violently alienated from society:

> Addiction seemed to offer a way of escaping from some of the unhappiness caused by the aggressive feelings. Most of the

Negro patients had strong ambitions but an equally strong bent not to succeed. Success amounted to a destruction of their justification for turning their hostility against society and perhaps also represented a betrayal of the whole racial group for the same reason. Many Negro patients had, upon achieving considerable success in artistic lines, immediately begun using drugs and had sunk rapidly into utter failure.[24]

But why do Negro addicts choose the so obviously damaging outlet of heroin? (The frequent exposure of ghetto people to addicts also teaches them early in life that addiction is an expensive, horrifying habit.) In background, the addicts rather closely resemble the Negro alcoholic or, as we shall show, the Negro schizophrenic. Why, then, this particular choice of heroin?

R. Knight has explained part of the difference.[25] Knight, in studying his Menninger Clinic patients, made the usual observation that the alcoholic presents a front of well developed "pseudomasculinity." As we have previously noted, the alcoholic tends to be loud, extroverted, and a "good fellow." Among drug addicts, on the other hand, "the strong pseudomasculine defense was rare, and most of the patients did not appear to have begun taking drugs to prove their 'masculinity.' "[26] The typical drug addict appears sensitive, interested in artistic matters, docile—in a word, feminine. The addict, it appears, gives in to his wish to be feminine while the alcoholic remains in conflict.

The specific differential between Negro addicts and other types of Negro escapists may, then, be traced to their feminine orientation and to the pharmacological effect of heroin. Since heroin deadens sexual desire—and since most addicts appear to feel great ambivalence about expressing their urges in the usual heterosexual manner—the choice of drugs may be due to a wish to avoid male-female entanglements. This is, undoubtedly, only one explanation of the disorder, but it may be the key to explaining why one Negro—a victim of poverty, a matriarchal family, and other pathological influences—becomes addicted to heroin while others who are superficially similar in background and character choose other escape routes.

THE PSYCHOTIC

Another form of withdrawal for the Negro whom the ghetto has crippled is psychosis, a painful world of delusions and hallucinations. One hardly "chooses" this path in the same way that one decides to take drugs, to drink, or even to commit suicide. Rather, the person involuntarily descends—either slowly or overnight—into a tormented dream world where reality takes on entirely new forms.

A mass of research has demonstrated that the poor urban Negro succumbs at least twice as frequently as do whites to schizophrenia.[27] These repeated findings must, however, be viewed with some caution. Whites, for example, as with alcoholism, can better afford to hide their condition. Some southern judges have a demonstrated tendency to commit Negroes to mental hospitals more often than whites. And, too, the term "paranoid" or "paranoid schizophrenia" may be applied too hastily since it is quite natural for Negroes "to see hostility in the environment.... We must guard against calling the Negro paranoid when he actually lives in an environment that persecutes him."[28]

Indeed, some studies flatly contradict the prevailing impression that Negroes suffer from more mental illness than whites. E. G. Jaco examined incidence rates of psychoses in Texas and noted that white rates actually exceeded those of Negroes. *[29] Nonetheless, the great majority of studies focusing on urbanized Negroes consistently reflect a higher rate of Negro psychoses.

What creates this tendency to have a complete personality breakdown? No one can propose a final answer since no consensus has been reached about the general causes of functional psychoses.

A few scientists attribute the disorder entirely to genetic and biochemical causes. This theory does not aid in explaining the Negro-white differential since most experts have found the

---

*In this chapter, we are examining so-called "functional" disorders, such as schizophrenia. Organic brain damage accounts for many illnesses, and perhaps this explains the discrepancy between Jaco's study and others.

genetic potential for mental illness distributed equally throughout the world.[30] And, in any case, Negro and white Americans
have a high proportion of similar genes in their gene pools.[31]

The majority of scholars believe that some type of genetic
factor—as yet undefined—does exist, but that environmental
factors trigger the disease. It seems to be these social
patterns—low economic status, a disturbed family structure,
racial discrimination—that account for the higher rate of Negro
mental disorder.

Two major studies have demonstrated beyond reasonable
doubt that a lower-class person, white or black, has a much
greater chance of being labeled as "crazy." August Hollingshead
and Fritz Redlich, in their classic book *Social Class and Mental
Illness*, examined a New Haven sample that included not only
hospital and clinic patients but also those who received care
from a private physician.[32] The researchers noted that lower-
class people become ill more frequently than those from the
upper strata and, once hospitalized, more often remained in a
chronically ill state. Considering only the lower class, they
found that Negro mental illness only slightly exceeded white
disorders.

A similar study in Manhattan utilized a questionnaire in
detecting signs of mental "impairment" in a sample of 1,700
New Yorkers. Thirty per cent of upper-class people were rated
as "well" compared to only 5 per cent of the lowest stratum.[33]
Even allowing for methodological biases (perhaps a tendency
for middle-class observers to view certain types of behavior
accepted in the lower class as "odd"), the evidence is overwhelming that urban poverty in America correlates highly
with mental disease. This finding partially explains the greater
propensity for urban Negroes—who are, of course, members of
the lower class—to fall ill.

On another level, various studies suggest that the Negro
family structure may be particularly conducive to psychosis. In
one longitudinal study, for example, it was possible to trace the
familial backgrounds of twelve schizophrenics from the age of
nine (before their illness) until their early thirties.[34] The subjects, both Negro and white, were matched to a "normal"

sample on the basis of age, sex, urban residence, several "social" factors (parental social class and ethnic group), for "heredity" (the psychiatric condition of the parents), and for certain "physical" characteristics (glandular and neurological status)—all variables which, at one time or another, have been demonstrated to be correlated with psychoses.

The results indicated that the prepsychotics were typically raised in an environment directed by an overprotective, smothering mother and were, in one way or another, forced into emotional dependence on her. Their fathers were either absent or appeared to be passive, relatively "deviant," ineffectual figures who left control of the family in the mother's hands and who showed few signs of active affection for their sons.

Theoretically, one can argue that this particular type of home has three major effects on a son:

1. The child is encouraged—indeed, forced—to become exceptionally dependent. He receives few rewards for independent behavior and little or no training in coping with problems unaided by his mother. Presumably this leads him to view dependent relationships as the normal form of human interaction and to develop a set of expectations that other human beings should and will treat him in a dependent fashion.

2. The child is deprived of a stable masculine model, and therefore does not have a responsible model of manhood that might serve to ameliorate the effects of the mother-child relationship. Instead, if he identifies with his father at all, he is presented with a model of passivity and withdrawal.

3. Because of this relatively sheltered existence—and the feelings of inadequacy that it apparently engenders—such a boy lacks training in human interaction. He is not allowed to participate in a variety of roles, to gain knowledge of others' reactions, or to practice different techniques for mastering his environment.

When he reaches adulthood, the prepsychotic is forced, by the nature of our society, to undergo a series of severe dislocations. Eventually, by death or separation, he is deprived of his dominating mother and he is unlikely to find a completely satisfying replacement for her. He is confronted with a number of situations—dating, marriage, military service, a career—for which he is ill trained. His response in the face of these demands for independence, responsibility, and masculinity is, presumably, a compound of confusion and fear.

It would seem only natural, therefore, that such a person would attempt to recapture the dependent relationship, either in actuality or in fantasy. Thus, by this interpretation, a psychosis is fundamentally an attempt to re-establish an early dependent environment, the only kind for which he has been trained and in which he feels relatively comfortable and secure. Unprepared to meet crises and perhaps hampered by genetic predisposition, he crumbles in the face of problems and seeks to return to a symbolic state of maternal domination—a condition for which he has been rewarded.

Unfortunately, because of the matriarchal nature of the Negro subculture, this "psychosis-producing" family is found very frequently. This factor—when added to the objective burdens of racial discrimination and low social status—may well help to explain the high incidence of mental illness of Negroes.

Viewing all the pathological factors in the Negro subculture has led one perceptive observer to ask, "Why don't all Negro men become schizophrenic?" The very fact that such a question can be formulated, psychiatrist Robert Coles has written, "suggests at once some of the problems facing both Negroes and social scientists. We do not know for certain the cause (or causes) of schizophrenia; but we do feel that consistently disorganized, brittle, tense, fearful parents in some way influence its development in their children. It does not seem fatuous, therefore, to inquire why *all* Negro men are not schizophrenic."[35]

One important study offers a plausible answer to this question and to the related issue of why a person withdraws in this fashion rather than through drugs, alcohol, or suicide. Seymour Parker and Robert Kleiner have conducted a large-scale investigation of the Negro mentally ill in Philadelphia, as well as a group of average Negro citizens.[36] They found that the mentally diseased person set unreasonably high goals for himself, and then when he could not achieve these aspirations experienced a great deal of stress. Rates of mental illness were highest

in those groups which had objectively achieved high occupational status as well as in those who were in the lowest occupational category. For those who were descending in social
status—say, by taking a job with a lower income—the chances
for mental illness were particularly high. Reasonably, Parker
and Kleiner interpret their findngs as confirming Robert Merton's theory that high rates of deviant behavior occur in situations where people are expected to "succeed" but where the
means for fulfilling their hopes are limited.[37] The Negro community, like the rest of America, generally accepts an ethic of
success, but for those who really try to achieve this goal it soon
becomes apparent that a "job ceiling" has been set. It is at this
point, apparently, that an extreme withdrawal from reality
begins.

We can hypothesize, then, that the Negro who collapses in a
psychotic state is a person who shares the American middle-
class dream but is frustrated in his search for fulfillment. He
differs in this sense, therefore, from the drug addict or alcoholic
since these avenues of escape are denied to those who wish to
lead "respectable" lives and strive to become copies of "the
man in the gray flannel suit."

Parker and Kleiner further discovered that native-born Philadelphia Negro adults—who presumably had become more
accustomed to the city than the rural migrant, or even migrants
from other cities—and young people were more highly suscepti-
ble to mental illness. This is indeed a discouraging finding, for
it suggests that the wave of urban migration—particularly
among young people—will lead only to further disillusionment
and greater mental illness.

THE SUICIDE

Any discussion of mental illness, defeatism, or escapism in the
Negro subculture must deal with a central problem: why do
Negroes take certain escape routes—which are, in reality, a slow
death—but avoid the final "solution" of suicide? Scholars have

almost totally neglected this paradox, and existing general theories of suicide hardly explain it.

Emile Durkheim's classic theory of suicide attributes the act partially to a condition of anomie—a social situation of normlessness, emptiness, apathy, and meaninglessness.[38] These conditions certainly prevail in the ghetto and yet the incidence of self-destruction remains low.*

A related position is that suicide results when social disorganization pervades a region. Thus, for example, some studies show that suicide reaches its peak in parts of a city where mental illness, divorce, and drug addiction are highest.[39] Again, this generalization does not apply to Negroes.

Other authors of the same persuasion have shown that population mobility correlates with suicide.[40] But since Negroes are perhaps the most highly mobile of Americans, this theory does not explain the facts either.

Andrew Henry and James Short have contended that suicides take place when people have high social status, weak relationships with others, and live in a culture that does not strongly prohibit suicide.[41] Once more the low incidence of Negro suicide cannot be fitted into the framework.

Admittedly, statistics concerning suicide cannot be trusted. In Catholic countries, for example, acts of self-destruction may be hidden from public view because of the family's shame. In America, as Jack Gibbs has pointed out, "the idea that non-whites . . . are 'naturally' immune to suicide is incompatible with the fact that certain groups of them may have a rate 189 times that of a particular segment of the white population."[42] Gibbs, of course, deals with "selected extreme cases." Still, urbanized Negroes in Seattle have a suicide rate of 10.2 per 100,000 while Mississippi whites kill themselves at a rate of 9.7 per 100,000. These anomalies should be taken into consideration by sociologists who examine the problem.

Nonetheless, study after study has demonstrated that the white rate of suicide, in general, greatly exceeds the Negro rate.

---

*An argument could legitimately be made that ghetto life does have some solidarity and mutual aid. If that were true, then Durkheim's theory of "altruistic suicide" might possibly apply.

The difference varies among the cities we have studied: in Los Angeles, white suicides exceed Negro suicides by about 100 per cent, while in Houston the rate is about 900 per cent greater for whites.

Why does this differential exist? Popular but too facile explanations have been proposed. It used to be said, for example, that rural people seldom committed suicide—and thus one could explain Negroes' "immunity" in terms of their once-rural background. But the facts are that Negroes now reside predominantly in cities and, in any case, the rural-urban gap in suicide rates has all but disappeared.

Some explain the difference by a simple recipe: all people feel aggressive, but some turn the hostility inward and some outward. Since Negroes proportionately commit homicide more often than whites, their destructive urges need not be turned against themselves. This explanation does not go far in explaining the phenomenon. As Alex Pokorny, among others, has shown, those who commit suicide differ radically in background and character from those who commit homicide.[43] They are not just the same type of person expressing aggression in apparently diverse (although "really" similar ways) but rather utterly different kinds of people.

Other scholars have offered other plausible, if unproved, explanations. Few Negroes, for example, hold high-status anxiety-producing jobs, and thus this particular form of stress does not affect many Negroes. As we have noted, other forms of "escape" are relatively more open to Negroes and, consequently, a man who might have committed suicide will take the path, say, of shooting heroin. The Baptist faith so prevalent among Negroes, with its emphasis on eternal salvation, may also serve as a deterrent. And the Negro subculture itself may generally act to prevent suicide in that the cultural emphasis on bravery has led to the rather common folk saying that "suicide is the white man's way of dying."

However inadequate our present state of knowledge, we believe that some clues to the nature of Negro suicide may be found in the case histories of the sixty-seven Negroes who committed suicide in Houston between 1957 and 1966.

Certain facts stand out about the Negro suicides:

• The Negro suicide rate was not notably affected by age in Houston, although the white rate steadily increased among older people. Since Negro suicides reached their peak between the ages of thirty and forty, at the very least this finding suggests that the suffering of old age played little part in motivating Negro self-destruction.

• Negro males more often used violent means (*e.g.*, firearms) to commit suicide than relatively mild ways of self-destruction (*e.g.*, sleeping pills). About 87 per cent of Negro suicides in Houston shot themselves as opposed to about 60 per cent of white suicides.

• Despite the general pattern of suicidal persons, Negro suicides were more often combined with the murder of another person. About 25 per cent of Negro suicides also entailed homicide compared to less than 4 per cent of white suicides.

The most salient characteristics of Negro suicide are perhaps best revealed in the case history of Glenn, a rather typical representative of the Negro suicide sample in Houston.

At the age of thrity-three Glenn shot himself. He had previously threatened suicide because, in his words, "everybody was against me." He had been raised in a large family. His father deserted the home when the child was an infant. In 1936 his mother became an hysterical aphasic during a hail storm. Although she suffered no organic damage, it was two years before her power of speech returned.

Outwardly Glenn appeared very normal. He completed high school with distinction and then joined the Air Force in 1946 with the intention of becoming a pilot. He served honorably (but as a cook and mechanic) until discharge in 1949. Upon the strong urging of his mother, he entered college and, six years later, graduated with a master's degree in psychology. During his college years he waited on tables at various Houston clubs and restaurants, a career he continued even after receiving his master's degree. His family wanted him to become a vocational counselor but he could not find such a job.

Glenn was married in 1959 to a woman who had previously borne a child by an unknown man, but left her in 1961 after they had two children of their own. He felt guilty about the desertion but also felt that circumstances had compelled it.

In 1961 his mother telephoned from California that she was sick, helpless, and in need of someone to care for her. Glenn volunteered to help her and went to Los Angeles for six months. Later he blamed his brothers and sisters: "My mother was bad off. She couldn't do much for herself. It was a dirty trick to play on me. She was just crazy. They [the siblings] led me to believe my mother was dying. . . . They wanted to shift the responsibility to me. . . . The older kids wanted the responsibility on me."

Glenn returned to Houston but stayed away from his wife, children, and brothers. By this point his wife had started to "run around" with other men. In 1962 he moved in briefly with a sister but soon began complaining that she was trying to poison him. Glenn became tearful, depressed, and suspicious that "everyone was watching him. He applied for various jobs but was not hired. On one application that requested his name, he wrote, "RUB . . . ask me to fight."

Late in 1962 his brother brought him to a local VA hospital. Glenn would not admit to mental illness but said that his stomach ached and that he could not sleep. At the hospital he received medication, group therapy, and job counseling. He seemed to improve and left the hospital, but in 1963 he killed himself.

In many ways Glenn conformed to the usual national pattern for suicides. He was isolated, divorced, male, forlorn, and mentally disturbed. Yet he differed from the common mold in several significant ways. Compared to most white suicides, he was young. He had given up all hope for happiness when he was in his thirties. Perhaps more importantly, he had objectively achieved a very high educational status compared to fellow Negroes. Despite an I.Q. of 100, he had pushed himself to the rather rarefied height of achieving a master's degree in psychology—but he had never been able to use his higher education in a meaningful way.

I put particular emphasis upon this latter point: Glenn had achieved a level of distinction denied to most Negroes. Nevertheless, the doors to "success" remained closed to him. Could it be that a person turns to suicide when his ambitions are outwardly achieved but his hopes for radical improvement in life are frustrated? Glenn had his master's degree, his mother's ultimate hope for him, and yet he still had to wait on tables. Further, his own aspirations precluded the common ghetto escapes of drugs or alcohol. When he found existence bitter, after all his strivings, suicide apparently seemed the only way to end his unhappiness. By this interpretation, then, the relatively "upper-class" Negro who has expended great efforts but still faces discrimination is the most likely candidate for suicide.

This opinion—hardly proved by a mere sixty-seven cases—does, however, fit well with a highly sophisticated theory proposed by Jack Gibbs and Walter Martin.[44] They suggest that people who occupy an unusual "cluster of social roles" (*e.g.,* older, divorced people) will most often kill themselves. Gibbs and Martin assume that such individuals undergo a high degree of role conflict and have few relationships with others. Such a theory helps to explain our cases, for a man such as Glenn did in fact have an unusual, isolated, and conflictful role in the Negro community.

If true, it could be predicted on the basis of this theory that the more a Negro takes on the attributes of white middle-class life, the more he will commit suicide. This dire possibility has been explicitly recognized by Kenneth Clark, but he rightly adds: "To deny the Negro the right to exchange lower-class suffering for middle-class suffering on the grounds, in certain ways defensible, that the good life is not so good after all, is to make for a group the kind of moral decision each individual has the right to make for himself, whether he chooses well or ill."[45]

"The Negro does not commit suicide," Dick Gregory once said, "because it is impossible to jump out of the window of a basement."

Glenn, for example, chose middle-class existence, cutting himself off from the ghetto, but it brought him to suicide. This hardly needs to be the fate of the "high achievers," as the next chapter shows, but we must face the fact that the few who do escape the black ghetto into an illusory, more gilded life may—in the short run—have to confront meaninglessness with wide-open eyes.

REFERENCES

1. Quoted in Kenneth Clark, *Dark Ghetto* (New York: Harper & Row, 1965), p. 95.

2. *Ibid.*, pp. 96-97.

3. Muriel W. Sterne, "Drinking Patterns and Alcoholism Among American Negroes," October 1966 Social Science Institute "Occasional Paper" No. 7, Washington University, St. Louis.

4. John A. Clausen, "Drug Addiction" in *Contemporary Social Problems*, R. K. Merton and R. A. Nisbet, eds. (New York: Harcourt, Brace & World, 1961).

5. For a perceptive discussion of the problem, see Ann Hallman Pettigrew, "Negro American Health" in *A Profile of the Negro American* by Thomas F. Pettigrew (Princeton, N.J.: D. Van Nostrand, 1964).

6. *Ibid.*

7. Samuel E. Wallace, *Skid Row As a Way of Life* (Totowa, N.J.: The Bedminister Press, 1965), p. 187.

8. William McCord, Joan McCord, and Jon Gudeman, *Origins of Alcoholism* (Stanford, Calif.: Stanford University Press, 1960).

9. Sterne, *op. cit.*, p. 30.

10. Lee Rainwater, "Work and Identity in the Lower Class" in S. H. Warner, *Planning for the Quality of Urban Life* (Cambridge, Mass.: Harvard University Press, forthcoming).

11. G. Madox and A. Jennings, "An Analysis of Fantasy: An Exploratory Study of Social Definitions of Alcohol and Its Use by Means of a Projective Technique," *Quarterly Journal of Studies in Alcohol*, 20, 1959.

12. Sterne, *op. cit.*, p. 40.

13. *Ibid.*, p. 9.

14. M. E. Wolfgang and R. B. Strohm, "The Relationship Between Alcohol and Criminal Homicide," *Quarterly Journal of Studies in Alcohol*, 1956, 17:411–25.

15. Claude Brown, *Manchild in the Promised Land* (New York: New American Library, 1965), pp. 271–72.

16. Abraham Wikler, "A Psychodynamic Study of a Patient During Experimental Self-Regulated Re-Addiction to Morphine," *Psychiatric Quarterly*, 26, 1952, pp. 270–93.

17. Brown, *op. cit.*, p. 334.

18. James Mills, "The Drug Takers," a special Time-Life report (New York: Time, Inc., 1965).

19. Isidor Chein, "Narcotics Use Among Juveniles," *Social Work*, Vol. I, April 1965.

20. *Ibid.*

21. John P. Fort, "Heroin Addiction Among Young Men" in *Narcotic Addiction*, John A. O'Donnell and John C. Ball, eds. (New York: Harper & Row, 1966).

22. *Ibid.*, p. 82.

23. *Ibid.*, p. 84.

24. *Ibid.*

25. R. Knight, "The Dynamics and Treatment of Chronic Alcohol Addiction," *Bulletin of the Menninger Clinic*, 1937, 1:233–50.

26. John Fort, *op. cit.*, p. 88.

27. Ann Hallman Pettigrew, *op. cit.*, p. 75.

28. Abram Kardiner and Lionel Ovesey, *The Mark of Oppression* (New York: W. W. Norton, 1951), p. 343.

29. E. G. Jaco, *The Social Epidemiology of Mental Disorders* (New York: Russell Sage Foundation, 1960).

30. See the various studies cited in Thomas F. Pettigrew, *op. cit.*

31. *Ibid.*

32. A. B. Hollingshead and F. Redlich, *Social Class and Mental Illness* (New York: John Wiley & Sons, 1958).

33. Leo Srole, *et al.*, *Mental Health in the Metropolis* (New York: McGraw-Hill, 1962).

34. William McCord, Judith Porta, and Joan McCord, "The Familial Genesis of Psychoses," *Psychiatry*, Vol. 25, No. 1, February 1962.

35. Robert Coles, "It's the Same, But It's Different" in *The Negro American*, Talcott Parsons and Kenneth Clark, eds. (Boston: Houghton Mifflin, 1966), p. 267.

36. Seymour Parker and Robert J. Kleiner, *Mental Illness in the Urban Negro Community* (New York: The Free Press, 1966).

37. Robert K. Merton, *Social Theory and Social Structure* (New York: The Free Press, 1957).

38. Emile Durkheim, *Suicide: A Study in Sociology*, trans. by John A. Spaulding and George Simpson (New York: The Free Press, 1951).

39. See Ruth S. Cavan, *Suicide* (Chicago: University of Chicago Press, 1951).

40. Calvin F. Schmid, "Suicides in Seattle, 1914–1925: An Ecological and Behavioristic Study," *American Journal of Sociology*, Vol. 39, July 1933.

41. Andrew F. Henry and James F. Short, *Suicide and Homicide* (New York: The Free Press, 1954).

42. Jack P. Gibbs, "Suicide" in *Contemporary Social Problems*, Robert K. Merton and Robert A. Nisbet, eds. (New York: Harcourt, Brace & World, 1961), pp. 306–7.

43. See Alex Pokorny, "Human Violence: A Comparison of Homicide, Aggravated Assault, Suicide, and Attempted Suicide," *Journal of Criminal Law, Criminology and Police Science*, Vol. 56, 1965, pp. 488–97.

44. Jack P. Gibbs and Walter T. Martin, *Status Integration and Suicide: A Sociological Study* (Eugene, Ore.: University of Oregon Books, 1964).

45. Clark, *op. cit.*, pp. 108–9.

CHAPTER 8

THE ACHIEVER

William McCord†

Frank Wright,* Negro, aged fifty, has been running all of his life to out-distance himself. "I am always competing—not to be better than other people, but just to be the best in whatever I do." Raised on an impoverished Iowa farm and later a hand in Pittsburgh's steel mills, Wright is now one of the nation's most distinguished lawyers.

His grandmother served as a washerwoman for a wealthy Chicago white family. She passed on this family's values of "success," leading one of her daughters to attend "normal school" and enter a teaching career. She in turn raised a son who went from honor to honor. At great financial sacrifice, she and her husband put her son through high school. Frank Wright finished as salutatorian. He still felt apologetic, in a 1967 interview, for not having been valedictorian and explained his "failure" as due to an illness during high school.

At college Wright served as class president for four years and

†Special recognition should be given to Douglass Price-Williams, who played a major part in gathering and analyzing the material in this chapter.
*Fictitious name.

was also student-body president, a track star, an orchestra leader, and editor of the school paper. He graduated six months ahead of his class with honors in a double major of mathematics and sociology. He published poetry, composed operettas, and learned fluent German.

Wright served as a pilot in World War II, and after the war he became a regional general manager for an insurance firm and simultaneously attended an Ivy League law school. After graduation he became one of the youngest law deans in the country. He was subsequently dean of several other law schools and then, at forty-five, decided to enter private law practice.

In his skyward leap to eminence Wright lost several wives, developed an ulcer, and suffered from hypertension. Today he is a rich man, accredited to the Supreme Court, and overwhelmed with civic commitments. "I know I will die of a heart attack," he said in an interview in 1967, "but I just cannot help myself from keeping going. I would like to go into retreat for a time—not to quit work but to sharpen my brain for more projects." He has, apparently, few regrets about the hectic pace of his life. He has not sought fame, but it has come to him.

In contrast to Wright, his older brother worked in a Pittsburgh steel mill and his younger sister took a low-paying secretarial position instead of attending college.

What motivates Frank Wright? Why should he have escaped the poverty, the sense of futility, the defeated attitude that affects so many Negroes?

During the interview Wright tried frankly to analyze his character. "I remember," he said, "a Negro spiritual which told of keeping your head high, of being proud despite what others think of you. Probably I just wanted social acceptance by whites."

Beyond this need, Wright observed, "I wanted to get even with the oppressor. I wanted to prove myself to be not only as good but better than the whites. I, like most middle-class Negroes, want to show our kids that you can make it, even if the whites try to keep you down."

Many Negroes undoubtedly share these desires, but few

develop into Frank Wrights. The difference, according to Wright, might be due to family background.

Wright's own background has a number of unusual features. He does not know his exact birthdate, since certificates were not issued for Negroes in Iowa. His father's family had long been "free Negroes," owning their own land, but his father felt dissatisfied with his meager lot as a yeoman. He migrated to a big city (Pittsburgh) so that his children might have a better life than he did. Outwardly, the bond between Wright and his father was slim; his father cared little for education (although he read a great deal) and left all business matters to Wright's mother (although he maintained a close check on expenses).

Retrospectively, Wright believes that his father loved his mother very much even though once in a while the older man formed liaisons with other women. Wright felt little empathy with him until his father became senile.

By any standard, Wright regarded his mother as the most important figure in his life. She taught him to love reading, music, and—above all—religion. She impressed upon him all the conventional Baptist virtues, including humility. While encouraging her son in the strongest terms to become a success, she always added that he must not degrade others while achieving his aims. Typically, his mother strongly disapproved of premarital sexual relations, and she impressed this standard so well on her son that some thirty years later he recalled: "I loved a girl very much. She thought that she would keep me with sexual relations. One night we tried. When she told me that she wanted to be a virgin for her husband, I stopped entering her. I did not feel like a martyr, only that I was doing right." Despite the mother's prohibition, Wright engaged in such "illicit" activities as masturbation. Now he apparently feels free from the sexual taboo imposed by his mother, but he is guided by other highly moral teachings.

Wright's mother admonished him, "Don't be just average; you must try all of the time." She also encouraged him, in conventional terms, to be a "sissy." He learned to cook, sew, embroider, clean house, and, as Wright puts it, "all of the virtues associated with 'Little Lord Fauntleroy.' " In school, however, his excellence in athletics protected him from any questions about his masculinity.

Wright, by his own admission, was the favorite in a family environment which he has described as "smoochy," because everyone was openly affectionate and kissed everyone else. His elder brother, who quit school to work in the Pittsburgh mills, wanted, above all, to put the young children through college and chose Frank as the beneficiary of his labor in the mills. "Even today," Wright recalls, "I care more for my brother than anyone. I cried more at my brother's funeral than at my mother's. He sacrificed everything for me. He knew a lot more than I did, but he just wanted to help me by paying most of my way through college."

The factors that pushed Frank Wright into his high achievements seem rather clear. First, his mother strongly encouraged him to better his lot, to attain a higher status than her or his father. She indoctrinated him with the "Protestant ethic" in its purest form. Second, his father and, particularly, his elder brother supported this drive with both moral encouragement and material support. Third, the family consciously shielded him from the most debilitating aspects of living in a ghetto and being a Negro.

Surrounded by foreign ethnic groups in Pittsburgh, Wright seldom thought of himself as a "Negro." One day, when he was twelve, he read of the lynching of a Negro doctor who had tried to help a wounded white woman. "Suddenly I knew there was a difference," he said. "I became a Negro." After reading of the incident, he went to see a Polish boy, who was his best friend. They had a habit of hitting each other in the solar plexus, supposedly to enhance the tone of their stomach muscles. Engulfed with anger, Wright hit the other boy with all his strength.

"I will never forget it," he recalls. "I had hurt my best friend, simply because I suddenly realized that I was a 'Negro' and he was white. I shall always feel guilty."

Another time, a white doctor refused to treat Wright's sister after she had been involved in an auto accident. Again, Wright said, "It was impressed on me that I was a Negro. I wanted to kill that doctor. Even today, I would still kill him."

Wright had learned what it means to be a Negro in America. Yet his mother kept preaching "Christian love" to him and he controlled or repressed his anger toward whites. Today Wright avoids involvement in the civil rights movement, although he maintains a token membership in the NAACP.

He is, in a very real sense, a "lone achiever" striving to improve his own situation in life but caring little about the condition of other Negroes. He regards himself as a contributor to the community as a whole rather than as a "race leader." His hopes for his children reflect his attitude: "I want them to be able to enter the best clubs in the nation and to regard association with whites not as a unique experience but as an expected, everyday occurrence."

THE PROFESSIONALS

From our data it is impossible to say whether Frank Wright is a typical representative of the Negroes who have achieved high status in American society. For that matter, the terms "achievement" and "achiever" can be understood in a number of ways. In a general sense these words indicate a syndrome of high aspirations and striving for goals, but they can also be used in a more precise way, for example, in relation to a theory such as McClelland's, in which the drive for achievement is viewed as a basic need, varying in intensity from man to man.[1]

The notion of achievement is undoubtedly culture-bound. In the framework of the Negro community in America, it may be that conventional even if minimal occupational achievement in white middle-class society counts very greatly, in terms of prestige, in the Negro ghetto. It is also probable that certain life styles in the Negro community are not acknowledged by whites as true achievements. The extraordinary feats of the Negro mothers, for example, who work, raise their children, support their church, and still manage to engage in civic activities are seldom recognized by whites.

One type of achievement in Negro society is clearly represented in the life of Frank Wright: his move from a relatively humble background to professional status. In *Black Metropolis*, St. Clair Drake and Horace Cayton describe many Frank Wrights, upper-class Negroes whose values are indistinguishable from upper-class whites.[2] Dewey and Humber, commenting on this material from *Black Metropolis*, identify a personality type among Negroes that they call the "striving, conforming personality."[3] Sutherland has also concerned himself with middle- and upper-class Negroes who are devoted to social climbing.[4]

Status-seeking is certainly not the sole form of achieving, but it does appear prominently in the motivation of people in the middle and upper classes of Negro society. Thus Pettigrew cites researches showing that "upper-status Negro youths harbor surprisingly intense needs for achievement and set for themselves very high levels of aspiration. Their needs are more intense and their levels of achievement are much higher than comparable white youths."[5] Elsewhere Pettigrew discusses McClelland's model and says that studies have shown that lower-status Negroes have less need for achievement than lower-status whites (from both the North and the South), but that this need is unusually strong among upper-status Negro boys.[6]

The strategies adopted by Negroes striving for personal achievement necessitate some kind of role playing. As Pettigrew states: "Negroes may handle tense interracial situations by attempting to separate their true selves from their role as 'Negro.' "[7] This type of conflict is highlighted in E. Franklin Frazier's *Black Bourgeoisie*, in which the author attacks the Negro middle class, maintaining that its members have rejected the mass of "grass roots" Negroes.[8] The conflict is especially crucial for the Negro professional man or woman. Back and Simpson have considered this problem and concluded:

> The position of the Negro in the United States can be and has been conceptualized as a question of overlapping group membership and conflicting norms. Negroes feel that the

official standards of the society promise them equal rewards, depending only on effort and ability, while at the same time they are forced to adapt to the realities of being a disfavored minority.[9]

Negroes who enter the professions become, in one sense, members of a privileged minority in this country and are confronted with a very specific set of norms, more specific than the general norms of American culture but compatible with them. These standards conflict drastically with those of the ghetto, however.

The problems of self-identification and the general status of Negro professionals has been stated well by G. Franklin Edwards, Horace Mann Bond, and in the book by Leonard Broom and Norval Glenn.[10] In an attempt to further illuminate the position of Negro achievers, we chose 118 persons in Houston who had a reputation for accomplishment, of whom sixty-three were professional men and women—doctors, lawyers, and teachers. For the moment, we will concentrate on the attitudes of this group as compared with Negro white-collar workers (nonprofessionals) and Negro blue-collar workers who were interviewed at the same time. The age and sex composition of the Negro professionals versus that of the other groups differed slightly.* Several questions seemed relevant in determining the differences between the professionals and others. We were interested, for example, in finding out to what degree a person believed he could control his own destiny, by asking: "Many things are changing in the world nowadays, in our daily life and in the society in which we live. Do you think that you could have a personal influence in the changes that are taking place?" A slightly greater number of professionals believed that they could exert influence on their lives and society:

---

*The professional sample consisted of thirty-three men and thirty women; seventeen were under thirty and forty-six were over thirty in age. The composition of the white-collar group was twenty-six men and fourteen women, seventeen being under thirty and twenty-three over thirty. Thirty-nine men and twenty-four women were in the blue-collar group; thirty-six were under thirty and twenty-seven over thirty.

CAN YOU INFLUENCE CHANGE?

	PROFESSIONALS (N:63)*	WHITE-COLLAR (N:40)	BLUE-COLLAR (N:63)
Yes	73 %	65 %	48.7%
No	11.1	15	17
Maybe	4.8	2.5	22.8
No opinion	11.1	17.5	11.5

A second question revealed that both the professionals and the white-collar group were slightly more inclined to believe that man can change his own destiny: "Some people think that there is very little that a man can do by his own efforts to change his destiny; other people think that a man can do much by his own efforts to change his destiny. What is your opinion?"

CAN MAN INFLUENCE HIS OWN DESTINY?

	PROFESSIONALS (N:63)	WHITE-COLLAR (N:40)	BLUE-COLLAR (N:63)
Can do much	58.8%	60.0%	47.6%
Can do some	7.9	12.5	10.0
Can do little	3.2	7.5	12.0
Can do nothing	7.9	2.5	2.7
No opinion/ Neutral	28.5	2.0	28.4

With both questions, the blue-collar group is less "affirmative" or "achievement-oriented" than the higher-status groups.

E. Franklin Frazier believed that the professional (or superstatus) Negro would incorporate the values of white society. Although we did not ask directly about reference groups, we did ask a question about whom the respondent admired most, and since the possible responses included both Negro leaders and white politicians, we hoped to gain some insight into this general issue. The actual wording of the question was: "Of all the people whom you know or have read about, whom do you admire the most?" The answers were as follows:

*N = number of respondents.

MOST-ADMIRED PERSON

	PROFESSIONALS (N:63)	WHITE-COLLAR (N:40)	BLUE-COLLAR (N:63)
Personal acquaintance	4.8%	2.5%	5.2%
Local Negro leader	9.5	2.5	3.0
National Negro leader	15.9	17.5	22.4
White politician	46.0	52.5	50.4
Sports or music figure	1.6	0.0	0.0
Other	6.3	5.0	5.9
No opinion	15.9	20.0	13.1

The results do not show any strong identification with white norms among the upper classes as compared with the blue-collar group, and, indeed, among the professionals there is slightly less identification with whites. There is a slope toward a national Negro leader as one goes from the professionals to the blue-collar group, but this is offset by the fact that the highest percentage of admiration for a local *Negro* leader is expressed by the professionals.

The influence of religion was noted in the brief biography of Frank Wright. An apparent devotion to religion can also be seen in the general sample of professionals. Compared with some of the other "ideal types" described in this part of the book, the achievers seem highly religious.

IMPORTANCE OF RELIGION

	ACHIEVERS (N:63)	ACTIVISTS (N:95)	RELIGIOUS STOICS (N:101)	REVOLU-TIONARIES (N:22)	THE DEFEATED (N:46)
Very important	70.0%	43.1%	77.0%	45.5%	24.0%
Somewhat important	12.7	25.3	15.0	31.9	20.6
Not important	3.0	19.0	0.0	18.1	35.0
No opinion	14.3	12.6	8.0	4.5	20.0

Since by definition religious stoics are church members, it is not surprising that religion is more important to them than to any other group, but it is interesting to note that the achievers rank almost as high. A possible double role of religion can be seen in these figures: for some of the stoics religion may be a consolation; for achievers it may be a spur to achievement.

NEGRO WOMEN

Too much emphasis on the upper-class Negro man may result in slighting another kind of achiever, one who is less oriented to occupational status or economic gain but whose achievement consists in maintaining stability in a situation of constant flux, of helping others, of being a mainstay of the community generally. We refer to Negro women, and specifically to Negro wives and mothers. It is her ability to cope with the day-in, day-out problems of ghetto life—no small achievement—that sets the Negro mother apart as an achiever. At the same time it has been noted that Negro women play an important part in the civil rights movement. As Jeanne Noble has written: "One can walk into any church on 'Movement Night' in the South and see hundreds of Negro women singing, exulting and putting hard-earned coins into the collection plates. They march, kneel-in, go to jail and do many of the chores necessary to keep a protest movement going."[11] The subject of the following case history is a woman who exemplifies the many achievements of the ghetto mother.

Mrs. Grace Adams* moved to Houston from Louisiana just after World War II. Her mother died when she was seven, and her father remarried a few years later. She left home when she was thirteen and worked for a white family until she was eighteen. Looking back, Mrs. Adams felt she had learned a lot about the interaction between black and white through this family, who, she said, had been good to her. As she put it, "People are just people. White folks are no different from black folks." At

*Fictitious name.

eighteen Mrs. Adams married, and eventually bore five children. The early years of the marriage were full of hardship. Her
husband was unemployed, and she had to provide for the
family by working as a domestic: "Things were pretty rugged."
She insisted that the children stay in school until they reached
at least the eleventh grade, and they did. While she was maintaining her family's integrity and doing the best for her children's future, Grace Adams also took part in community activities. She was the leader of the tenants' association of her particular area, worked with the Boy and Girl Scouts, became a precinct watcher, and was captain of the March of Dimes for her
district. Subsequently, as a result of her efforts in the community, she was elected to the Board of Directors of the local
O.E.O.

Mrs. Adams was never interested in civil rights as such. She
could think of no reason for this except that she was so terribly
busy with all her other activities, but it did not mean that she
would not protest if she felt protest was necessary. Indeed, she
organized people to become interested in voting and to go to
City Hall when repairs were needed in her neighborhood. She
was emphatic on school integration because she felt that her
children and those of her relatives and friends would have a
better education, and thus a better future, in integrated schools.
When protests were held against the school board in Houston
on this issue, Mrs. Adams was prominent, but demonstrations
as such, and even organizations like the NAACP, were not her
way.

Although she had only completed the seventh grade, Grace
Adams filled in her own education by voluminous reading. "I
was always interested in things," she said, "and I would read
anything I could lay my hands on: Sinclair Lewis, political
stuff, the life of Michelangelo—anything which happened to
interest me." Indeed, her own struggle was closely linked with
her children's welfare, particularly with their education. She
was sensitive to her children feeling inferior, as she herself had
been made to feel. "They feel inferior if they do not have a
decent shirt," she said, "so I had to work to get them that."
Working as a domestic for whites helped her realize that

Negroes were often exploited in their own neighborhoods: "I had to go shopping for the lady I worked for, and found that in the white stores there was a vast difference in the price and quality of meat."

Grace Adams spoke of the role of the Negro man as father. "Papa puts the responsibility on Mama" was the way she summed it up. The mother pays the bills, helps the children with their school work, and keeps them from being dropouts. The father, she said, without any note of complaint but just as a matter of observation, is truly unconcerned with kids: "Let Mama worry about it" was their attitude, she said. Negro mothers, she went on, are "real good parents," but they tend to keep things to themselves. Often they feel ashamed of the way their children behave. "Why did it happen to me?" they say. They are very concerned about what happens in the neighborhood, she said, but they feel "kind of hopeless: don't know what to do or where to go" when their children or husbands get into trouble.

Nearly fifty now, Mrs. Adams evaluated her own struggle so far. She is still doing heavy domestic work, still has children in school, and her husband has stayed away for several years, but she feels that "I haven't done so badly. I still hope for the best. I've had a lot of hard knocks, but with all the knock downs—and I've had plenty—I never give up."

Grace Adams is hardly atypical. As we have already noted, public-opinion polls have revealed that Negro women are generally as concerned about all types of civic affairs as men. Eliminating factors such as age, occupation, and belief in religion, Negro women consistently exhibit both discontent with the Negro's lot and great interest in community improvement. In fact, compared with men, they are more concerned about their neighborhood, the adequacy of the family income, and the unfairness of police, and they even have a slightly greater tendency to support the black-power movement.

Some years ago John Dollard stated one of the reasons for this greater verbal involvement of women in "race" issues:

It is worth noting as a general point that within the caste situation Negro women can be somewhat more expressive of their resentment than can Negro men. In comparing life-history data of Negro men and women, it was quite clear that much more antagonism is tolerated from the women; they can do and say things which would bring a severe penalty had they been men.[12]

While our own studies have not concentrated upon achievers among Negro women, the part they play in the internal affairs of the Negro community and in the struggle for Negro emancipation is important and needs further intensive study.

THE ACHIEVER AND CIVIL RIGHTS

As we have noted, the Negro white-collar classes sharply divide on civil rights issues. Holding other factors constant, we found that the white-collar classes produced the highest proportion of people committed to the civil rights cause *and* the highest proportion who said they had no interest whatsoever. Of the sixty-three professionals whom we questioned, twenty claimed to have participated in some type of protest but the rest had apparently done nothing regarding civil rights. Nonetheless, both the protesting and nonprotesting professionals held essentially the same opinions about the speed of the civil rights movement, the utility of violence, and the justification for riots. On the surface, therefore, the protesting and nonprotesting professionals exhibited similar opinions.

Thus, in the case of the professionals one is forced to fall back on an impressionistic analysis and take into consideration what is *not* said or expressed as well as what *is* stated. This is sometimes made very manifest, as it was in an interview with a Negro City Hall official who, as soon as the interview started, made it clear that he was willing to talk about his work but absolutely refused to discuss anything of a racial nature. The statements of many upper-status Negroes are often tinged with heightened sensitivity, suspicion, and wary attention.

Frank Wright represents this type of person. He has more or less chosen to cut himself off from the civil rights movement and, indeed, the mainstream of Negro life. Another fledgling lawyer, however, has taken a different route: Stanley Sanders has committed his life to improving the conditions of his home town, Watts.

Sanders was born and schooled in Watts. He played football at David Starr Jordan High School and later received a scholarship to Whittier College, where he won academic distinction, became student-body president, and received a Rhodes Scholarship to study in England. After two years he entered Yale Law School. He returned to Watts just in time for the riots, in August 1965. During the summer of 1967 he served as a director for summer projects for the Westminster Association in Watts, and has decided to practice law in the ghetto in the future.

When he first left Watts for Whittier he hardly intended to return:

> The Watts-as-a-way-station mentality has a firm hold on both those who remain and those who leave. Such as it is, the ghetto is regarded as no place to make a career for those who have a future. Without exception, the prime American values underscore the notion. Negroes, inside it or out, and whites too, behave toward the ghetto like travelers.[13]

At Whittier, Sanders denied his connection with Watts. He felt its stigma was too much to bear:

> I followed the instructions of those who fled Watts. I adopted the language of escape. I resorted to all the devices of those who wished to escape. I was from South Los Angeles thereafter, not Watts. "South Los Angeles," geographically identical to Watts, carried none of the latter's stigma. South Los Angeles was a cleaner—safer—designation. It meant having a home with possibilities.[14]

Sanders forgot his conflicts about Watts during his two years as a Rhodes scholar in England; he lived in a relatively tolerant atmosphere, and the distinction between Watts and South Los Angeles had no meaning there. Treated solely as a "Yankee" and as a man, he let down all his defenses about race. This happy period ended, however, when, while he was attending the University of Vienna during the summer of 1964, news of Harlem rioting reached Vienna. The reactions of his fellow European students surprised him: they asked him why Negroes didn't riot more often in America. Said Sanders:

> My own lack of shame in the rioting then taking place in America surprised me. In one sense, I was the archetype of the ghetto child who, through hard work and initiative, was pulling himself toward a better life. I was the example, the exception. . . . In another sense, however, my feelings toward the rioting were predictable. I had always been bothered by the passivity of the ghetto. The majority of black men in the North had remained outside the struggle. Nothing was happening in the ghettos. No one was making it happen. Ghetto rioting then was the first representation I perceived of movement and activity among the mass of Negroes in the North. . . . The ghetto wanted legitimization. That was a beginning.[15]

When Sanders first returned to Watts in 1965 those who remembered him thought he must be an FBI agent or, at best, "crazy" to return. Little seemed to have changed in the community; it still seemed to be the ramshackle, "unacknowledged child" of an otherwise proud city. When he went on to Yale, however, Sanders did not turn his back on Watts, and subsequently decided to devote his life to working there:

> I suspected at the time and now realize that the riots were perhaps the most significant massive action taken by northern Negroes. It was a watershed in the ghetto's history. Before the riots the reach of the Negro movement in America seemed within the province of a small civil rights leadership. Now Watts, and places like Watts, were re-defining the role of black men in their city's life. . . .
>
> The problem of the poor and of the city in America, simplified, is the problem of the ghetto Negro. I regard it as *the* problem of the last third of this century. Plainly, Watts is where the action is. If there is no future for the black ghetto, the future of all Negroes is diminished. What affects it, affects

me, for I am a child of the ghetto. I'll never escape from the ghetto. I have staked my all on its future. Watts is my home.[16]

Clearly, Frank Wright and Stanley Sanders are two quite different types of human beings. They have in common a drive to overcome extraordinary obstacles imposed on them by white society, but Wright has chosen the customary path followed by the "black bourgeoisie" while Sanders represents a more militant and, one suspects, a more constructive force in the Negro ghetto.

Tragically, some Negroes attain their high achievements by exploiting their own people. In the next chapter we examine this anomalous, rarely studied style of ghetto life.

REFERENCES

1. D. D. McClelland, *The Achieving Society* (Princeton, N.J.: D. Van Nostrand, 1961).

2. St. Clair Drake and Horace R. Clayton, *Black Metropolis, A Study of Negro Life in a Northern City,* revised edition (New York: Harper & Row—Harper Torchbooks, 1962), Vol. II, Chap. 19.

3. Richard Dewey and W. J. Humber, *An Introduction to Social Psychology* (New York: Macmillan, 1966), p. 387.

4. R. L. Sutherland, *Color, Class and Personality* (Washington, D.C.: American Council on Education, 1942), p. 44.

5. Thomas F. Pettigrew, *A Profile of the Negro American* (Princeton, N.J.: D. Van Nostrand, 1964), p. 31.

6. Thomas F. Pettigrew, "Negro American Personality: Why Isn't More Known?," *The Journal of Social Issues,* 1964, XX, pp. 4–23.

7. Pettigrew, *A Profile of the Negro American, op. cit.,* p. 29.

8. E. Franklin Frazier: *Black Bourgeoisie* (New York: The Free Press—paperback, 1957).

9. Kurt W. Back and Ida Harper Simpson: "The Dilemma of the Negro Professional," *Journal of Social Issues*, 1964, XX, pp. 60–70.

10. G. Franklin Edwards, "Community and Class Realities: The Ordeal of Change" in Talcott Parsons and Kenneth B. Clark, *The Negro American* (Boston: Houghton Mifflin, 1966), pp. 280–302 (especially pp. 294–95). *See also* Edwards' previous book, *The Negro Professional Class* (New York: The Free Press, 1959); Horace Mann Bond: "The Negro Scholar and Professional in America" in *The American Negro Reference Book*, John P. Davis, ed. (Englewood, N.J.: Prentice-Hall, 1966), Chapter 14; Leonard Broom and Norval Glenn, *Transformation of the Negro American* (New York: Harper & Row, 1965).

11. Jeanne L. Noble, "The American Negro Woman" in John P. Davis, *op. cit.*, p. 546.

12. John Dollard, *Caste and Class in a Southern Town* (New York: Doubleday—Doubleday Anchor Books, 1957), p. 289.

13. Stanley Saunders, "I'll Never Escape the Ghetto," *Ebony*, August 1967, p. 31.

14. *Ibid.*, p. 32.

15. *Ibid.*

16. *Ibid.*, p. 36.

CHAPTER 9

THE EXPLOITER

William McCord

"I am sick and tired of all these Jew business places in Harlem. Why don't more colored business places open? This is our part of town. They don't live here but they got all the businesses and everything."[1] This complaint, in one form or another, is echoed throughout the American Negro community, and some nationalist journals like *The Liberator* directly express anti-Semitism.[2] In Houston, as it happens, Negroes direct much of their antagonism toward Chinese, rather than Jews. Historically, in Houston, the Chinese and, to a lesser extent, the Koreans, Italians, and Lebanese own many of the small service stores which characterize the ghetto. They are noticeable targets and are naturally open to charges of "exploitation."

The value-laden terms "exploiter" and "exploitation" are, of course, hard to define objectively and, even if it can be defined, exploitation is a difficult charge to substantiate. In this chapter, I am labeling an exploiter as 1) a person who economically discriminates against the poor by charging them higher prices, interest rates, or rent than he could or would charge in richer districts, or 2) a person who consciously perpetrates a fraud.

Most of the exploiters in the slums are *not* Negroes, and certainly not all of the businessmen or professionals who work in the ghetto treat their clients unfairly. Yet there is a small group of the "black bourgeoisie" who bilk their fellow Negroes. As E. Franklin Frazier noted years ago:

> With the emergence of the new black bourgeoisie, the standards of consumption which the 'sporting' and criminal elements are able to maintain have become the measure of success among the black middle class. The standards which they set are emulated by Negroes in the professional classes— doctors, dentists, and lawyers, and even teachers as far as they are able to do so.[2]

Most significantly, Frazier went on to observe that "in order to secure the money necessary to maintain these standards, Negro professional men engage in the same 'rackets' as the successful Negroes in the underworld."[3]

The exploitation of one's own social group is a common phenomenon throughout the world. It was practiced by Benedict Arnold, by a few Jews in the concentration camps, by Cabinet ministers in Ghana, to mention only a few. Consequently, as with all the life styles we discuss, one should not draw the conclusion that this is a uniquely *Negro* way of adapting to a difficult situation. If people have traditionally been closed off from the usual avenues to "success," it is hardly surprising that a minority will turn to illegitimate (or semilegitimate) ways of earning a living.

BACKGROUND OF NEGRO "EXPLOITERS"

Although exploiters come from a variety of ethnic backgrounds, we have chosen to examine the attitudes of some of Houston's Negro exploiters. We selected thirty-four Negro men who— justly or not—had gained a reputation in the Negro community as "exploiters."* We found direct evidence that sixteen of these

*Twenty of these men were originally interviewed in the spring of 1966. An additional fourteen were contacted in the fall of 1966. We owe special thanks to Miss Charleen Jackson for arranging the interviews and tabulating the responses.

men were guilty of unfair pricing, fraud, etc.; the others merely had a reputation for such practices. Since we could not verify this information—some interviews were conducted anonymously and certain activities (such as who runs the "numbers racket") are well-kept secrets—our data may be contaminated because some of the presumed exploiters may possibly have reputations they do not deserve. This seems unlikely, however, since Houston Negroes could easily accuse more visible targets (*e.g.*, the Chinese) of exploiting them rather than naming fellow Negroes.

All the Negro exploiters studied apparently had high incomes and all but two lived in well-to-do residential sections of Houston south of the Third Ward. The sample included one reputed head of the "numbers racket," five grocery-store owners, three real estate salesmen or apartment-house owners, three undertakers, two doctors, one minister, two night-club owners, one architect, two liquor-store owners, one house painter, two pharmacists, two policemen (who, supposedly, ran "shake-down rackets" on the side), four loan brokers, two insurance salesmen, and three owners of remodeling, carpet, and aluminum-siding concerns.

When compared with a random sample of Negro Houstonians, the exploiters were (by definition, of course) better off financially and were both older and better educated:*

AGE

	"EXPLOITERS" (N:34)†	RANDOM SAMPLE (N:572)
Under 20	3%	17%
21–30	20	31
31–40	10	21
41–50	23	17
Over 50	44	12
No answer	0	2

*As in other chapters, the percentages are rounded off and consequently may, at times, be slightly over or under 100 per cent.

†N=Number of respondents.

EDUCATION

	"EXPLOITERS" (N:34)	RANDOM SAMPLE (N:572)
8th grade or less	10%	15%
Some high school	14	30
High school graduate	14	44
Some college or more	62	4
No answer	0	2

As noted in Chapter 5, these differences in occupation, age, and education may well explain why exploiters have a somewhat different view of life than the average Negro Houstonian. It may also be that the very practice of exploiting one's own group engenders contrasting attitudes.

OPINIONS OF EXPLOITERS

Predictably, the exploiters are generally more content with life in Houston than average Negro citizens are. For example, they usually approved of the existing political leadership of the city and state, while the average Negro ordinarily disapproved:

OPINION OF GOVERNOR

	"EXPLOITERS" (N:34)	RANDOM SAMPLE (N:572)
General approval	66%	21%
General disapproval	17	11
Disapproval because of racial policies	0	50
No opinion	17	18

OPINION OF MAYOR

	"EXPLOITERS" (N:34)	RANDOM SAMPLE (N:572)
General approval	59%	21%
General disapproval	10	11
Disapprove because of racial policies	14	50
No opinion	17	18

In their specific opinions about civil rights, the exploiters did not differ greatly from the general Negro population. Approximately equal proportions of the exploiters and the random sample believed that the pace of integration was moving too slowly (38 per cent vs. 44 per cent) and about the same proportion believed that integration was coming at "about the right speed" (48 per cent vs. 51 per cent). Equal proportions of both groups (82 per cent) had apparently never participated in civil rights demonstrations, protests, or picketing.

The exploiters, however, deviated from the general population in their beliefs about which groups would be most effective in aiding the Negro cause. Most of the exploiters put their faith in the efficacy of the NAACP, while they generally had little respect for either the churches' influence or that of "militant" groups (*e.g.*, PUSH, SNCC, and CORE):

MOST EFFECTIVE CIVIL RIGHTS GROUPS

	"EXPLOITERS" (N:34)	RANDOM SAMPLE (N:572)
NAACP	62%	17%
Religious organizations	14	35
"Militant" organizations	3%	33%
Other (*e.g.*, federal government)	14	5
No opinion	7	10

Predictably, the exploiters more often condemned the use of violence. Specifically, more of them said that they would never use violence in defense of civil rights and more of them believed that the Watts riot had hurt the Negro cause.

USE OF VIOLENCE

	"EXPLOITERS" (N:34)	RANDOM SAMPLE (N:572)
Never justified	56%	·45%
Generally justified	7	24
Justified in self-defense	34	26
No opinion	3	5

OPINION OF THE WATTS RIOT

	"EXPLOITERS" (N:34)	RANDOM SAMPLE (N:572)
Helped	23%	30%
Hurt	67	37
Both	7	10
No opinion	3	23

In their general opinions about life, the exploiters disagreed with the average Houston Negro in a number of ways. Among the most interesting of these contrasts was the fact that "exploiters" more often claimed that religion was an important factor in guiding their lives:

IMPORTANCE OF RELIGION

	"EXPLOITERS" (N:34)	RANDOM SAMPLE (N:572)
Very important	70%	22%
Somewhat important	10	49
Not important	0	26
No opinion	20	3

Strong adherence to a religious faith might, of course, reduce whatever guilt the "exploiters" feel concerning their day-to-day operations, and it is also possible, of course, that they were lying, either to themselves or to the interviewers.

There is some evidence to support the inference that another mechanism the exploiters utilize in psychologically justifying their behavior is to reject the Negro world and identify with whites. When asked whom they admired most, the exploiters more often named a white person such as John F. Kennedy rather than a Negro person such as Martin Luther King:

MOST-ADMIRED PERSON

	"EXPLOITERS" (N:34)	RANDOM SAMPLE (N:572)
Negro personality	32%	65%
White personality	50	26
No opinion	18	9

In the next chapter we note that violent Negroes ("rebels without a cause") also most often choose white people with power as their most admired figures. Perhaps the exploiters and the violent criminals have one element in common: an over-weening desire for power and a consequent admiration for those who possess it.

PORTRAIT OF AN "EXPLOITER"

The contemporary Negro exploiter tends to accept the status quo and, for economic reasons, prefers society in its present form. While he claims to favor more speed in civil rights and at least gives lip service to religion, he in fact thrives on a segregated system. Compelled by circumstances or his own character, such a person truly leads a double life. Clifford Vaughn*

*Fictitious name.

illustrates this particular dilemma. On the one hand, he is supposedly head of the numbers racket in Houston, owns several Negro tenements, runs a mortuary, and is a "loan shark." On the other, he serves as a deacon of his church, contributes large sums to the NAACP, and calls the governor by his first name.

A rather corpulent man of fifty-six, Clifford Vaughn directs his varied activities from the paneled study of his $80,000 home. He officially lists himself as "self-employed" and is naturally reticent about describing his business operations. Police sources, however, provide some idea of the nature of one of Mr. Vaughn's presumed activities, the "numbers" or "policy" racket. The business is quite simple. Cards are distributed in the Negro districts bearing twenty-five numbers (or symbols). A person bets any amount from ten cents to $21 that the number he picks will be chosen in a lottery held each week. Theoretically the winnings can be as much as $15,000. There are various "fronts"—small stores throughout Houston—where one may place a bet. About 25 per cent of the profits go to the front owners who, in turn, must pay various employees. According to some Houston Negroes, another slice of the profits goes to policemen or sheriff's deputies in the form of "protection." The remaining profit goes to "The Company" which, according to police and to general Negro opinion, is essentially Clifford Vaughn. He in turn has other expenses since he admits openly that he contributes a great deal of money to various politicians. No one knows how much Vaughn actually keeps after everyone else has been paid off, but he owns an expensive home, a Rolls-Royce, a Jaguar, and a forty-foot cabin cruiser. While he will not acknowledge any connection with the numbers racket, he was willing to comment generally about it during an interview. "As a religious man, I suppose I should condemn the numbers," he said, "but, frankly, I see little harm if a man wants to play the game. He gets some fun out of it, never loses very much, and—if he wins—can take it easy for a year."

Vaughn was equally tight-lipped about his other businesses. He owns property in the Fifth Ward, but refused to specify the extent of his holdings. His mortuary is apparently one of the most successful in Houston; around 300 Negro families a year choose to have their funerals handled there. (The cost of a Vaughn funeral, according to our survey, averages 14 per cent higher than that charged by ten morticians who serve whites.[4]) Reputedly, Vaughn also owns a number of apartments used by prostitutes in Houston's well-known red-light district. We were able to establish that he does own at least one apartment building frequented by prostitutes and their pimps.[5] Clearly, Vaughn's operations skirt the boundaries of legitimate business, yet he has never been convicted of a felony and has not been publicly rebuked by an organization such as the Houston Better Business Bureau.

Outwardly he seems to be a model of respectability. He has been elected president of various Negro business groups in Houston and he says he is well received at city hall and is listened to attentively at the state capital. He plays an active political role and, he claims, exercises power in the Negro "Council of Organizations," a Houston grouping of civic clubs that either supports or condemns various political candidates.

He is also apparently a model husband and father. He has been married to the same woman for thirty years and she seems to be happy. Although Vaughn himself had only one year of college, his three children have successfully graduated from several institutions of higher learning.

Vaughn is active in certain community causes. In addition to serving on a local NAACP board, he participates in Negro lodges, a fraternity, and charitable causes. The center of his life, he claims, is his local Methodist Episcopal Church. "I enjoy stately, dignified religious services," he says; "it gives me comfort to know that I am in touch with the Lord."

He believes that the civil rights movement is moving at "about the right pace." "Many of these hot-heads like Stokely Carmichael just stir things up," he says. "The way to achieve progress is to work with the system. I have done more to advance my race by just talking with the right officials than 100 demonstrations could have accomplished." His proudest moment, he claims, occurred in 1963 when a local civil rights group was demonstrating for school integration. "Why, those people could have gone on for days and nothing would have happened. All I had to do was pick up the telephone and call a good white friend of mine who heads ——— [a prominent department store]. We got the Negro leaders together in a hotel with the school board members. At first they wouldn't be in the same room, but after I talked to the Negroes, they agreed to negotiate. As a result, we won more integration."

Vaughn attributes his success to "hard work, careful planning, and keeping my nose to the grindstone." He believes that many Negroes "are just plain lazy" and that their salvation lies in "pulling themselves up by their bootstraps."

In a completely free and open society, Clifford Vaughn might have been a successful businessman without having to resort to questionable methods to obtain his high income. We must always remember that Negro exploiters exist because the ghetto exists, and that American whites have created the ghetto. In a perceptive discussion of "blockbusting" (another activity in which Clifford Vaughn reputedly engages), Eunice and George Grier have observed:

> Technically speaking, blockbusters represent an unscrupulous minority of the real estate industry—"outlaws" in a moral if not a legal sense. However, their activities would not prove profitable if racial restrictions on place of residence were not accepted and enforced by the large majority of builders, brokers, and lenders, backed by the supporting opinion of a large segment of the white public.
>
> By restraining the Negro market and permitting its housing needs to be satisfied only on a waiting-list basis, "reputable" members of the banking and housing industries have helped perpetuate the conditions under which their less-scrupulous colleagues can flourish.[6]

The Clifford Vaughns of this world can exist, in other words, only so long as "reputable" white businessmen allow them to, only so long as white policemen close their eyes to the existence of prostitution, and only so long as white politicians lend their "protection" to such exploitive activities as the numbers racket.

What can Negroes do about "blockbusting," or other forms of exploitation? In Houston, at least, several fairly effective measures have been employed. The Houston Legal Foundation (a group of volunteer lawyers serving poor people) has, for example, exposed fraudulent house-buying operations and brought their perpetrators to justice. The Houston Civic Association (an organization of Negro and white home owners) has vigorously fought the attempts of blockbusters to ruin a particular neighborhood by joining together to prevent unscrupulous real estate practices. They did not try to keep Negroes out of the area, but worked to create a truly integrated neighborhood. Those whites who did not want to leave their old, well-established neighborhood put signs on their lawns saying, "This house is *not* for sale. It is our home." This refusal to panic in the face of rumors circulated by blockbusters has resulted in Negroes and whites working together to establish a harmonious community.

Perhaps the most effective weapon against exploitation by local merchants, Negro or white, is the economic boycott, or "selective buying," which, if properly conducted, can bring enough pressure to bear to cause a store owner or manager to make him give up his unfair practices.

Exploitation can be reduced, if not eliminated, within the Negro community, then, by educating consumers, by the use of such legal measures as tough prosecution of the numbers game, and, particularly, by selective-buying compaigns, even though the Clifford Vaughns of this world—and their more numerous white colleagues—can be eliminated only when poverty and the ghetto itself are eliminated.

The ghetto also spawns another type of person—"the rebel without a cause." Frustrated and goalless, the rebel, like the exploiter, usually takes his vengeance out upon his own people. He does so, however, in a violent fashion without any pretense of staying within the boundaries of the law. It is this type of person whom we next examine.

REFERENCES

1. Quoted in Kenneth Clark, *Dark Ghetto* (New York: Harper & Row, 1965), p. 29.

2. E. Franklin Frazier, *Black Bourgeoisie* (New York: The Free Press—paperback, 1957), p. 128.

3. *Ibid.*

4. George Hammond, "Economic Discrimination in the Negro Community," unpublished paper, Rice University.

5. *Ibid.*

6. Eunice and George Grier, "Equality and Beyond: Housing Segregation in the Great Society" in *The Negro American*, Talcott Parsons and Kenneth Black, eds. (New York: Houghton Mifflin, 1966), p. 534.

CHAPTER 10

THE "REBEL WITHOUT A CAUSE"

William McCord

In recent years white Americans have often pictured Negroes as dangerous, switchblade-wielding savages leading a rampage of "crime in the streets." As with many prejudicial beliefs, reality lends some credence to the stereotype. As the famous sociologist E. Franklin Frazier—who happened to be Negro—noted some years ago, "There is every reason to believe that as long as the Negro is discriminated against in employment and is forced to live in ghettos where there is considerable social disorganization, criminality among them will continue to be high."[1]

This chapter is primarily concerned with the "rebels without a cause"—people who aggressively lash out at their world in an apparently senseless way, who express their rage through overt violence. On the surface, their crimes may appear to be motivated simply by a desire for money or sexual release. Yet prior studies have shown that the rapist, for example, is more interested in dominating his victim than in achieving a sexual climax.[2] Even murderers who may be able to say what their conscious motives were at the time of the act are largely unaware of the unconscious factors operating within them, often since childhood, that *really* motivated them to commit murder. In fact, murderers can be accurately predicted on the basis of the tangled web of social conditions from which they emerge.[3] In other worlds, subconscious forces which may have little to do with the overt purpose of the crime can drive the violent person to his actions. These violent individuals are "rebels without a cause" in two senses of the word: 1) they seldom know the basic reasons behind their actions and 2) even though they reject the existing code of the dominant social order, they do not "rebel" under the flag of some movement or "cause."

Any statistics concerning such Negro "rebels" must, of course, be taken with a grain of salt. Police, juries, and judges obviously share the prejudices of other white Americans; middle-class whites can better afford either the bribes or the fees which will release them from a charge; "duck-pond" raids, such as those conducted in Watts, certainly label more people as "criminal" in ghettos than in the white suburbs. All these factors could inflate the presumed Negro role in American crime.

Nonetheless, other variables should be considered. For one, official statistics may often underestimate the amount of crime. Either because of fear of retaliation, hostility toward the police, or guilt about being a "stool pigeon," ghetto residents report far fewer crimes than actually occur. The President's Commission on Civil Disorders, for example, studied three precincts in Washington and showed that at least six times as many crimes had been committed than were reported to police.[4]

It must be recognized, too, that the American system dispenses one type of justice for Negroes and another for whites—sometimes in ways that work to the advantage of the Negro criminal. As Roy Wilkins, executive secretary of the NAACP, has observed, "If a Negro steals from another Negro, that's just a misdemeanor. . . . But if he kills a white man, why that means electrocution."[5] Austin Porterfield and Robert Talbert have demonstrated that when someone commits a crime in a Negro district, the police quite often "make a perfunctory inventory of the scene, go on about their business and never make any attempt to discover the perpetrator of the act."[6]

These various biases balance each other in some unknown

fashion, rendering suspect almost any statistic. Nonetheless, since study after study—as well as numerous autobiographies—have come to the same conclusion, it seems reasonable to assume that there is a high incidence of violent crimes in the Negro ghetto.

To achieve a balanced picture of ghetto violence, one must consider certain facts that racist orators often overlook:

1. The victims of Negro "rebels without a cause" are largely Negroes themselves. The Chicago police department has indicated that approximately 85 per cent of crimes committed by Negroes involved Negro victims. If you happen to be reading this book in the comfort of a crime-free white, middle-class district, contemplate these facts:

• Your chances of being the victim of any major felony are 78 per cent less than if you lived in a ghetto.

• A white woman's chances of being raped are almost 400 per cent less than those of Negro females.

• The probability of your being robbed is 3.5 times less than if you were a Negro.

Naturally, then, most ghetto residents suffer from a deep sense of insecurity, for they can never enjoy the safety afforded by living in a white suburb.[7]

2. The rate of crime in a Negro ghetto drops sharply when a nonviolent civil rights protest is taking place there. Well-documented reports from Cambridge, Maryland, and other cities suggest that the peaceful civil rights movement may drain off some of the rage felt by rebels, temporarily directing their energies—or at least their attention—to constructive efforts.

3. Except during periods of nonviolent protest, there seems little reason to believe that the rate of crime in Negro ghettos will drop in the future. In fact, one can foresee an increasing incidence of Negro crime, simply on the basis of projecting existing trends into the future:

• Even allowing for inadequate statistics, most experts agree that the crime rate in general has been going up in America. Violent crimes have apparently risen 37 per cent in the short period between 1960 and 1966.[8]

• Young people commit a disproportionate number of

violent crimes. In 1966 people under twenty-five committed 37 per cent of the nation's murders, 60 per cent of the rapes, and 71 per cent of armed robberies. And the President's Crime Commission has projected that the number of Negroes between fourteen and twenty-four in America's core cities will increase by about 63 per cent from 1966 to 1975, while the total Negro population in the same cities will increase by only 32 per cent.[9] To the degree, then, that violent crimes remain correlated with youth and urbanization—and no changes are made in the structure of our society—the incidence of Negro "rebels without a cause" will probably grow.

4. Segregation of Negroes, particularly in northern ghettos, apparently goes hand in hand with high crime rates.* In desegregated areas the rate of Negro crime drops.[10]

5. Negro crime has not always been disproportionately high; the gap between the Negro and white crime rate has apparently arisen only during the last century.[12] This finding should serve as a definitive disproof of those who have held to a theory that Negroes are somehow innately or biologically predisposed to violence. In an exhaustive study of antebellum New Orleans, Mark Hepler not only reviewed arrest and court statistics on Negro-white crime, but checked the reliability of his sources by consulting the records of three newspapers operating in New Orleans at that time (since the newspapers were in intense competition, they presented as much material as possible about crime). Counterchecking his sources, Hepler found that the rate of Negro and white crime was the same in proportion to their distribution in the population. To disprove any belief that slavery held the Negro "in check," Hepler compared the incidence of crime among whites, freed Negroes, and slaves. Again he found that the rate for each group was the same in relation to their numbers in the New Orleans population.†

Another study covering the first three decades of this century

---

*Earlier studies done in the South suggest that the crime rate is lower in segregated than in integrated areas.[11] Perhaps there is a true northern-southern difference in this matter; the segregated Negro in the South might, for example, be more insulated from such influences as the mass media that might motivate greater criminal activity.

†It is likely that there was a higher incidence of crime among slaves than was recorded, however, as slaves were tried before courts run by slavehold-

has shown that in Chicago the juvenile delinquency rates of Negroes increased seven times while the Negro population rose by only three times.[13]

Why, today, does the ghetto have such a high incidence of violent crimes? Why has it increased and why does it show every sign—including the new release found in riots—of growing still further?

THE GENESIS OF THE
"REBEL WITHOUT A CAUSE"

What produces the "rebel without a cause" in the urban ghetto? Why does the subculture of crime flourish there? Why has the ghetto crime rate increased since the early 1920's and show every sign of increasing still further? A brief look at the theories about ghetto crime can help answer these questions.

THE SUBCULTURE OF CRIME

American society has sentenced most of today's urban Negro to live in neighborhoods that are breeding grounds for crime. These are the "ports of entry"—transitional, dilapidated, economically deprived areas—that have always been the way stations for generations of newly arrived immigrants to American cities until they are able to move to better quarters. In an interesting study, Pauline Young demonstrated that if immigrants moved into a high-delinquency area the incidence of crime among them was 5 per cent during their first five years of residence, 46 per cent after another five years, and 83 per cent after another twenty years.[14]

Irish and Italian immigrants suffered the same fate as the Negro migrant in being consigned to these areas when they first arrived, but the Negro has a problem in the United States that other immigrants did not have: his skin color. Because of racial

---

ers, who would have been anxious to protect their property. On the other hand, the crime rate among freed slaves might have been exaggerated, since they probably received unusually harsh treatment from the white courts.

discrimination he cannot leave the ghetto as easily as his white predecessors. Whether decreed by law, by economic considerations, or simply by "gentlemen's agreements," most Negroes must remain in the urban slum areas where crime has traditionally flourished and even been condoned.

Robert Merton has noted that all Americans, poor or not, are inculcated with a drive toward "success," particularly in terms of material achievement.[15] Deprived groups, however, are not equipped with the means to achieve success through channels approved by American society, but there *are* a number of alternatives open to them for achieving "success." Many of these means are deviant or illegitimate, and one of them is, of course, crime.

The problem of status is particularly acute for American males, as Albert Cohen has pointed out in his brilliant book, *Delinquent Boys*.[16] Often the solution lower-class males choose is to reject the middle-class "rules of the game" as far as achieving status goes and create their own subculture with its own rules about what constitutes status. There are many different kinds of gangs in the criminal subculture, as Richard Cloward and Lloyd Ohlin have pointed out, depending on the context in which they emerge.[17] One of the types of gang is the "violent" gang, in which conventional values are spurned in favor of a new ethic emphasizing courage, defense of the group's honor, and aggressive behavior.

The motivations of the violent gang range from defending its "turf" to pure sadism, but those who have most closely studied bedrock rebels have generally concluded that a drive for power—especially as manifested in a desire to establish a reputation and thereby gain a sense of identity—motivates most of the violent rebels. Lewis Yablonsky argues that the rebel robs or attacks people primarily because he wishes to achieve status, or a "rep," without any particular interest in the victim's characteristics or material possessions.[18]

Lee Rainwater has ably explained why this search for identity among Negroes often takes the form of violent rebellion. He has noted that the ghetto child is "constantly exposed to identity labeling by his parents as a bad person,"[19] and that there is a tendency among lower-class Negroes to denigrate each other. This constant emphasis on being a "nobody" and being "bad" leaves many Negroes without a positive sense of identity. In their efforts to counteract this negative self-image and establish some sense of personal power and dignity many lower-class Negroes resort to physical force, because one way for a "nobody" to prove his importance is to dominate another person through violence.

Yet although most urban Negroes are exposed to all of the cultural conditions that promote violence, only a minority become "rebels without a cause." Admittedly, these broad social factors contribute strongly to the high rate of violent ghetto crime, but one must probe into the nature of the family to find out why one young Negro becomes a rebel while another chooses a different life-style.

THE FAMILY AND CRIME

Two studies have particular relevance in explaining why one slum child turns to crime while another does not. The first, a classic study by Sheldon and Eleanor Glueck, matched 500 delinquents and 500 nondelinquents from the same ghetto area of Boston.[20] A meticulous examination of their personalities and backgrounds revealed striking differences between the two groups, although both had been exposed to the influences of a delinquent subculture. Apparently, in the case of both Negro and white nondelinquents, their families provided a shield against the criminogenic elements existing in their neighborhoods. The delinquents, on the other hand, had been raised in an atmosphere characterized by extreme parental conflict, rejection or neglect by parents, and erratic, brutal, or negligent discipline. Deprived of love, security, and dignity, these children went to the streets and joined gangs which offered them some satisfaction for the basic needs which their families had frustrated.

A second study, the Cambridge-Somerville experiment, essentially confirmed the Gluecks' findings, but went one step further by examining a small sample of truly violent rebels.

Since the experiment has been described in various publications, I will give only a brief sketch of its background.[21]

In 1935 Dr. Richard Clarke Cabot of Harvard selected 650 boys, Negro and white, from Cambridge and Somerville, Massachusetts. Half the children were given social counseling, medical and educational aid, and various other help. As a control group the rest were left to the usual community services.

For a period of some seven years, social workers kept records of their regular visits to the boys' homes, psychiatrists and psychologists examined the children and their parents, physicians checked them, and various social agencies contributed information about the boys and their families.

Then, beginning in 1956 the boys—now men—were traced through a variety of community agencies. Approximately 40 per cent of the men had public criminal records, while the majority did not, and fourteen of the men had committed murder or assault with intent to kill.

Despite the severe limitations imposed by the small number of men examined, the results of the Cambridge-Somerville study made it clear that the backgrounds and personalities of the deviants—before they became deviant—differed substantially; that distinct differences appeared between the violent rebels and both the noncriminals and "property" criminals; and that the differences applied to both Negro and white offenders.

1. The potential murderers came from homes devoid of love. Their parents hated each other and their children. From early childhood onward, therefore, the violent rebels intimately experienced a world full of conflict and hatred.

2. Their mothers either neglected them or tried to dominate every aspect of their lives. Consequently, in their early lives, these men had not experienced a feminine environment in which they were treated warmly yet allowed some identity of their own.

3. Their fathers, if present in the home at all, were generally highly aggressive men who quite often had criminal records themselves. They taught the child, at least implicitly, that one could express violent tendencies without inhibitions and they offered the child a model of violence.

4. Typically, the parents disciplined the potential violent criminals in an extraordinarily erratic manner: sometimes they overlooked a transgression entirely while at other times they brutally punished the boy for the same action.

When violence-prone children eventually do commit an act of extreme violence, their behavior can best be understood as an act of symbolic revenge against their parents—and, by extension, against all human beings. The violence is a way of repaying the world for the beatings, cruelty, and domination they experience as children. Such children are naturally predisposed to join a gang which sanctions their violence and gives expression to their inner rage.

Sophisticated observers can easily diagnose these violent tendencies early in the life of the child. Counselors of the Cambridge-Somerville project, for example, had access to various psychological tests of the children. The counselors had predicted that sixteen boys would commit acts of aggression later in life. Of the fourteen persons in the sample who had become violent criminals twenty years later, only one was not included in this group of sixteen.

The factors promoting violent crime apply equally to Negroes and whites and yet Negro children are more often subject to a climate of familial violence, disorganization, and neglect which draws them into a subculture of "senseless" brutality and revolt. David Walters* is one example of the products of the "jungle of pathology" that can entrap the young Negro male.

PORTRAIT OF THE "REBEL WITHOUT A CAUSE"

"This child wishes to kill himself." So commented David Walters' teacher when he referred the boy to the Cambridge-Somerville program. "He frequently wishes he might be run over. Three times he has been hit by an automobile. We do

*Fictitious name.

not know whether he stepped in front of them deliberately, but we do know that he has attempted to jump out of a school window."

In 1938 David Walters, a chubby, oversized boy of twelve, came into the project. Another teacher described him as "belonging to our worst nigger bunch. He often gets into trouble when he is saucy or aggressive; at other times, he daydreams and lives in a world of make-believe." The psychologist who first interviewed him found that David had normal intelligence and that he was a "very unhappy, frustrated child." He added, "Unless he can secure understanding and affection, I am certain he is headed for difficulty. He will simply explode."

A social worker went to the Walters' home and later described the father as a vain, aggressive show-off. He had readily agreed to let David become a subject: "Someone needs to do something about him!" During various home visits, David's family fought continuously. His mother was a large, lethargic woman who worked as a maid. She described David (one of three sons) as "having too much pep. He's very hard to manage. I have trouble with him when he goes and acts smart. He is a big, old coward—he thinks about himself but nobody else." The social worker recorded her reaction after the first visit in this fashion: "I felt the queerest sensation in this home, something strange and unhealthy."

Interviews with school officials filled out a picture of David as "destructive, dull, lacking in attention. He cries easily, daydreams and is moody. He is a very restless boy."

Miss Casey,* a nurse turned social worker, decided to accept the case. In January 1939 she made her first visit to the family. David's father told her that his constant beatings failed to give the boy any "gumption." Mrs. Walters broke in, "You know how you would feel if people made fun of you and didn't like you." Mr. Walters looked up and sadly commented, "You know, I feel a lot like that myself."

Welfare officials and neighbors concurred in describing David's mother as a strange and mentally disordered woman. A minister whose church helped support the family observed,

*Fictitious name.

"The last time I went to their home, the mother was drunk. The little boys clung to me. They were mortally afraid of their mother." In her talks with the mother, Miss Casey noted a pervading feeling of tension: "She made a great effort to keep herself under control. She tried to appear at ease, but one could not help feeling that there was real tension and emotional disturbance under all the acting." Mrs. Walters' rejection of David became more and more apparent; she talked constantly of beating him, refused to get glasses for him after they had been recommended, and informed the boy's teacher that he could whip him whenever he wanted because "David is such a brat."

Meanwhile, David increasingly withdrew from his family and rose in prestige with his gang, the Tigers. He became war leader of the junior branch of the gang and led them in battles against an Italian gang that was trying to take over the Tigers' territory

In late 1939 David was wounded in a gang fight and hospitalized. Complications, including pneumonia, kept him confined for more than five months. During that time his parents seldom visited him. Mrs. Walters confessed to a nurse, "I just don't love that kid. When he was a baby, I could kiss him, but not now. I seen all them mothers doing it, but I can't." As the time approached for his release from the hospital, the Walters were reluctant to take him back. Miss Casey finally convinced them to let David return, under her nursing supervision, the boy was brought back to good health.

By late 1940 Mrs. Walters reported that David had become concerned about sex. He had just entered puberty. "David's getting very modest," the mother said proudly. "He won't let no one in the bathroom when he is there. He is just like me—I like to be alone."

One day David suddenly said, "Mother I have a question. I hate to ask because it is a dirty question. Where do babies come from?"

The startled mother said quickly, "Why do you want to know?"

"Jimmy said that you should not take that baloney that they

come from heaven. He said your mother and father do dirty things to each other and then they have a baby."

"Well, that's not a nice thing for boys to discuss. Just forget it." And then she slapped him.

Mrs. Walters informed Miss Casey about the incident and pleaded for her help. The counselor convinced her that David should be given some information about sex and volunteered to do it herself, to Mrs. Walters' relief.

In weekly interviews, Miss Casey broached the subject with the boy, who responded with apparent eagerness. Nonetheless, he revealed strong anxiety about sex: "I don't want to get married ever!"

"But why not?"

"Because I don't want to do those dirty things that Jimmy told me about." The interviews continued, but David showed continued anxiety despite some progress. Just before a hospital examination, David said, "I don't want the doctor to look here," pointing to his penis.

In one tape-recorded interview, David indicated many of his fears: "I want to tell you now something about my fears. I am afraid to swim—afraid I might drown—once I nearly did drown in deep water. My father doesn't understand me. He gets cross all the time. I want the boys to like me, but sometimes they call me stupid. I don't know what's wrong with me. I guess I am queer. Oftentimes I ain't got nothing to say. I won't turn out very well. No one will want to have me. No one will want to marry me. I just can't do nothing . . ."

In 1942 Miss Casey wrote in her annual report, "I am not discouraged with him. He has improved more than any boy in my group. . . . He keeps away from his gang friends. I am delighted with him."

The day after Miss Casey had written, "I am proud of David and think he is worth the effort of the whole study," she received a telephone call from the police. They informed her that David Walters had been arrested on suspicion of murder. A fellow gang member, Richey Jones,* had disappeared and

---

*Fictitious name.

David was the last person known to have been in Richey's company.

As the police questioned him, David admitted that he had frequent sexual relations with other boys. He had also boasted to his gang that he would "get" Richey for some insult. David confessed to having had sexual relations with Richey Jones on the day of his disappearance, but he stubbornly denied having killed him. Four months later, when the ice broke on the Charles River, the police recovered Richey's body. Circumstantial evidence pointed to David Walters, yet there was no proof that he had pushed Richey into the river.

The police booked David on a charge of sodomy, and psychiatrists recommended his commitment for observation at the Boston Psychopathic Hospital. There, examiners found David to be essentially sane. A Rorshach analysis, however, showed pronounced obsessional qualities and a sadistic trend in his personality: "He is obsessed with sucking and blood letting, the touching of fluffy textures, and the killing of chickens."

Miss Casey visited David in the mental hospital, and David insisted on his innocence: "The cops tried to make me say that I pushed Richey into the river. I did not. I liked Richey. Why should I kill him? I finally said to the police, 'What are you trying to do, frame me?' I did not kill Richey."

He was released from the hospital in 1942 and diagnosed as "without psychosis." The next year David was shifted from mental hospital to reform school and back to the hospital. Finally Miss Casey arranged for his placement at a center for disturbed children, where he was once caught wringing the neck of a chicken. Several times he threatened children with a knife. The center, complaining strongly about his seducing other children and his sadism, soon returned him to the city.

Miss Casey questioned David about his behavior. He answered candidly: "I like to use knives and I guess I feel like sometimes cutting chickens down the middle and watching their guts spew out. Sometimes I feel that way about people."

"Do you try to control these feelings?" Miss Casey asked.

"Yes, I guess I do, but when people make me mad I want to do something!"

With David's permission, Miss Casey arranged for the boy to be placed in a state hospital. He corresponded with her often and seemed relatively content. An older inmate, a former forger, became friendly with him. Yet in 1945, when the older man cast some aspersion on his masculinity, David knifed and killed him.

THE REBEL AND NEGRO PROTEST

Clearly, people like David Walters seldom participate actively in the civil rights movement. Yet to the degree that urban riots can be considered part of the Negro protest, the rebels do play a part. Once a disorder has erupted, such men play a prominent (although not dominating) role in looting, vandalism, and sniping.

To tap their attitudes about civil rights, in the spring of 1968 we interviewed 100 Houston men between fifteen and twenty-five who had committed violent felonies unconnected with civil rights issues. They were interviewed randomly as they entered a Houston police station.* Their backgrounds, as they reported them, were similar to that of David Walters.

To see how they differed from the general population, we compared them to the random sample drawn in Houston. We asked both groups, "Do you think the riots in Watts helped or hurt the Negro's cause?"

OPINION OF THE WATTS RIOT

	"REBELS" (N:100)†	RANDOM SAMPLE (N:572)
Helped	42%	30%
Hurt	27	37
Both	28	10
No opinion	3	23

*A police station is hardly the ideal place to interview men about their attitudes on such subjects as violence, and we made every effort to assure them of their anonymity. Nonetheless, it would be unwise to take their responses at face value.

†N=Number of respondents.

One of the most interesting aspects of these findings is that almost three times as many rebels thought the riot both helped *and* hurt, possibly the most objective assessment of the effects of the explosion as one can reach. Further, it should be noted that only a handful of the rebels expressed no opinion whatsoever, perhaps indicating that they pay more attention to violent events than the average urban Negro.

Expectedly, even in the context of a police-station interview, the rebels more often condoned the use of violence. Asked, "In what situations, if any, do you think violence is justified in defending Negro rights?" they responded:

USE OF VIOLENCE

	"REBELS" (N:100)	RANDOM SAMPLE (N:572)
Never justified	11%	45%
Generally justified	36	26
Justified in self-defense	50	24
No opinion	3	5

The rebels apparently picture their own actual violence and the potential violence of a riot as simply defending oneself, a convenient way of rationalizing their behavior.

The rebels and the random population did not differ in their attitudes toward the police; here, one must assume that the rebels were simply lying:

OPINION OF POLICE

	"REBELS" (N:100)	RANDOM SAMPLE (N:572)
Generally good/Neutral	43%	46%
Generally bad	41	31
Bad/Racial discrimination	1	8
No contact	0	15
No opinion	15	0

Both groups again agreed on what they regarded as the main problems facing Negroes in Houston:

MAIN PROBLEMS FACING NEGROES

	"REBELS" (N:100)	RANDOM SAMPLE (N:572)
Jobs	42%	55%
Education	9	14
Housing	7	11
Police, discrimination, other problems with "power structure"	21	10
Internal problems of the Negro community	5	10
No opinion	18	10

The only possibly significant area of disagreement lay in the greater tendency of the rebels to blame the "power structure" rather than Negroes themselves for basic problems; the rebels again appear to be a more volatile element of the general population than the average man.*

Finally, on the basic question of the speed of civil rights progress, the rebels exhibited much more discontent than the average person. When asked, "In attempts of Negroes to gain their civil rights, have things been going too slowly, about right or too fast?" they responded in this fashion:

SPEED OF INTEGRATION

	"REBELS" (N:100)	RANDOM SAMPLE (N:572)
Too slow	62%	44%
About right	37	51
Too fast	0	4
No opinion	1	1

*It should be noted in passing that the rebels exhibited a deep distrust of others. When asked about how trusting they should be toward someone whom they meet for the first time, 26 per cent of the rebels would trust him, 42 per cent would treat him with caution, and 33 per cent would distrust him on sight. This question was not asked of the random sample, but we do know from the selected responses of the "activists," "achievers," etc., that only a tiny handful would definitely distrust another person immediately.

While none of the rebels had actively forwarded the cause of civil rights, their high level of dissatisfaction suggests that they could easily become absorbed into a movement which—in the name of Negro advancement—would use violence to achieve its means. Bred in a subculture of crime, reared in brutal families, and acting in "self-defense," they could be transformed into the shock troops of an insurrection.

REFERENCES

1. E. Franklin Frazier, *The Negro in the United States* (New York: Macmillan, 1957), p. 647.

2. William McCord, Joan McCord, and Paul Verden, "Sexual Deviance Among Lower-Class Adolescents," *International Journal of Social Psychiatry*, 8, 1962, pp. 165–79.

3. William McCord, "The Personality of Social Deviants" in *The Study of Personality: An Interdisciplinary Appraisal*, Edward Norbeck, Douglass Price-Williams, and William McCord, eds. (New York: Holt, Rinehart & Winston, 1968).

4. *Report of the National Advisory Commission on Civil Disorders* (Washington, D.C., 1968), p. 268.

5. Roy Wilkins, as quoted in Bradford Daniel, *Black, White, and Gray* (New York: Sheed & Ward Inc., 1964), p. 34.

6. Austin Porterfield and Robert Talbert, *Crime, Suicide and Social Well-Being* (Fort Worth, Tex.: Leo Potishman Foundation), p. 69.

7. *Report of the National Advisory Commission, op. cit.*, p. 268

8. *Ibid.*

9. *Ibid.*, p. 269.

10. Donal Cressey, "Crime" in *Contemporary Social Problems*, Robert Merton and Robert Nisbet, eds. (New York: Harcourt, Brace & World, 1966), p. 153.

11. *Ibid.*

12. Mark Hepler, *Urban Negro Crime*, unpublished Ph.D. dissertation, Rice University, 1968.

13. Earl R. Moses, "Community Factors in Negro Delinquency," *Journal of Negro Education*, Vol. 5, April 1936, pp. 220–27.

14. Pauline V. Young, "Urbanization as a Factor in Juvenile Delinquency," *Publications of the American Sociological Society*, Vol. 24, 1930, pp. 162–66.

15. Robert Merton, "Social Structure and Anomie," *Social Theory and Social Structure* (New York: The Free Press, 1957), pp. 131–60.

16. Albert Cohen, *Delinquent Boys* (New York: The Free Press, 1955).

17. Richard Cloward and Lloyd Ohlin, *Delinquency and Opportunity* (New York: The Free Press, 1960).

18. Lewis Yablonsky, paper presented at the American Association for the Advancement of Science meeting, Philadelphia, December 1962.

19. Lee Rainwater, "Crucible of Identity: The Negro Lower-Class Family," *Daedalus*, Winter 1966, p. 204.

20. Sheldon and Eleanor Glueck, *Unraveling Juvenile Delinquency* (Cambridge, Mass.: Harvard University Pres, 1950).

21. See, for example, Edwin Powers and Helen Witmer, *An Experiment in the Prevention of Delinquency* (New York: Columbia University Press, 1951); and William McCord, Joan McCord, and Irving Zola, *Origins of Crime* (New York: Columbia University Press, 1959).

CHAPTER 11

THE ACTIVIST

John Howard

The activist has committed himself to changing the role of the Negro in America—indeed, to reorganizing American society itself. He is a rebel but he has chosen the reformer's path rather than the way of individual or mass violence. Men like Martin Luther King, Roy Wilkins, and Whitney Young have in the past best exemplified this approach.

The reformist orientation has dominated the civil rights movement throughout most of its history, but recently, it has come under attack by critics who charge that reform cannot be achieved within the framework of existing American society. This dispute has profound implications, for if the reformers are wrong the only option for the movement would seem to be increasingly militant activity, perhaps including terrorism and guerrilla warfare. It becomes crucial, then, to examine the reformist perspective. What are the activist's goals? What are his assumptions? What are the sources of his support?

THE REFORMIST PERSPECTIVE

The way of the reformer is not an easy one. Within weeks after his election as the first Negro mayor of Cleveland Carl Stokes was being attacked as a sellout by the radical Black Panthers. Regarded by traditionally Democratic whites who voted against him as an upstart, it was Stokes's fate to be seen by some Negroes as too conservative. We are not concerned here with shades and varieties of orientation among whites; therefore, let us examine the reformist outlook by contrasting it with the black radical orientation.

The essential assumptions of racial reformism can be spelled out as follows:

1. Significant improvements in the Negroes' position can be achieved within the framework of the existing political system, *i.e.*, the legal process, the acquisition and use of the ballot, and coalition politics. Reformers have a more optimistic view of American society than revolutionaries. They assume that its fundamental structure is basically sound and that the major problem is one of gaining full participation for Negroes. Thus, while black-power spokesmen such as Stokely Carmichael and H. Rap Brown charged that the Vietnamese war was symptomatic of basic pathologies in the American social system, Roy Wilkins of the NAACP refrained for a long time from criticizing it. The orientation of the reformers is analogous to that of the "bread-and-butter" trade unionists, those members of organized labor who do not question the fundamental structure of the economy but simply seek more for labor within it.

2. The reformers place their major emphasis on achieving integration. They assume that all-black schools or communities are inherently undesirable and that the ultimate goal of the Negro should be the loss of a sense of racial self. By contrast, the radicals argue that the Negro not only has a heritage within this country but an ultimate heritage rooted in Africa that should be preserved. The sense of a unique American heritage finds expression in the concept of "soul," which refers both to certain concrete things—cultural artifacts, in the language of anthropology—and to a certain *geist*. Substantively it embraces certain kinds of music and food, and in terms of ethos it compels a joyful acceptance of being black. The radical also argues that the ingrained nature of American racism and the realities of American politics will not permit the black man to be

accepted as an equal by the larger white society and that prag-
matic considerations dictate some plan for the survival of the
black man in America that takes cognizance of this fact.

The black reformer is the equivalent of the white liberal, as
their outlook and assumptions are similar. Liberals tend to
accept the premise that the basic institutional system is sound
and that problems arise from the persistence of a few anachronistic practices here and there (discrimination, for example)
and/or the manipulations of corrupt or incompetent men.
Thus the white liberal and the black reformer take the position
that the removal of discrimination in housing would constitute
a major step toward coping with the housing problems of the
ghetto. Neither would question the premise that housing
should be a market commodity nor examine the possibility that
bad housing is endemic in the system in that tax laws and the
operations of the marketplace decrease incentives of the slum
landlord to upgrade the quality of his dwellings.

On issues, reformers can be differentiated from radicals as
follows:

Education. The reformer favors integration, both on moral
grounds and in the belief that it is the only way black children
will receive quality education. The radical argues that the
increasing black population in many big cities makes school
integration an impossibility and that, in any event, the notion
that quality education cannot exist in all-black schools is
implicitly racist. They argue that blacks should control their
own schools, since they believe that the inferiority of black
schools does not spring from the racial make-up of the students
but from the fact that nonblacks control them and divert
resources away from them.

Housing. The reformers argue for integration, while the radicals assume that the persistence of the black community is not
only inevitable but desirable.

Politics. The reformer assumes that traditional activity (i.e.,
lobbying, voting, and the like) are viable and, by and large,
opts for participation in the Democratic Party. The radical feels
that blacks should organize as an independent political force,
forming alliances with the traditional parties only on terms

which it deems favorable. They argue that if blacks automatically give their allegiance to the Democrats they lose their leverage to bargain for concessions.

Broader tactics. Reformers countenance the use of the courts to seek redress of grievances and advocate certain kinds of direct action. Radicals are much more willing to talk about violent confrontations between whites and blacks. They are unequivocally in favor of armed self-defense and occasionally talk in terms of guerrilla warfare.

The reformist orientation is typified by the NAACP, which was founded in 1909 to combat the extremely harsh and repressive anti-Negro legislation and social intimidation that grew out of the post-Reconstruction "white backlash" of the late 1800's. At the time of its inception, the NAACP was regarded as radical, but within a decade it was attacked by the black-chauvinist Garvey movement as "too conservative" and was accused of being dominated by the middle class and by mulattoes who had no roots in the ghetto. Within two decades it was being attacked by the Communist Party as being bourgeois-dominated and insensitive to the revolutionary potential of the "black masses." On the other hand, throughout most of its history white segregationists have attacked it as being extremist. Its approach is essentially reformist, however, and at least for quite a while it probably reflected the outlook of the great majority of Negroes.

Despite its prominence, the NAACP and other activist groups have never enjoyed full participation by the Negro community. Even though Negroes in the United States are continually subjected to unfair treatment because of race, relatively few have ever been associated with any civil rights organization. It seems, for example, that the membership of the NAACP has never exceeded 500,000, and if one totaled the number of Negroes who took part in the many demonstrations and sit-ins of the early 1960's it would come to considerably under 1,000,000.

The question, then, is: since all Negroes face the same problems, how do we account for those who do engage in reformist types of protest while so many others do not?

Numerous "theories" of the Negro movement are to be found in the literature of the social sciences. The most common hypotheses are the following:

1. The Relative-Deprivation Hypothesis states that although things may be getting better for Negroes they still fall considerably behind whites in terms of income and standard of living. Insofar as Negroes increasingly compare themselves with whites they come to feel relatively more deprived despite certain objective gains in income and status.

2. The Rising-Expectation Hypothesis is similar to the explanation used to account for colonial uprisings. Briefly, it states that modest gains cause Negro expectations to exceed the pace of progress and this gap between expectations and advances produces frustration that leads to protest.

3. The Status-Inconsistency Hypothesis is that an individual is likely to feel frustration if he ranks high along one dimension of status and low along another. For example, a female engineer would be in a low-status position in a profession dominated by males, and to some extent in the larger society, but in a high-status position insofar as engineering is a prestigeful occupation.

WHO ARE THE ACTIVISTS?

Following the publication of E. Franklin Frazier's *Black Bourgeoisie* it became fashionable to condemn the Negro middle class for, among other things, its lack of leadership in the struggle against segregation and discrimination. Such accusations notwithstanding, however, insofar as there has been sustained active opposition to American racism it has come from the black bourgeoisie. This can be accounted for not in terms of any special virtue of this group, but probably in terms of status inconsistency.

Historically, members of the middle class took the lead in mounting the first protests against the crippling confines of caste at the turn of the century, and fifty years later middle-class Negro college students initiated the sit-ins which in turn gave impetus to the massive assault on racism of the early and middle 1960's. If these middle-class reformers—from W. E. B. DuBois to the students of the early '60's—did not turn to radicalism and condemn the basic political and social system in the United States in toto, it was because so many of them had enjoyed a certain degree of educational and occupational mobility, which convinced them that the system was not inherently defective but needed reform rather than complete transformation.

POST-SELMA REFORMERS

Following the passage of civil rights legislation in 1964 and 1965 many people, black and white, had the feeling that the corner had been turned as regards Negro rights. The Watts riot of August 1965, however, graphically demonstrated that the game was not even close to being over. The massive march in Selma, Alabama, and the 1965 voting rights act were only turning points. After Selma the focus shifted from the largely nonviolent, relatively integrated demonstrations and confrontations in the South to the ghettos of the North and West.

The post-Selma struggle has been much more complex than the pre-Selma struggle—the issues are more involved, the identity of major actors less clear. It is the purpose of this section of the chapter to analyze the post-Selma phase of the movement, which in many ways is more important than the pre-Selma phase. The early movement dealt with narrowly defined racial issues such as discrimination at lunch counters. The later movement has tended to focus on class deprivation and has called for remedies relevant not only for blacks, but for all class have-nots—Puerto Rican, Mexican-American, American Indian, and white.

In very broad terms, three groups have emerged in the post-Selma movement—the ghetto rioter, black students, and the politically mobilized poor. Riots and rioters are dealt with in other sections of this book. Let us deal here with the other two groups. Both have been militant but as of the spring of 1968 neither has turned to violence (except for sporadic student rebellions).

The data on which this section of the chapter is based were gathered via field work at South Carolina State College at Orangeburg, South Carolina, the scene of prolonged black student protest, and at the Poor People's March on Washington in 1968.

In the first part of this section I shall discuss black student activists and in the last half the mobilized poor. The discussion will attempt to identify the issues around which these post-Selma activists have mobilized and account for the strategies they employ.

ORANGEBURG, SOUTH CAROLINA: IN THE HEAT OF THE NIGHT

It is not easy to get to Orangeburg. It is an out-of-the-way place, but twice in the last decade, South Carolina State College at Orangeburg has in a dramatic way marked the mood and trend at black schools. In that sense this out-of-the-way place is significant.

Orangeburg is a small town, with a population of about 14,000. Railroad tracks run through town and there is a monument to the Confederate dead in the town square. One senses that life in Orangeburg—with its obsession with race—teeters between tragedy and the theater of the absurd.

South Carolina State and Claflin, a religious school, sit side by side on Watson Street near the edge of town. South Carolina State, the only state-supported black school, has a student body of just under 2,000. Claflin has just over 800 students. The killing of three black students by the police had brought me to town. There had been several nights of student protest over the continuing refusal of the owner of the All-Star Bowling Alley to admit Negro patrons. On the night of February 8, 1968, three blacks, two of them students at the college and the third a high school student, had been shot and killed by the police. Twenty-eight students had been wounded. The next day the local paper spoke of "rampaging Negroes" and Governor

McNair attributed the tragedy to the incitement of black-power advocates. A few weeks after the shooting I arrived in Orangeburg to find out what had happened and estimate the dimensions and direction of the black-student movement. What emerged was not simple, but it did help clarify the nature of the post-Selma movement.

In *The Invisible Man* Ralph Ellison provided a devastating portrayal of the Negro administrator at the Negro college. He might have drawn his portrait from the administrators at South Carolina State prior to 1967.

A certain concept dominated administrative policy at State. There were rigid standards of dress and attendance at vesper services was compulsory. The relationship between students and administration was highly authoritarian. The system seems to have been predicated on the idea that one of the major functions of the school was to "civilize" the students, to transform them from niggers into Negroes.

South Carolina State's former president, D. C. Turner, was viewed in essentially this manner by the students at State to whom I spoke. The system began to come apart in 1967. One student described the situation as follows: "In the last few years a lot of job recruiters have come in here who never came before. They are all trying to get their token Negro—their 'count' Negro, you know. Anyway, these students began to find the education they were getting was not all that good. The employer's representative would say you need this and you need that—and these kids had not had the stuff. In the past you were trained to be a teacher or a preacher and what you got was good enough for that but not a whole lot else."

So the students began to ask, "Why is the administration concerned about whether we go to vesper service, but not whether we get a good enough education in this place?"

Student discontent with the quality of education and the authoritarianism on the part of the administration crystallized in a 98 per cent effective boycott of classes over the issue of the failure of the administration to renew the contracts of three white instructors. Turner resigned and an acting president, a younger man, M. Maceo Nance, was appointed in his place.

Apparently the students had expected significant improvements when they returned to school in the fall of 1967 and when they found none their disappointment generated a sense of discontent in which a number of specific grievances began to be articulated.

There were a number of perspectives represented among the students that fall. First, there was a small number who were essentially "New Left" in their orientation. They turned out to picket when the Dow recruiter came to State and they talked about "imperialism" and "militarism."

Second, there was a slightly larger group, numbering perhaps a dozen, who called themselves the Black Action Coordinating Committee. The group was formed in the spring of 1967 and sought courses in black history and a greater emphasis on Negro contributions to the national culture.

Third, there was the campus branch of the NAACP, which seemed to be run by only one or two students.

Finally, there was the great mass of students who were politically apathetic but increasingly discontented with the old regime and the quality of the education they were receiving. The students at State were not in any sense radical.

The immediate cause of the shooting on campus was police reaction to student demonstrations directed at the All-Star Bowling Alley, which refused to accommodate blacks.

As early as 1965 a complaint had been filed with the Justice Department as a result of owner Harry Floyd's refusal to admit Negroes. Three years later there had still been no change in policy.

Finally, between February 5 and 10, 1968, the matter came to a head.

On Monday evening, February 5, a number of blacks sought admittance to the bowling alley. Proprietor Harry Floyd sought to have them arrested but Chief Roger E. Poston demurred on the grounds that the students were not committing a crime. He did clear the place, however.

On Tuesday evening arrests did take place when several hundred students gathered in the parking lot in front of the bowling alley to press their claims. Several students were clubbed by the police, and bricks were tossed by the students. M. Maceo Nance, the acting president of South Carolina State, declared the next day, "I do not condone destruction of property, but for the record, it happened after young ladies were hit."

The next day the mayor, the city manager, and the head of the Chamber of Commerce met with the students at an assembly. The meeting was a disaster. The mayor and the city manager reportedly either denied that problems existed or said they had no authority to deal with them. Only the head of the Chamber of Commerce seems to have made an impact when he agreed to read student grievances to a meeting of the Chamber the next day.

There were twelve demands, including closing the All-Star Bowling Alley until its segregationist policy was changed, the establishment of a biracial human-relations commission, integration of drive-in theaters, and the encouragement of the Orangeburg regional hospital to accept Medicare.

The Chamber as a whole, like the mayor and the city manager, either denied having the authority to deal with particular problems or claimed that there was no problem. Thus, by Thursday evening, there was no resolution in sight.

That evening, three eighteen-year-olds—Samuel Hammard, of Fort Lauderdale, Florida, Henry Smith, of Marion, South Carolina, and Delano Middleton, an Orangeburg high school student—were shot and killed when Orangeburg police and state police converged on the campus. Twenty-eight students were wounded. There had been a rally on campus that evening and the police claimed they had been fired upon, although this has never been verified.

In the immediate aftermath of the tragedy the All-Star Bowling Alley was desegregated when the Justice Department finally mobilized itself to act.

There are a number of currents astir on black college campuses. In the context of the Orangeburg tragedy, let us try to sort them out for what they say about one kind of activist.

1. The Enemy Within. In the early 1960's black college students engaged in protest against whites who discriminated. They initiated the sit-ins and provided the spirit and bodies

that sustained the drive. In the late 1960's black students are still active, but—at Texas Southern University, Howard, South Carolina State, and other schools—black administrations are their targets, charged with failing to provide quality education for black students, with failing to allow students to participate in the decision-making process, and with maintaining rules that unnecessarily circumscribe the student's social life.

At South Carolina State post-Selma activism seems to have been a consequence of the successes of pre-Selma activism. In all probability the black student did not fully realize how bad an education he was getting until job opportunities had improved to the point where he could consider offers from a wide range of firms. It is also probable that exposure to students from northern schools during the feverish days of the civil rights movement in the South in the early 1960's brought home to him the restrictiveness of his campus rules, *e.g.*, compulsory vesper attendance and ten o'clock curfew hours for girls.

2. Old Enemies. Following the tragedy on the campus of South Carolina State the Orangeburg newspaper, the *Times-Democrat*, declared that Floyd (the bowling-alley proprietor) and black power were on a collision course. Governor Robert McNair attributed the violence to the presence of Cleveland Sellars of SNCC. Neither of these interpretations is accurate. Discrimination rather than black power was the issue at the bowling alley. Student protest was directed at the same kind of issue that had inspired the early sit-ins. To some extent, then, the post-Selma activist has the same concerns as pre-Selma activists.

The essential thrust and meaning of the movement among black students is obscured by using the phrase "black power," because it has no clear meaning. In one sense this generation of black student activists are lineal descendants of the students of the early 1960's. Both have gone into action against discrimination as practiced openly in places of public accommodations. In another sense, their protest is more radical, as they have openly and directly taken on their black elders.

One must separate rhetoric from action. The rhetoric of student activists has occasionally borne elements of something called "black power"; in practice, however, they have sought to do away with anachronistic social relations on campus and authoritarian decision-making systems.

The black student activists have not, as a group, given up hope in America or in the efficacy of nonviolent action. In Houston, for example, we selected a sample of 141 Negro college students. Sixty-four were "activists" in the sense that they claimed to have participated in such nonviolent activities as picketing and boycotting. A similar sample of seventy-seven students said that they had never participated in civil rights activity.*

Predictably, the student activists were more dissatisfied with the speed of the civil rights movement than other students. When asked, "In the attempts of Negroes to gain their rights, have things been going too slowly, about right or too fast?" the students responded in this fashion:

SPEED OF INTEGRATION

	STUDENT ACTIVISTS (N:64)†	STUDENT NONACTIVISTS (N:77)
Too slow	75.6%	50.6%
About right	20.3	19.5
Too fast	3.1	19.5
No opinion	1.0	10.4

In their views about riots and violence, however, the student activists seemed somewhat less bellicose than the presumably more apathetic students:

* Our results here may be legitimately questioned since, for example, students who said they hadn't participated may actually have been involved in some clandestine, even violent, movement.

† N=number of respondents.

OPINION OF THE WATTS RIOT

	STUDENT ACTIVISTS (N:64)	STUDENT NONACTIVISTS (N:77)
Helped	23.81%	31.17%
Hurt	36.51	38.96
Neither	36.51	27.27
No opinion	3.17	2.60

USE OF VIOLENCE

	STUDENT ACTIVISTS (N:64)	STUDENT NONACTIVISTS (N:77)
Never justified	34.38%	24.68%
Justified in self-defense	56.25	58.44
Justified for other reasons	6.25	6.49
No opinion	7.91	10.29

Another question indicated that bitterness and pessimism did not motivate the activists but that they seemed definitely more hopeful about the future than other students. When asked, ' Do you think your children's lifetime will be better, worse, or just about the same, as yours?", the response was:

WILL YOUR CHILDREN'S LIFE BE BETTER?

	STUDENT ACTIVISTS (N:64)	STUDENT NONACTIVISTS (N:77)
Better	95.31%	77.92%
Worse	0.0	2.60
Same	0.0	6.49
No opinion	4.69	12.99

Donald Mathews and James Prothro examined a somewhat different sample of students, but our research bears out their basic conclusion: "The more active students are more tolerant

understanding and optimistic about white people and segregation than are the inactive students. . . . The student protesters
apparently were not 'the children of despair' but of hope and
optimism."[1]

The other set of post-Selma activists, the black poor, are all
too consistent in status, at the low end of all the dimensions of
power and prestige. They have become increasingly active,
however, and are seeking to significantly change the structures
and assumptions of the American economic system. Let us now
discuss the mobilized poor.

THE POOR PEOPLE'S CAMPAIGN

The more one thought about it the more one had to conclude as a social scientist that it could not work. The plan was
to bring some large but unspecified number of poor people to
Washington and to camp out while conducting a campaign
whose tactics ranged from conventional lobbying through possible civil disobedience for (1) the passage of various kinds of
legislation intended to improve the economic situation of the
poor, and 2) changes in administrative policy yielding greater
use of things like surplus food for benefit of the poor.

Who were these new marchers? From where did they come
and what did they hope to achieve?

Into early June there were at least the following kinds of
persons at Resurrection City.

1. The Rootless Young. There were young people between
the ages of eighteen and twenty-five who, being out of school
and out of work or having jobs of only a marginal nature
(domestic, busboy, etc), were willing to go to Washington
D.C. They were motivated by a genuine desire for something to
be done to help the poor, but had little notion as to what that
might be beyond simply "good jobs" or "decent pay." The
intricacies of the negative income tax or the food-stamp program escaped them. Equally important were their hopes for
bettering their own situation, and many had said they might
not return home. Young people have always been mobile; it

was simply that in this case the mobility had an element of social protest built into it.

A minority within this group had an ideology and to some extent a program. They were personified by "Sweet Willie" Hines and the "Invaders." Sweet Willie was the first person I met at Resurrection City, when he rushed up to me and asked if I had a car and could give some of the camp residents a ride to an important meeting. I had seen his picture in the paper that morning in a story alleging that he and some of the Invaders had sought to take over a local high school. I volunteered my car and my services as driver and as it turned out Sweet Willie and the Invaders were going to another high school.

They had come from Memphis and had been among the early arrivals at the camp. Some newspaper stories had alleged that they had been responsible for the violence during the last march in which Martin Luther King had participated in Memphis. To the average high school principal Sweet Willie's appearance must have invoked fear and trembling. He was a tall, dark youth in his early twenties with "natural" (unstraightened) hair and a gold earring in his left earlobe. He wore a sarape, hurachs, and a brightly colored shirt. He did not look like a young Republican.

As we barreled across the bridge toward the Anacostia High School I asked Sweet Willie about the newspaper story.

"That story is not true—we didn't try to take over any school. The principal got scared because he had read that we are a gang—but we're not a gang, we are an organization. What I wanted to do was . . ."

We had reached the Anacostia High School. A crowd of students was out front as the noon lunch break neared. Sweet Willie, the Invaders, and I advanced on the schoolyard as a police car pulled up and two officers got out. An assistant principal emerged from the school building. We were surrounded.

A crowd gathered as Sweet Willie and the principal came face to face. Sweet Willie, virtually taking up where he had left off in our conversation in the car, said he wanted to address an assembly of the students. The assistant principal, Mr. Lom-an assembly on short notice and so close to the end of the bardi, said it would be difficult, maybe impossible, to arrange school year with examinations coming up so soon. From the ensuing dialogue it emerged that Sweet Willie wanted to talk about nonviolence and the need for it. He said that the "militants" were exposed to the students all summer and that unless a program was established before school let out to run through the summer the game was left to the other players. Lombardi agreed and a kind of rapport began to develop between them. Eventually it was arranged for Sweet Willie to talk to several social-studies classes, as the combined enrollment in these classes was greater than the number of people who could be brought together at an assembly.

As we rolled on to the next high school I asked Sweet Willie how he had come to accept nonviolence. He said he had been persuaded by Martin Luther King of its meaning and effectiveness and that he was now carrying on his beliefs.

A car had been following us, and when we reached the next school one of the Invaders wondered if the driver was a detective. Whoever he was, he was easily decoyed. Sweet Willie spoke loudly of confronting the principal of this school and of another school immediately after. He rushed into the school, presumably to confront the principal, and we piled into the car and headed for a different school from the one that was to be "hit" next.

It appeared that it was simply the idea of surveillance that was repugnant.

At the next school we were met by two Negro administrators who were obviously frightened, too frightened to put us out but unhappy to have to talk to us. They agreed to meet with Sweet Willie (who had arrived in another car) while the rest of us waited. An hour passed and more black administrators were called into an inner office where the conference was taking place while a husky uniformed fellow from the juvenile division was hanging around the outer office where the rest of us waited.

When Sweet Willie emerged he was followed by one of the black administrators, who followed us out to the front steps.

"You got to understand," he said, "that our man [the principal negotiator] is a middle-class Negro—he gets scared easily. I'll work out the rest of the details with him."

An assembly for early the following week had been arranged.

Sweet Willie was one kind of rootless young person at Resurrection City. The Invaders were all in their teens or early twenties. Were they a gang or an association? Who can say?

2. The Ghetto Country People. On Saturday, May 25, the first town meeting was held at Resurrection City. Several hundred people gathered in one of the large tents and after being "warmed up" with some singing they began to air their thoughts and feelings about the campsite. Several speakers talked about "cold food," and then an old black man trudged to the microphone.

The meeting had been raucous up to that point. George Wiley and the Welfare Rights Organization and Reverend James Bevel had opened the affair by saying that "the people" were going to be encouraged to speak, but when they had attempted to quiet the gathering so that people could speak there were cries of outrage from some quarters that they were attempting to "run the same slick game that people downtown run."

Even when people from the floor spoke, their remarks had been punctured by bellows of support and cries of anger from the floor. Up to that point, urban militants had dominated the meeting, and the old man provided quite a contrast to them. He did not strut down the aisle and snatch the microphone as if he were going to hurl it at the audience.

"I been hearin' about cold food in the morning and long lines to get it," he began, "but if you can't put up with a little discomfort—a little waiting and meals that aren't hot—then why did you come here in the first place? I been poor all my life and I had to put up with ten times, twenty times, worst. For some people who are poor the meals they get here and the places they have to live in are better than they ever had before." He spoke quietly. He was not engaged in any of the games that militants sometimes play, such as "I'm more radical than you are," in which each speaker sees who can go farthest in verbally excoriating "whitey," "Uncle Toms," and various enemies of "the people." "I've been here every day and I'm going to stay," the old man concluded.

In general, the country people were older and less frenetic than the urbanites. Neither group had very clear notions of what form or shape legislation benefiting the poor might take, but the country people were less given to warnings of apocalypse.

3. The Other Ethnic Groups. It was the intention of the organizers of the Poor People's Campaign to involve poor whites, Mexican-Americans, Puerto Ricans, and American Indians in the struggle for legislative reform. There were some Puerto Ricans in Resurrection City, but they blended in with the blacks.

Late in May large contingents of Mexican-Americans and American Indians began to arrive, and when they did the political problems became more complex. Almost immediately Rijas Tijerina, the presumed spokesman for the Mexican-Americans, denounced the leadership of the Southern Christian Leadership Conference for excluding Mexicans from decision making. A hurried conference with Ralph Abernathy, successor to Martin Luther King as head of SCLC, resulted in a reconciliation with Tijerina.

Soon the American Indians held a news conference to denounce the blacks *and* the Mexican-Americans for ignoring Indians in making decisions. These denunciations and reconciliations allowed the leadership among the Mexican-Americans and Indians to demonstrate their importance. A leader could show his people that he was not just another nobody but a man important enough to be counted by Abernathy when he expressed dissatisfaction.

Poor whites were vastly underrepresented. Most of the whites present were students or clergy, and they were there not because they were poor but because they supported the goals of the campaign.

4. The Professionals. It was the task of the professionals to solve the logistical problems of setting up and running the camp, to maintain a sense of community among the participants, and to direct the program to put pressure on Congress, and to do all this while faced with continual financial problems and with accusations by conservative whites of being radicals and firebrands and by so-called militant blacks as Uncle Toms. In addition, most got barely more than subsistence for their work.

Who, then, were they?

They were a potpourri.

F. W. J. was a black Baptist minister in his early thirties who had for a while lived in Houston. He had supported students at Texas Southern University and had been arrested by the police as an alleged fomenter of discontent. At Resurrection City he was in charge of "entertainment." His most important function was to provide some relief in the day-to-day grind. He organized songfests and played his own compositions and standard civil rights and religious songs. His life was in the movement, but he was not a paid functionary. Rather, he involved himself in varying capacities in the central actions and struggles of his time.

A. H. was a black student from Cleveland. He had been involved off and on in the movement, particularly in CORE in the early 1960's when it was a leading exponent of nonviolence. He had been recruited for the campaign by a minister whom he knew from those days. In the camp he worked the security force. A low green picket fence surrounded the campsite, and infiltration by provocateurs for the purpose of vandalism, theft, or agitation would have been easy. To protect against this, Resurrection City had a security force made up of young men who by twos and threes patrolled the fence at night. A. H. reported that they occasionally had to rouse drunks or quiet rowdies but that in general the night patrols did not encounter problems.

The publicly visible leadership was made up of people who have for some period of time been involved in the movement. Abernathy went to jail with King on a number of occasions and

Julian Bond had been deeply involved in the peace and civil rights movements as well as in Georgia politics. The City's twenty-six-year-old "city manager," Jesse Jackson, had been involved in the movement since the early 1960's.

The professionals, then, had been involved before Selma and had been largely successful in eroding the legal edifice of caste. Here they were involved in a struggle which focused basically on class deprivation.

SUMMARY

To summarize this chapter briefly, post-Selma reformers have been largely drawn from the ranks of middle-class black students and the mobilized poor. Although the student activists deplored the slow speed of integration more than those students who had not participated in the civil rights movement, in some significant ways the activist and the apathetic students resembled each other. Neither group, for example, thought that the Watts riot had advanced the Negro cause but a majority of both samples said they would turn to violence, if necessary, to help the black community. This last fact may cause some concern, since it suggests that certain historical conditions might mobilize previously apathetic students into a violent movement. Contrary to the usual opinion, bitter hopelessness did not seem to motivate the student activists, since they evinced greater optimism about the future.

The mobilized poor, at least as they emerged from the Poor People's March on Washington, came from a variety of backgrounds. They seek different goals than the students and their grievances call into question the adequacy of the entire economic and political system.

If both the students and the poor fail in their campaigns for reform, then one can probably say, without being dramatic or overwrought, that the American system will fail and that the path of "the Revolutionary" will be followed to its tragic end.

REFERENCE

1. Donald R. Mathews and James W. Prothro, *Negroes and the New Southern Politics* (New York: Harcourt, Brace & World, 1966), p. 422.

CHAPTER 12

THE REVOLUTIONARY

John Howard

"We will govern Newark—or no one will." So proclaimed LeRoi Jones to a packed auditorium on the campus of the University of Oregon in 1968. Ninety per cent of the audience was white. Most of the Negroes were in the first five rows on the left and applauded vigorously at each verbal salvo. Two "bodyguards" accompanied Jones, standing at opposite ends of the stage facing the audience. They were wearing dark glasses and kept their hands jammed in the pockets of their black overcoats; later there was speculation on whether they had guns in their pockets. Jones had been invited to the campus as one of five Negro participants in a three-day conference on social revolution. The other panelists that evening ranged from Goldwater conservatives to members of the American Communist Party. Four of the five Negroes were black nationalists and the fifth, curiously enough, was an officer in Young Americans for Freedom.

Jones and the other three nationalists obviously frightened and disconcerted many of the thousand or so whites in the auditorium. He was not a Negro to whom they could easily "relate." He was not essentially a white man with a dark skin like Senator Edward Brooke or a calm and analytic advocate like Roy Wilkins or Whitney Young. He was a short, bearded black man wearing a loose-fitting African shirt and making threats.

Jones was strange and frightening to the whites largely because they were not aware of the social and historical process-es that had led him from poet and esthete to revolutionary. In this chapter I shall attempt to account for the Joneses and the Huey Newtons and the Albert Cleagues. They and other black revolutionaries have emerged as major figures in the unfolding drama of the nation's struggle to avoid dissolution. Who are they? What do they want? From what historical context do they emerge?

This chapter takes up, first, the history of black radicalism in the United States from World War I through the early 1960's. There are vast and dramatic differences between contemporary black radicals and their immediate predecessors. The con-temporary revolutionary can be better understood if he is contrasted with the radicals of previous periods.

The second part of the chapter is given over to a discussion of those elements in the civil rights movement (and the white response to them) which generated the nationalist orientation. Following there is an analysis of the tactics and programs of contemporary revolutionaries. The chapter closes with a discus-sion of the extent and intensity of the support commanded in the ghetto by black revolutionaries.

REVOLUTIONARIES
AND OTHER MALCONTENTS

As has been frequently pointed out, the so-called "Negro revolution" has actually been very modest in its goals: full cit-izenship rights for American Negroes. Both its goals, and, in some respects, its tactics, make it more like the feminist move-ment in the United States during the first two decades of this century than the movement which yielded the American revolution. Many civil rights activists, in supporting civil disobedience, cite the precedent of the Boston Tea Party. A more accurate analogy would be between the demonstrations and hunger strikes carried out by the suffragettes to obtain the ballot for women and marches and demonstrations in the South in the early 1960's to overturn the overtly segregationist system there.

The civil rights movement of the 1950's and early 1960's was not really very revolutionary, but by the middle of the 1960's Negroes had emerged who were true revolutionists in their outlook. There are not many black revolutionaries, as there are not many white revolutionaries, but the matter of numbers is not wholly meaningful. One might recall that both Castro and Christ had only twelve at the beginning. Often what revolutionaries lack in numbers they make up for in zeal.

The following general statements can be made about recent American radicalism and American Negroes:

Prior to the mid-1960's there was no independent revolutionary orientation on the part of American blacks. Before then, black revolutionaries were members of radical Marxist organizations, the Communist Party, the Socialist Workers Party, etc., and espoused the doctrines and goals of these organizations. Nevertheless, despite frequent and intensive efforts, these organizations never established a solid base of support in the black community. The number of blacks in Marxist organizations always remained small.

Let us briefly review some of the reasons for the failure of the white political radicals to impress the black community.

First, since the Communist Party was outside of the political system and did not have any power in its own right, it could not deliver pay-offs to a population standing in need of all rewards it could get. Unlike the political machines in the big cities of the North, the radicals could not deliver turkeys at Christmas and jobs on the public payroll.

Second, the radical political ideology of the Party contrasted sharply with the fundamentalist Christian orientation of much of the black population.

Third, insofar as Negroes were also Americans they probably accepted the prevailing notions about communism and stood as much in fear of its adherents as most other Americans.

Fourth, the great majority of Negroes were excluded from politics in the South and were deflected from it by poverty and apathy in the North. Thus they tended to disregard politics as a means of problem solving.

Left radical parties continue to make appeals to the black population and to try to secure a foothold in the ghetto, but without much success.

Throughout American Negro history there have been episodes of black chauvinism. The period following World War I witnessed the birth of the so-called "New Negro" and the surge of the Garvey movement. This episode ran its course, however, in less than a decade.

A radical black ideology independent of the ideologies of radical Marxist orientations reappeared in the mid-1960's. The major exponents of these new ideologies appeared to have a stronger base of support in the ghetto than their Marxist predecessors. They still, nevertheless, probably entertained considerably less than mass enthusiasm.

Nationalist organizations have been products of the cities, and particularly of the urban ghettos. They first became a major phenomenon in the period during and after World War I, a period which saw the mass migration of Negroes from the South to the cities of the North and the brief emergence of the Garvey movement.

These migrants met the usual problems of rural people in an urban setting and in addition had to cope with racial discrimination. Probably three factors account for the development of separatist organizations in this period: 1) the relative disappointment experienced by the migrants in encountering some severe forms of discrimination in the cities, 2) the relative inadequacy of opportunities for improving class status, and 3) the relatively greater amount of freedom for the expression of discontent.

Separatism, as we noted in discussing the Black Muslims, has frequently been a component of nationalism. The thinking of the separatists can be summed up as follows: We have tried the South, we have tried the North. We are mistreated in both places. This is because whites are unredeemedly racists. In any event, we are morally and intellectually superior to them and we must, therefore, seek separation in order to escape the inequities which they visit upon us and in order to once again realize the high standard of culture and achievement we once enjoyed.

To briefly summarize thus far: there have been Negroes who espoused left radical ideologies but the parties advocating such ideologies have never had a solid base in the ghetto. Separatist organizations with millenialist ideologies have been much more successful in mobilizing ghetto support.

Against this background let us now discuss the contemporary black revolutionary.

PROFILES OF CONTEMPORARY REVOLUTIONARIES

There are many kinds of black revolutionaries. The alarmed white, listening to voices from the ghetto, hears only bits of the various revolutionary cantos. To the white they seem to be a single chorus of hate. His ear is not attuned to the differences of style and tempo from one revolutionary to the next, and to the clashing and discordant notes that separate them.

Let us attempt to identify the varying revolutionary orientations by discussing their proponents. The revolutionaries share with other blacks a growing belief in the importance of black pride, an interest in re-examining African history, and in reaffirming the importance of the Negro's contribution to American culture. Unlike other blacks, however, they are more likely to repudiate nonviolence and to seek black control of institutions in the ghetto, and some even demand actual geographical separation of the races. The major themes shift from one revolutionary to the next. Let us elucidate these themes by discussing particular revolutionaries.

ROBERT WILLIAMS: VISIONS OF URBAN GUERRILLA WARFARE

The letter-sized envelope was post-marked Peking. I knew it was from Robert Williams, a man with whom I had debated at the Berkeley Community Theater in March 1961. At that time he was touring the country after a visit to Cuba, and our debate was about Cuba. He took the position of supporting all facets of the Castro government, while I, although adhering to the values and goals of the left, expressed reservations about particular aspects of the Castro regime.

He was a good speaker and carried the audience with him. He said he had served in the Marine Corps and, upon his discharge and return to Monroe, North Carolina, had encountered the same kind of racial oppression he had experienced before going into the service. His response was to join the NAACP and become chairman of the local chapter and a thorn in the side of local segregationists.

It is instructive to follow the events that led Robert Williams from Monroe to Peking. It was not inevitable. By examining what happened we may be able to understand how the larger society itself makes revolutionaries out of mild reformers.

On May 5, 1959, after a jury had acquitted two white men of brutal assaults on two Negro women and a Negro of limited intelligence had been convicted and sentenced to two years imprisonment for a lesser offense, Williams, then president of the Union County Branch of the NAACP, issued a statement to the effect that the traditional channels for redress were inadequate and that Negroes must defend themselves, meeting violence with violence.

In the context of the times this statement was regarded as radical and Williams was suspended from his NAACP post for a period of six months. At that time Williams was an integrationist, concerned about equal access to public accommodations, better housing, and greater educational opportunities. His aspirations were no different from those of Roy Wilkins or any other integrationist.

Williams broke with conventional integrationists solely on the issue of whether blacks should defend themselves if the authorities failed to provide protection. In the late 1950's even the mild integrationist goals of the NAACP were widely regarded by the white community, particularly in the South, as radical. Its decision to suspend Williams was probably a defensive maneuver to ward off attacks by segregationists accusing it of advocating violence. Ironically, by 1965 the goals Williams was advocating in the late '50's had been enacted into law in the 1964 and 1965 civil rights bills, but by that time he was in exile, issuing manifestos calling for the violent overthrow of the American government.

Within a matter of months after our debate Williams became involved in the conflict that led to his flight. He had formed a rifle club in Monroe and spoke of the need for blacks to defend themselves. This alarmed those whites who did not like the idea of Negroes responding to violence with anything more vigorous than spirituals. Tension between the white and black communities finally threatened to break into violence, and in an incident whose details are still clouded Williams was accused by the authorities of kidnapping a white couple. Williams contended the couple had inadvertently strayed into the black community at a very critical time and he had given them temporary shelter for their own protection.

Williams fled, first to Cuba and then to Red China. In exile his tone and message changed. He had put out a newsletter called *The Crusader* in Monroe and it continued to come out even after he fled. Sometime in the early 1960's I had taken out a subscription to it and thought my money lost after Williams went to Cuba. But then it began to come again via Toronto, and later, after he had gone to China, it still found its way to me from Peking.

As riots engulfed American cities Williams began to evolve a theory of urban guerrilla warfare. At one time he had attacked only segregation and discrimination. Now he began to place these two evils in the context of a broad theory.

> The capitalist system was predicated on the abuse and dehumanization of black people. It was partially designed and fashioned to glorify white supremacy and to liberate the European from feudalism at the expense of colored people. The pitiful

cases of the American Indian and Mexico offer ample evidence that Americanism is an evilly constituted authority fashioned to generate brute power and to institutionalize the white man's right to exploit, rape, rob and plunder in the name of white civilization. Yes, poor whites are exploited too, but the supreme white authority has been careful, even from the beginning, to afford them escape hatches built into the system. Even their slavery, what little of it that existed, was not of a permanent nature. They elected to call it indentured. Even today a white skin still carries a certain significant premium. It is still a badge of status in the system of racial caste.[1]

The alternatives for the oppressed, Williams believes, are either submission or revolt, but he argues strongly that a minority can overcome a majority in carefully planned guerrilla warfare. The nature of American society, he contends, makes this possible.

The urban guerilla fighter must rely on the elements of mobility, speed, surprise, terror, a friendly environment, knowledge of the community, concealment and cover when possible. He must consciously concentrate on the enemy's weakness, attack him at his weakest point and avoid becoming a target of his massive power.[2]

Robert Williams was a precursor of the black revolutionaries of the 1960's. Unlike earlier blacks associated with the radical left, he had some roots in the black community and he did not deal solely in an esoteric ideology but evolved a set of strategies and tactics intended for use here and now. Also unlike earlier black revolutionaries Williams' name is known to at least some people in the ghetto, and at least some of his thinking has been influential.

Let us now focus on a group which has to some extent drawn on Williams—the Black Panthers.

THE BLACK PANTHERS

It began with one sixteen-year-old boy in 1966. I spent the last three months of 1966 in Oakland studying his ghetto. I talked with a number of people ranging from those in the mayor's office to black militants. No one mentioned an organization called the Black Panthers, which first came to public attention on February 1, 1967, when twenty Panthers, with pistols and shotguns, marched through San Francisco's International Airport to escort the wife of the late Malcolm X to a speaking engagement. On May 2, 1967, a number of armed Panthers entered the California state capitol building to protest proposed gun-control laws. Within a year and a half they had attracted around 1,000 members throughout California, were running candidates for political office, had formed an alliance with the Peace and Freedom Party, and were the subjects of attention in a number of publications. In addition, one of their members, Eldridge Cleaver, had written a book, *Soul on Ice*, which has been widely hailed as a masterpiece.

Whites regarded the Panthers with horror, seeing them as raving blacks bent on burning and destroying. As Charles Howe stated in the *San Francisco Chronicle*, "They are black and they are young and they go forth into a white and frightened and hostile world."[3] In essence, however, they have simply taken over the "self-defense" position advocated by Robert Williams a decade earlier. Most whites would view the Panthers as revolutionary because they choose to arm themselves, but many of their goals are distinctly nonrevolutionary. "We want your goods," Howe quoted one young Panther as saying. "We want a fine home and a car; what they got up in Piedmont. We don't want to take your stuff away from you; but if you come down here and mess with us, we'll give you one up side the head." They have voiced a desire for full employment and decent housing. Most of all, the Panthers are in revolt against the Oakland police, seeing them as *the* instrument of ghetto oppression.

Some Panther demands are most extraordinary. They seek the removal of white businesses from the ghetto, military exemption for all blacks, and the release of all blacks presently in jail. Their program is a pastiche of traditional civil rights proposals and newer, less orthodox demands of dubious practicality and doubtful popularity in the ghetto.

The Panthers began as a kind of community-alert patrol patterned after the Los Angeles citizens' group of that name which used to patrol the streets of Watts at night on the lookout for any police mistreatment of blacks. If the words of an intelligence agent who infiltrated the Panthers can be taken at face value, the Oakland police pushed the organization over the line from stern criticism of police activity to armed militancy:

> It started out as something of a shuck. . . . Then the police took them seriously; stopped Panther cars; hummed Panthers in [arrested them on spurious charges]. This, naturally, scared the Panthers, who then really started to arm. Self-defense, as they saw it, wasn't just something to talk about any more.

They started to organize in earnest and by the spring of 1968 had set up two headquarters—one public and one "underground."

In terms of structure, the lowest position is that of the subsection leader, who is responsible for organizing a city block. A section leader supervises ten square blocks and a captain oversees ten section leaders. It is not clear how closely the actual structure approximates this ideal.

Any one who is black can join, and dues are twenty-five cents a week "if a cat has it." The rank-and-file membership is made up mainly of the "disenfranchised black teenager, unsure of himself, already with a police record, and with a feeling of utter desperation."[4]

Huey Newton and Bobby Seale, the two Panther leaders, were students at Merrit Junior College in Oakland when they founded the organization in 1966. At that time they had no idea what it was to become. Their ideas about self-defense grew out of the realities of their own lives. That they reached the position Williams had come to a decade before was due more to circumstance than design. Whether they eventually reach the position Williams moved onto after leaving Monroe depends, in large part, on the response of the larger community to their demands for justice and equal opportunities.

The intelligence agent who did undercover work among the Panthers articulated this in terms which may be simplistic but are nevertheless accurate:

If conditions get rougher in the ghetto—any ghetto—they're going to get more recruits. Then a hard-core element may escalate the gun business again. If the federal government, on the other hand, makes a serious attempt to pump lots of money into the ghetto, you can likely kiss the Panthers good-by. You simply can't agitate happy people.

Let us now turn to a discussion of the third kind of revolutionary. Although the Black Muslims are, in a certain sense, a retreatist organization, some of the members have an orientation and stance *vis-à-vis* the larger society that is revolutionary in tone.

THE MUSLIM MILITANT

We have previously discussed the "cultist stoic," one type of person who joins the Black Muslims in hopes of reinforcing his strong drive toward respectability. Other Muslims, however, have adhered to Muslim teachings in the hope of achieving a revolutionary change in American life. In interviews with fourteen of these militant Muslims, in spite of substantial differences in background, certain broad similarities appeared among them.

At some point each one had experiences that led him away from the institutionally bound ties and commitments that lend stability to most people's lives. Nine had been engaged in semilegal or criminal activities. Two had been in the military, not as a career but as a way of postponing the decision of what to do for a living. None had a stable marital history. All of them were acutely aware of being outsiders by the standards of the larger society, and all had come to focus on racial bias as the factor which denied them more conventional alternatives.

Bernard X* grew up in New York City:

As a kid . . . you always have dreams—fantasies—of yourself doing something later—being a big name singer or something that makes you outstanding. But you never draw the connection between where you are and how you're going to get there. I had to—I can't say exactly when, thirteen, fourteen, fifteen,

*Fictitious name.

sixteen. I saw I was nowhere and had no way of getting anywhere. Race feeling is always with you. You always know about The Man but I don't think it is real, really real, until you have to deal with it in terms of what you are going to do with your own life. That's when you feel it. If you just disliked him before—you begin to hate him when you see him blocking you in your life. I think then a sense of inevitability hits you and you see you're not going to make it out— up—away—anywhere—and you see The Man's part in the whole thing, that's when you begin to think thoughts about him.

Frederick 2X* became involved fairly early in a criminal subculture. His father obtained a "poor man's divorce" by deserting the family, and his mother had children by other men. Only a tenuous sense of belonging to a family existed. He was picked up by the police for various offenses several times before he reached his teens. The police patrolling his neighborhood eventually restricted him to a two-block area. There was, of course, no legal basis for this, but he was manhandled if seen outside that area by any policeman who knew him. He graduated in his late teens from "pot" to "shooting shit" and eventually spent time in the addict-rehabilitation hospital in Lexington, Kentucky.

William 2X,* formerly a shoeshine boy, related the development of his perspective this way:

You know how they always talk about us running after white women. There have always been a lot of [white] servicemen in this town—half of them would get around to asking me to get a woman for them. Some of them right out, some of them backing into it, laughing and joking and letting me know how much they were my friend, building up to asking me where they could find some woman. After a while I began to get them for them. I ran women—both black and white. . . . What I hated was they wanted me to do something for them [find women] and hated me for doing it. They figure 'any nigger must know where to find it . . .'

Amos X* grew up in an all-Negro town in Oklahoma and

*Fictitious name.

attended a Negro college. Because of this, he had almost no contact with whites during his formative years.

> One of my aunts lived in Tulsa. I went to see her once when I was in college. I walked up to the front door of the house where she worked. She really got excited and told me if I came to see her anymore to come around to the back. But that didn't mean much to me at the time. It is only in looking back on it that all these things begin to add up.

After graduating from college, Amos joined the Marines. There he began to "see how they [the whites] really felt" about him; by the end of his tour of duty he had concluded that "the white man is the greatest liar, the greatest cheat, the greatest hypocrite on earth." Alienated and disillusioned, he turned to professional gambling. Then, in an attempt at a more conventional way of life, he married and took a job teaching school.

> I taught English. Now I'm no expert in the slave masters' language, but I knew the way those kids talked after being in school eight and nine years was ridiculous. They said things like "mens" for "men." I drilled them and pretty soon some of them at least in class began to sound like they had been inside a school. Now the principal taught a senior class in English and his kids talked as bad as mine. When I began to straighten out his kids also he felt I was criticizing him. . . . That little black man was afraid of the [white] superintendent and all those teachers were afraid. They had a little more than other so-called Negroes and didn't give a damn about those black children they were teaching. Those were the wages of honesty. It's one thing to want to do an honest job and another thing to be able to.

With the collapse of his career as a public-school teacher and the break-up of his marriage, Amos went to California, where he was introduced to the Muslim movement.

> I first heard about them [the Muslims] in 1961. There was a debate here between a Muslim and a Christian minister. The Muslim said all the things about Christianity which I had been thinking but which I had never heard anyone say before. He tore the minister up.

Finding an organization that aggressively rejected the white man and the white man's religion, Amos found his own point of view crystallized. He joined without hesitation.

Norman Maghid* first heard of the Muslims while he was in prison.

> I ran into one of the Brothers selling the paper about two weeks after I got out and asked him about the meetings. Whether a guy could just go and walk in. He told me about the meetings so I made it around on a Wednesday evening. I wasn't even bugged when they searched me. When they asked me about taking out my letter [joining the organization] I took one out. They seemed to know what they were talking about. I never believed in nonviolence and love my enemies, especially when my enemies don't love me.

Muhammad Soule Kabah,* born into a family of debt-ridden Texas sharecroppers, was recruited into the Nation of Islam after moving to California.

> I read a series of articles in the Los Angeles *Herald Dispatch*, an exchange between Minister Henry and a Christian minister. It confirmed what my grandfather had told me about my African heritage, that I had nothing to be ashamed of, that there were six thousand books on mathematics in the Library of the University of Timbuctoo while Europeans were still wearing skins. Also, my father had taught me never to kow-tow to whites. My own father had fallen away. My parents didn't want me to join the Nation. They said they taught hate. That's funny isn't it? The white man can blow up a church and kill four children and the black man worries that an organization which tells you not to just take it is teaching hate.

In microcosm, the career of a revolutionary Muslim can be illustrated in the life of Leroy X,* a typical member of the revolutionary branch.

Leroy was forty-two and married. He had in the past been at one time or another a waiter, a thief, a pimp, a dope peddler, a fence, and a porter. He had been a Methodist and Catholic

*Fictitious name.

before becoming a Muslim. His evolution as a kind of revolutionary can best be suggested by recounting in detail two interviews with him.

INTERVIEWER: When did you first become aware of the race problem?

LEROY X: I was always aware of it. I grew up in Kansas City, Missouri, and Missouri is a segregated state. Negroes in Kansas City were always restricted to the menial jobs. I came out here in 1940 and tried to get a job as a waiter. I was a trained waiter, but they weren't hiring any Negroes as waiters in any of the downtown hotels or restaurants. The best I could do was busboy and they fired me from that when they found out I wasn't Filipino.

The war had broken out then and they drafted me to fight for "my country." I was sent down to the hospital at Monterey because I had gonorrhea. Now down there the major came around in the morning and the sick men were supposed to get out of bed and stand at attention. Well, my first day in there the major came around and the other guys crawled out of bed and stood at attention. I just lay back and took it easy. The major got to my bed and looked at me and said, "What's your story, soldier?" I told him I wasn't a soldier, they had sent me there, I didn't want to come. He told me to get up and stand at attention and I told him to go to hell. A nurse ran out and came back with four big Mississippi M.P.s with clubs and guns so I reached over and took a milk bottle off the stand next to my bed and smashed it. The major tried to sweet talk me into putting down the bottle and I told him I would if the M.P.s put down their clubs and guns. He sent the M.P.s out and I put down the bottle. Later that day they came back and told me they had a special room for me upstairs. The special room turned out to be a cell. I told them that was all right—like having a private room with room service. They came back a few times and tried to sweet talk me but I chased them out every time.

They sent me from there up to the Presidio—the S-1 ward—the psycho ward. The first day I was there they took me down to see some little psychiatrist. He saw me at the door and said, "Come right in, Henry." I told him, "You know my name ain't Henry, and you know damn well I'm not crazy." He told me to get out, which I did.

They had me up for three court martials because I wouldn't fight. They would ask, "Why won't you fight for your country?" I asked them, "What country? You're my enemies." They asked me what I wanted and I told them "to get out of the damned army."

A couple of times they threatened to send me to the south but they never did. Finally they let me out as psycho.

INTERVIEWER: What happened then?

LEROY X: Well, I tried to get a job but I couldn't so I started stealing. There was nothing else to do. I couldn't live on air. The peckerwoods didn't seem to give a damn whether I lived or died. They wouldn't hire me but didn't seem to worry how I was going to stay alive. I started stealing.

INTERVIEWER: How did your family compare economically to others?

LEROY X: We were poor like everybody—I came up during the Depression.

INTERVIEWER: Did you ever belong to CORE or the NAACP or any other civil rights groups?

LEROY X: No—I never joined any of them. I went to the NAACP once when I didn't have a job and they talked a lot of funny talk but I still walked out without a job. All those organizations are run by whites. Farmer, Wilkins, King—they are all puppets. What kind of nonsense is it to let somebody whip your head and not fight back? "We will make them love us through our capacity to suffer," says King. What kind of nonsense is that? The white man likes King because all he is saying is "the harder you kick my ass the more I love you." You saw what happened to Robert Williams. He said, "White man, you kick my ass and I'll kick yours," and he had to flee the country. Look at it from the white man's point of view; isn't it much safer to have somebody like King or Farmer around telling the so-called Negro to be nonviolent and endure than it is to have somebody telling them to stand up like men? That's why I said these people are only puppets. I saw Walter White on television once. He looked white, talked white, and had a white wife. As far as I was concerned he was white. I was watching TV last night—watching those cops down in St. Petersburg whipping heads—and those people weren't fighting back. If King told them to fight back what do you think would happen to him? What happened to Robert Williams? He would be dead or run out of the country like Robert Williams.

INTERVIEWER: Did you feel that other Negroes had much the same view that you had on the race problem? When did your views come to differ?

LEROY X: I always knew that something was wrong. My uncle worked for a white family out on a farm in Missouri. They took out insurance on him. My aunt who lived with us said they might kill him to collect the insurance money. Sure enough my uncle died. He was burned up—but they probably killed him before burning the body. They sent my aunt the burnt husk. My aunt didn't get a cent of the insurance money and had to turn around and pay to have that piece of burnt-up garbage they sent her buried.

INTERVIEWER: What about other Negroes when you were growing up?

LEROY X: Other so-called Negroes? They seemed to get along. They were brainwashed. In the grave. The white man and the big Negroes kept them down.

INTERVIEWER: What do you mean "the big Negroes"?

LEROY X: The preachers and politicians. I remember when I was a kid seeing the preacher sneak a drink and I asked my mother, "Why does he drink when he tells us not to?" My mother told me, "Hush up, boy, you didn't see the preacher drinking." These people are corrupt. You read all the time about this or that preacher having sex relations with some teenage member of his congregation then you hear nothing more about it. The white man doesn't want to get the preachers into trouble. Do you think if they had anything on Mr. Muhammad they would suppress it? Most of our people know that something is wrong but they don't know exactly what. I felt that way for a long time.

INTERVIEWER: How—what happened after you got out of the service?

LEROY X: I told you—they said I was psycho and let me go and I started stealing.

INTERVIEWER: How long did you steal for a living?

LEROY X: Well, I could get—I did a lot of things. I could get you anything you wanted—a car, drugs, women, jewelry. Crime is a business like any other. I started off stealing myself. I wound up filling orders and getting rid of stuff. I did that for fifteen years. In between I did a little time. I did time for things I never thought of doing and went free for things I really did.

INTERVIEWER: You mean your lawyer would fix it for you?

LEROY X: It never got to the lawyers—you take care of things with the arresting officer.

INTERVIEWER: This was approximately between 1945 and 1960—did you have any legit jobs during that period?

LEROY X: Yes—I mentioned I was a trained waiter. When the heat was on I waited tables sometimes. Once I shipped out with the merchant marine. We went to Japan. I remember talking to a guy there—a Jap—who asked, "Why do you people put up with it?" I didn't know what to tell him.

INTERVIEWER: What was your life like before you became a Muslim? What was your position in the community?

LEROY X: I lived in a room. I—in my business you had no friends, only associates and not very close ones at that. It was always best not to let a person know any more about you than you knew about him so that if he turned you in he would know that you could turn him in too. I had plenty of money. I could get anything I wanted without working for it. It wasn't enough though.

INTERVIEWER: When you first became bothered by the race problem whom did you blame for it? Did you feel there was something wrong with Negroes or that whites were in the wrong?

LEROY X: Our people have been misguided and misled by whites and by their so-called leaders. Our people are very strong up here [taps side of head] and the Messenger is trying to wake them up. No one else is doing it—King is not doing it—no one else is doing it. Did you read about this football player—what was his name—Powell—with his white wife living in Richmond and complaining about the treatment he got. I have been out there selling *Muhammad Speaks*. There are a lot of them living out there with their—the whites they married and these brown babies. Are they helping the so-called Negro Mr. Muhammad is trying to help. These other people, like the football player, are doing nothing for us. The white man is afraid—afraid of Mr. Muhammad for what he is trying to do. For 400 years they have held us down and now a man comes along to wake us up and they are scared to death of him.

INTERVIEWER: Do you think that most Negroes could do better if they worked harder?

LEROY X: That depends on how you mean it—now that Mr. Muhammad has brought us the Message we cannot simply sit back and wait for things to change, we have to work and make sacrifices ourselves in order to bring about the changes. But until people have some knowledge of themselves and their own history they cannot be blamed if they do nothing. Before the Messenger came the so-called Negro was in the grave. He could not help himself because he did not know to what end nor did he have any faith in himself. Now that the Messenger has shown the way we can change ourselves and change the world.

INTERVIEWER: When did you first hear about the Nation? What did you think about them?

LEROY X: I first heard about them in 1957 through reading the Messenger's column in the *Pittsburgh Courier*. It seemed to me he was telling the truth. I tell you the only other person to impress me that way was W. E. B. DuBois. I had read DuBois years before. You see what happened to him—the white man shut him up.

INTERVIEWER: When did you attend your first meeting?

LEROY X: Not until 1960—March of 1960. In between I did a lot of things—just never got around to going. I went in March of 1960 to the temple over in Oakland.

INTERVIEWER: When did you first begin to think of joining?

LEROY X: I had made up my mind to join before going to the first meeting. I took out my letter that night.

INTERVIEWER: What was the attitude of your family toward your joining?

LEROY X: I didn't have any family. I was living with a woman. She wasn't opposed to my joining. We had talked about it and she understood why I wanted to join. Later she joined herself and we got married. She is at a meeting tonight—you might have seen her leave as you came in.

INTERVIEWER: Yes, I did—what was the attitude of your friends toward your joining?

LEROY X: As I said, I had no friends. If anyone had really gotten to know me they would have had too much on me. I mentioned to the guys I used to know that I might join and they respected me for it. They said, "If you join you'll be serious about it." I still see them every now and then, they say, "When you coming back man, we're not making as much money now."

INTERVIEWER: You mean you quit?

LEROY X: No, it wasn't quite like that. Quit is not the right word. In the line of work I was in you drift in and out. Things go great for a while then you get sent up or the heat is put on and you cool it for a while—you get a job until things cool off. I thought for a long time about joining the Nation. I drifted out of the other world.

INTERVIEWER: Did you belong to a church—I suppose not.

LEROY X: I gave up being a Baptist after I got old enough so that my parents couldn't force me to go to church. I tried being a Methodist once and being a Catholic, but it didn't work. When I was a Catholic I would see the priest every week. I would ask him questions which he couldn't answer.

He told me I shouldn't ask the questions, I should just have faith. What kind of nonsense is that?

INTERVIEWER: I see. You took your letter out at your first meeting?

LEROY X: Yes, but I didn't become really involved until 1961.

INTERVIEWER: Did you know any one already a member?

LEROY X: Yes—I knew a member—between reading the paper and talking to him I decided to join.

INTERVIEWER: How big a step did joining seem to be at the time?

LEROY X: One has to make many sacrifices for the Nation—in time, in money. Sometimes I get discouraged. It doesn't seem that we are getting anywhere, but when I look back over the last four years and see how much we have accomplished since then things look different. Day by day it does not seem like much but when you look at it over the long run it is. It takes discipline though, it is not easy.

INTERVIEWER: What exactly do you do as a member of the Nation?

LEROY X: It takes a great deal of time; first, there are the lessons to study.

INTERVIEWER: Lessons?

LEROY X: Yes, we receive lessons from Chicago which we study. Then I sell the paper. It is surprising how many so-called Negroes are afraid to be seen buying it. There is more truth in that paper than in anything else, yet they are afraid to buy it openly. Many times if they buy it they stick it in a shopping bag or under their coat. Then I go to meetings three or four times a week. Then there are other things to do like keeping records.

INTERVIEWER: Records?

LEROY X: Yes, how many people come to the Temple at each meeting. Who has taken out a letter and who has not. Who has returned his letter. Sometimes we have to check up on people.

INTERVIEWER: How do you mean?

LEROY X: People like you.

INTERVIEWER: Oh!

LEROY X: When the day comes everyone will have to pass muster.

INTERVIEWER: About how much time a week do you spend at it?

LEROY X: You can't look at it that way. It's not a job on which you spend so many hours a week, it's a way of life. I think it will be the way of life for more and more of our people. In the next few years you will see us coming up, up, up and the white man going down, down, down. This would be a better world if there were no white people in it. Then you would have true peace. Until there are no white people left in the world things will not be right. Mr. Muhammad teaches us that their time has come. When the world is rid of them we will have true peace.

HOW MUCH SUPPORT DO THE REVOLUTIONARIES HAVE?

Every survey of Negro opinion suggests that only a small percentage of ghetto residents subscribe to the values and goals of the revolutionaries, but the magnitude of support is not a wholly meaningful index of their influence for two reasons: 1) Those most likely to support the revolutionaries, namely the rootless, drifting young men in the ghetto, are least likely to be seen by opinion pollsters, and therefore the various opinion polls probably underestimate the amount of support the revolutionaries have; 2) In riot situations the old normative system no longer operates and the revolutionary may then be able to command the support of people who otherwise might find his message unappealing.

Ultimately the base of support for the revolutionaries will be determined by the seriousness of purpose and degree of humanity with which the larger society responds to the ghetto's grievances.

Let us enlarge on each of these points.

None of the surveys of black attitudes in the 1960's gives comfort to the revolutionaries. All indicate mass support for the older, established civil rights organizations. For example, in *Protest and Prejudice* Gary Marx dealt with the relative popularity of some of the traditional organizations and the Black Muslims. He stated, "Some observers suggest that relatively large segments of the black community had withdrawn allegiance from the conventional civil rights groups in favor of the Muslims,"[5] but his data undermined that contention.

COMMENDATION OF CIVIL RIGHTS ORGANIZATIONS[6]

	METRO-POLITAN AREAS IN GENERAL	NEW YORK	CHICAGO	ATLANTA	BIRMING-HAM
NAACP	79%*	70%	84%	87%	92%
CORE	11	12	6	2	3
Muslims	3	8	3	0	1
None	2	6	2	1	0
No opinion	6	5	7	10	5

*Percentages may add up to more than 100 because some individuals are counted in more than one group.

The same data indicated that Martin Luther King was the leader most admired by blacks, followed by Roy Wilkins of the NAACP.

It is undoubtedly true that the great majority of ghetto residents are not revolutionaries, but this is not wholly relevant in a discussion of the impact of the revolutionaries. Jack Newfield has used the term "prophetic minority" to characterize that segment of each generation of young people which gives the generation its imprint. That most young people are conformist is meaningless in terms of discussing the impact of young people on the course of events.

THE HIDDEN REVOLUTIONARIES

In the nature of things black revolutionaries are not easy to study. Often access is closed to white social scientists and there are not that many black social scientists around. Certain things do emerge, however, from the literature on revolutionary organizations in the ghetto. They seem to appeal most strongly to the most dispossessed of the ghetto's young men. The typical Muslim and the typical Panther are alike in being young, unskilled, in trouble with the law, and out of school. These are individuals who are failures even by the standards of the ghetto, and even the modest legitimate aspirations most ghetto residents have are closed to them.

These rootless young men are precisely the people least likely to be seen by polltakers. They are not residentially stable and if caught at home by a polltaker would probably think he was a bill collector or a policeman and refuse to be questioned. It follows, then, that their opinions are probably underrepresented in the various surveys of what people in the ghetto think. Ghetto support for revolutionary organizations is probably a little broader than survey research efforts would have us believe.

The amount of influence the revolutionaries have is probably related to the type of atmosphere in which they attempt to exercise influence. In general their influence is limited, but in a riot situation, for example, where the usual norms are suspended, they may be able to sway individuals who ordinarily would not find their message appealing.

Participation in the affairs of revolutionary organizations probably allows these alienated and dispossessed young men to assume a male role. As Patrick Moynihan has pointed out, discrimination and segregation deny many black men the opportunity to meet the conventional expectations of the man's role. He cannot achieve occupationally if his education has been stunted. He cannot support his family if his income is low. The kinds of handicaps Moynihan discusses seem to apply most directly to the typical rank-and-file recruit to the Muslims and

Panthers, which provide opportunities to fulfill at least some of the dimensions of the male role. They are paramilitary in structure and their use of uniforms, titles, and arms undoubtedly gratifies a certain sense of manliness for individuals denied more conventional forms of achievement. This is not to say that the Panthers' resort to arms for purposes of self-defense might not be a realistic adaptation to the particular situation they face (it probably is), but only to indicate that there are psychodynamic dimensions to their behavior that are also relevant.

It has been suggested at several points in this chapter that the larger society makes the revolutionary. Like the mad scientists in horror movies, society then becomes fearful of its own creation. The white community's response to the revolutionaries seems to be a mixture of fear, hatred, and paranoia. A more useful response would be to attempt to develop creative opportunities to channel the revolutionaries' drives. If the revolutionaries are damaged individuals due to no fault of their own, those responsible might at least accept the challenge and inconvenience of developing the kinds of programs that would open up possibilities for life without deprivation or despair.

REFERENCES

1. *Crusader Newsletter*, Vol. 9, No. 2, p. 3.

2. *Ibid.*, p. 9.

3. Charles Howe, "The Black Panther," *San Francisco Chronicle*, May 17, 1968.

4. *Ibid.*

5. Gary Marx, *Protest and Prejudice* (New York: Harper & Row, 1967), p. 25.

6. *Ibid.*

CHAPTER 13

COLLECTIVE STYLES
OF LIFE

William McCord & John Howard

Because of the impact of urbanization and other factors, new *collective* styles of life, new avenues of expression, have been opened for urban Negroes: specifically, a greater tendency toward mass use of violence, the emergence of new groups (such as the black-power coalition) aimed at changing the Negro situation, and more participation of Negroes in the usual political processes of American life. Admittedly, blacks as a civic body have united in the past. Slave revolts erupted, political clubs lobbied for their rights, the NAACP strove to end legal segregation, and a handful of Negroes voted. But today, our research indicates that many of the traditional Negro organizations—most prominently the churches—have lost much of their appeal. And the riots of the 1960's, the new concern with poverty, and the millions of additional voters represent a mass expression of power which has never before characterized the Negro community.

Sheer knowledge of individual life styles would be relatively useless unless one could relate it to these new collective modes of life in the ghetto. In this last chapter, therefore, we shift our focus from the individual and attempt to analyze the sources, nature, and impact of collective trends, as well as their relevance for public policy. Specifically, we address ourselves to four issues:

1. Who riots, and why?

2. Who allies himself with the black-power movement (in one of its various manifestations), and why?

3. Who responds to measures for ghetto economic improvement?

4. Who takes the political path as a means for change, and what may they expect as their rewards?

RIOTS

Clearly, Negroes have suffered from worse oppression in the past than exists in America today. Yet mass violence in the ghetto has emerged as the decisive symbol of the decade of the 1960's. Beginning with Watts, these riots had certain elements in common: they expressed a rage which blacks had previously suppressed; they occurred in urban areas; and they were usually directed against symbolic representatives of white society (*e.g.*, police and merchants). As in every revolutionary situation, the objective lot of Negroes has been improved but they have been left in a state of "relative deprivation." As Alexis de Tocqueville first recognized, if an oppressing class (in this case, the whites) begins to allow some latitude toward its victims, and then closes the door to freedom, revolution occurs.

In viewing the last decade of ghetto revolts, we have found it useful to distinguish three types of violence:

Expressive riots: Violent confrontations that involve all segments of the Negro community in a diffuse form of protest.

Class riots: Violent clashes in which poor blacks and whites join together in looting. (This type of riot has particular appeal, of course, to "rebels without a cause.")

Guerrilla warfare: Ideologically motivated attacks on highly selected targets of the white "Establishment." This activity is undertaken by revolutionaries, often allied with "converted" rebels without a cause.

In a fragile urban society such as our own, it is of the utmost importance to understand each of these three manifestations of violence. First, the expressive riot, which was classically epitomized in Watts.

Watts: An Expressive Riot

The events of August 1965 in Los Angeles markèd a decisive turning point in the Negro's struggle for dignity—a change in focus from South to North, from Mississippi plantations to urban ghettos, from pacifist suffering to violent reprisal. The name Watts had seldom been used by residents of the area because of their shame about living in a ghetto. During the riots, however, people scrawled Watts in big letters on storefronts, demonstrating a newly achieved pride. Americans must respond to this assertion of black power with reason and compassion, for the Watts riot could have an even more profound significance. Future historians may come to regard it as the flaming signal that the Negro "revolt" of the 1950's had ignited into a genuine revolution.

I* witnessed those stormy, historic days when the Los Angeles ghetto exploded into flame and gunfire. On August 15, 1965, I disobeyed the police injunction to stay out of the ghetto, for I realized that the often-prophesied "fire next time" had literally started. The riots were not just an unplanned explosion of hoodlumism. They were an armed marshaling of the Negroes' hatred for whitey, a true, if hopeless and unwise, insurrection. As a sociologist, I felt compelled to witness this new and perhaps ultimate stage of the Negro revolt.

After dodging the various Army blockades, I found myself deep in the devastated section of Los Angeles. "If them gangs come after you, just run to this house," an elderly Negro told me. He pointed to a trim cottage on one of the attractive side streets. I welcomed this act of hospitality and honored the courage which prompted it. To aid a man of white skin during

*William McCord.

the August days of madness in Los Angeles required unusual kindness, even valor. I knew for the first time the feeling which every American Negro experiences: the sense that one's skin color alone can evoke hatred, humiliation, and violence.

In the midst of the holocaust, jeeps armed with machine guns patrolled the streets while police huddled together protecting themselves from snipers. Around them, on the main streets, the hulls of stores smoked and let out occasional flames. Burned automobiles lined the streets. Young Negroes, often stripped to the chest, slipped from building to building. They signaled each other by holding up one, two, or three fingers, indicating the section (and gang headquarters) to which they belonged. They obviously felt a joyous release in fighting back. They joked, yelled, drank, looted, and burned—asserting, they thought, a sense of manhood which had been denied them. Even when they were arrested, their faces shone with a quiet dignity and calmness, unknown to me in the police line-ups which I had witnessed in the past.

I had to keep moving as quickly as possible to locate Negroes who would not automatically recognize my white face as a symbol of tyranny. And I did find them. Even in the midst of the flames (a hundred major fires had been set that day), I discovered many Negroes—some terrified, some aiding the wounded, some trying to calm the mob—who would talk with a lone white and offer to help him.

One black whom I encountered had seen the incident which triggered the riots. By a devious route, he took me to the spot on Avalon Boulevard—then spattered with glass and charred remnants—where three days before police had arrested two Negroes for drunken driving. The two men, Marquette Frye and his brother Ronald, had resisted arrest. Their mother, a typical religious stoic, joined them, swearing at the police. "Those cops called us all 'dirty niggers,'" my informant said.

In the sweltering heat of that Wednesday evening, the conflagration began. "My husband and I saw ten cops beating a man," a Negro woman testified. "My husband told the officers, 'You've got him handcuffed.' One of the officers answered, 'Get out of here, nigger. Get out of here, all you niggers.'" Hundreds gathered at the scene. After the Fryes had been dragged off, the mob broke loose. "I threw bricks and rocks and anything I could get my hands on to hurt them," an eighteen-year-old girl said. "We were throwing at anything white."

This initial passionate hatred of the white man *per se*, contrary to the original lurid press reports, soon abated. On Thursday, August 12, 7,000 Negroes rioted in the Watts ghetto. Their antagonism, however, was selectively directed against white policemen. The rioters smashed cars and looted the district of clothes, food, liquor, and guns, but the victims were almost invariably the white businessmen regarded as parasites in Watts. Signs saying "Colored-owned" saved the smaller establishments. Except for the exploiters, Negro businessmen received explicit advance warnings that riots would begin at a particular hour on their street.

Further, the few white people who lived in the district and had earned a reputation for decency were not molested. One white woman with whom I talked had lived in Watts for twenty-one years. "On the thirteenth, mobs ran up and down my street," she said, "with the police coming after them in droves. But my neighbors, who are all colored, made sure that no one disturbed me." The astonishing element in the Los Angeles riot was not the pillage and passion, but the respect for decent white men.

This restraint suggests that the riots had a more important aim than sheer revenge. Dr. Harold Jones, a Negro psychiatrist in charge of a Watts clinic, reported that "the rioters showed a common motivation by their actions—a determination to show their strength by using violence." Jones believed that the riots were "an attempt to give Negro leadership a bargaining position with white authorities."

On August 14, as the battle gained in intensity, Negroes—including some from the white-collar class—came from all over the city to join the attack. "There were a lot more 'outsiders' here than regular residents," one old-timer in Watts remarked. "People came from all over—some for profit, I suppose, but a lot came because they thought we were really accomplishing something." The rioters had, in fact, forced the police to admit defeat; 18,000 National Guardsmen moved into the twenty-one-square-mile area, declared a curfew, and opened fire with machine guns. The world knows what happened: thirty-five killed, hundreds wounded, 4,000 arrested, and some $100,000,000 in property damage.

As I saw the area on August 15, 1965, southeastern Los Angeles, ravaged by hundreds of blazes, resembled an embattled city under artillery fire. Tooting the slogan on their car horns, groups of Negroes cruised the neighborhood chanting "burn, baby, burn!"—a phrase made popular by a local disc jockey. Even Negro reporters, trying to infiltrate the area, joined in beating out the rhythm.

On Monday, the Army announced that it had won control over the riots. Yet as news reports came in, one wondered whether the end had come; in Long Beach, riots resulted in the death of another policeman; in Orange County—the home of Disneyland—roving cars of Negroes attacked some whites; and in San Diego, 120 miles down the coast, the Logan Heights ghetto exploded in its own riot.

Well-printed pamphlets, mysteriously distributed in Los Angeles, declared on August 16: "The song has ended, but the melody lingers on." And Marquette Frye, whose arrest had ignited the violence, told a Black Muslim rally: "These troops don't mean a thing. They haven't seen anything yet."

The subsequent riots throughout America between 1965 and 1969 indicate the truth of this prediction. We saw the beginning of armed insurrection in northern, western, and even southern cities. All of the ingredients of a classic revolutionary situation were there: an objective lessening of oppression; a consequent spiraling of the oppressed's aspirations; and, as reality dashed these new hopes, a heightening of frustration.

To the superficial white observer, Watts seemed a most unlikely place for mass violence to erupt, for its inhabitants benefited from most of the civil rights advances of the last decade. The neighborhood was composed of clean, if modest, dwellings enclosed by clipped lawns—far from the diseased shacks of Mississippi. Children attended legally integrated schools (98 per cent Negro). Parents had the vote. Public accommodations were open to all. For a man from the Deep South, Los Angeles would seem a haven of comfort and freedom. And this very promise attracted 2,000 Negroes a month, 65 per cent of them originally from the South.

But the reality of Watts hardly fitted the dream of the southern Negro. Over 30 per cent of the men were unemployed wanderers. Some 40 per cent of the families were broken by divorce or desertion. The area was three times as crowded with human beings as any other quarter of Los Angeles. The breakdown of the family had predictable results: if children saw their father at all, they saw him sitting around the kitchen drinking beer with his buddies while their mother worked. Because their inactive fathers, lacking effective control, still attempted to dominate the children, the average boy came to despise authority.

Many Negro adults in Watts regarded the white merchants and police as their most visible oppressors. The area was ruled by 272 policemen, 90 per cent white, who acted like troops occupying enemy territory. White landlords owned 70 per cent of the homes and apartments. White businessmen controlled all but a handful of the stores, bars, and gas stations. "Here you have to pay that white man, jump when the white cop calls you 'nigger,' " a Negro labor union official told me. "Here is where the Negroes' hopes were to be fulfilled. When they find life so empty, what can they do? Where can they go?"

The Negroes in Watts have sought release in drugs, rackets, sex, and crime, a fact which the late Police Chief William Parker claimed Negro leaders ignored. (Actually, the area has been the crime center of Los Angeles. A gangland tradition, established by whites, surrounded the Negroes who were first forced to move into the district thirty years ago.)

A year before the Watts riots, California had passed a law legalizing housing discrimination and insuring that Negroes would be kept in their ghettos. Proposition 14—that ironic product of democracy's hope, the referendum—repealed a fair-housing law and made it clear that California whites did not want Negroes as neighbors. Although the amendment has since been declared unconstitutional—and few Watts Negroes would have had the means to move to better neighborhoods anyway—this demonstration of white contempt deeply hurt even the stoics in Watts. "They told us that they didn't want no niggers living near them," a Negro bricklayer told me. "Now we are showing them that we don't want them sucking our blood in our own neighborhood."

One may speculate upon the underlying causes of the riots in Watts, but the most obvious fact is that the riots started spontaneously as the citizens' response to an instance of what they regarded as "police brutality." Once in the streets, the people came under the control of a variety of groups (none of them truly "revolutionary" or "activist") drawn from the various segments of the community. The Black Muslims, I was told, wore red armbands to identify their members, harangued the crowds, directed them to appropriate targets, and bailed out comrades who suffered arrest. Various criminal gangs also intervened. These gangs, operating independently of each other, went on a looting spree. Other groups within Watts—rallying around the cry, "We'll get them for Bogalusa"—attacked the most Scroogelike white merchants.

The riots, therefore, were neither an expression of pure lawlessness nor the product of civil rights demonstrations. The activist leaders had repeatedly warned the city government that a rebellious situation was building up in Watts. They requested, but did not receive, police cooperation. "We knew months ago what was coming," one leader told me. "Gangs of young men cruised these streets aimlessly every night. There was ample warning, but no action."

Watts has, of course, been expertly analyzed since the events of 1965, perhaps most intensively by a UCLA team headed by Nathan Cohen, Raymond Murphy, and James Watson. The excellent UCLA study and our own research have tended to dispel some common myths about the nature of expressive riots.

• Everyone from cultist stoics to achievers can be found in a riot crowd. Perhaps the only groups that abstain are highly religious stoics and the activist leaders.

• The studies challenge the notion that the white-collar class will somehow act as a stabilizing influence. The UCLA workers, canvassing a number of districts which ranged from very poor to middle class, found about the same proportions of people who favored the riot. Similarly, we found in Houston that the white-collar group split dramatically: they had the highest number of people who exhibited unrest but they also had the highest proportion of people who had no interest whatsoever in civil rights issues.

• The UCLA study concluded that increased contact between Negroes and whites did not moderate racial antagonisms. The researchers concluded: "We expect that continued contact with white persons by those Negroes who have made economic gains would serve to increase their impatience and frustration at not being able to enjoy the same freedom of movement and opportunity taken for granted by white persons in their quest for the 'American Dream.' "[1]

• The UCLA group found that "the idea that recent migrants from the South, bitter and frustrated at their lack of success in Los Angeles, helped to stimulate the riot may be a myth."[2] The researchers noted that 70 per cent of the men involved had lived in Los Angeles for ten years or more when the riot took place, and, further, that southern migrants tended to be older, while the rioters were young. Again, it appears that the urban ghetto itself creates revolutionaries.

• The antagonism of rioters may, in some situations, be as strongly directed against members of their own ethnic group as against whites. During the Texas Southern University riot in Houston, the militants expressed as much—or even more— anger at Negro university administrators and Negro campus police as they did toward whites. The converse also held true, according to William McCord's observations. The few Negro policemen in Houston who participated in suppressing the riot seemed more eager than other officers to attack the student rioters.

The selection of only white stores for looting (as occurred in Watts in 1965) was not seen in either Detroit or Newark in 1967. John Howard, who was on the scene, found that Negro-owned stores were attacked with the same frequency as white-owned stores.

Presumably many rioters feel that certain Negroes have "sold out" to the whites or are exploiting them with the same techniques as whites.

• As the FBI has confirmed, "outside agitators" played little or no role in riots between 1965 and 1968. In the major riots—Watts, Detroit, Newark, Cleveland—the explosions occurred spontaneously. With the possible exception of riots on Negro campuses (which have sometimes followed closely after the visit of some "revolutionary" speaker), the sinister vision of plotters setting off a riot is a myth.

• The black-power ideology (at least until 1968) had little significant influence in sparking the major riots. John Howard's interviews in both Newark and Detroit revealed that few people claimed that the black-power ideology had any effect on their actions. Further, Howard found that none of the more militant groups were identified as playing a leading role in instigating the riots in Newark and Detroit.

Thus, it is most difficult to construct a theory of expressive violence which explains the phenomenon. We do not, at this stage, know a great deal about several essential questions: What role do the mass media play in either promoting or controlling a riot? What role do rumors have? Exactly what effect do the actions, reactions, or nonaction of civic authorities have in creating the conditions for a riot and precipitating one?

We can really make only one generalization. In reviewing the 1967 riots, psychiatrist Alvin Poussaint concluded that "rage is common to all of them."[3] The targets of attack may differ, but in Poussaint's view, rage motivates all of the people: "The rioters range from the plain damn angry to those with fantasies of taking over, to those who want a TV set, to those who are angry at their father and mother, to those caught up in hysteria, to those who will act only when they see the cops shoot someone."[4] Graham Blaine, an acute observer of adolescent behavior, also sees the violence in riots as emerging from "a boiling rage combined with a deep contempt for law and order."[5]

At this point in our knowledge, it is as difficult to generalize about expressive rioters as it is to discuss the "typical" American Negro. Studies of people who have been arrested during a riot, for example, can seldom offer an accurate profile. Robert Conot, in his brilliant history of the Watts explosion, has amply demonstrated that many utterly innocent people were caught in a network of confusion and hauled to jail.[6] In fact, in the case of the thirty-six homicides, only one man was actually brought to trial—and he was found not guilty. Of 2,249 adults who were arrested in Watts, the court found only 350 guilty of felonies.

We must, then, fall back on the impressions gathered by observers during the riots themselves. Admittedly, because of the very nature of a riot, our reports are often biased, confused, and contradictory. Nonetheless, a compilation of first-hand observations of the riots of 1965–1968 serves at least to dispell some common myths:

• Rioters are not all young, bare-chested men carrying flaming torches. In Watts, the generation aged fifteen to twenty-five did take the lead, but they were joined by many women, children, and older men. Conot, for example, reported old men throwing rocks and children of eight simultaneously pleading with them to be allowed the same privilege. As we have indicated, neither sex nor age divided the majority of our sample that favored violence.

• Many rioters have previously been law-abiding citizens, true stoics. To cite Watts again, 54 per cent of the adults and 41 per cent of the juveniles who were arrested had no prior criminal record. Juvenile gangs, like the Rebels, took a highly active part in the conflagration, but did not by any means comprise the majority of those who were incarcerated.

• Rioters are not drawn just from the ranks of unemployed, defeated, "shiftless" types of people. In Watts, William McCord witnessed many well-dressed people, apparently "responsible" and highly achieving, throwing rocks and looting. In Detroit and Newark, John Howard (and police reports) confirmed that a number of people who participated in the 1967 events held well-paying jobs.

• People who participate in riots are not just an insignificant minority of the population. The UCLA report on Watts indicated that 15 per cent of adult Negroes claimed to have taken a hand in the riot and an additional 35 to 40 per cent said they were "active" and approving spectators.[7] And our study suggests that a majority of Negroes in American cities approve the use of violence under certain conditions.

It appears, therefore, that rioters can be drawn from almost any stratum of urban Negro society. Once inflamed, the oppression of centuries breaks out in a revolt which makes no distinction of age, "respectability," or income.

Our own observations suggest, too, that different types of people take part in different stages of a riot. Specifically, one may make a distinction between three types of rioters: "violent" rioters (those who, through sniping, fire bombing, or rock throwing, are truly out to "get whitey"); "carnival" rioters, who simply enjoy the excitement of the riot and may also wish to get their share of the loot; and "ideological" rioters, who act on the basis of a more or less coherent doctrine which condemns the status quo.

While lacking in definitive evidence, our observations in Watts, Houston, Detroit, and Newark offer some clues as to the differences between these types of rioters:

THE VIOLENT RIOTERS

Robert Conot has well described this type of man in his account of the spread of the Watts riot to the South Park area of Los Angeles. The Businessmen, a juvenile gang, hung out on a corner of the park. They had seen fires burning in Watts but had not yet joined in the fight. Toward the end of the riot, a police car pulled up to the gang and the officers (one of them Negro) wanted to investigate the trunk of a car belonging to one of the Businessmen, a known passer of dope. The gang taunted the officer. What follows typifies the entrance of "rebels without a cause" into a riot:

The officers ignored their taunts.

"Hey, you motherfuckers! You're chicken!" A young man fired a Coke bottle against the side of the car.

The Negro officer leaped on him like a cat. Grabbing him by his T-shirt he spun him around and slammed him backward across the hood of the car. "You goddam punk! I ought to let you have it!" he ejaculated. Another police car, responding to the Help call, turned into the parking lot.

"Hey, man! That's brutality!" an onlooker protested.

He was arrested also, and, together with the bottle thrower, driven off. To the south, the northward drifting smoke from the fires along Avalon Blvd. was now visible. "Man! We gonna take this lying down?" someone asked.

"Shit, no. They want a riot. We give them a riot."

"Like man! The blood down in Watts need our help."

"Three for one. Three for one." They began their chant of revenge.[15]

And so they entered the fray. Of course, no one knows what damage they may have done in 1965, but young men like these formed the hard core, the "elite," of the rioters. These were men who felt no compunction about fighting back against the "blue minority," the police.

In addition to having had prior experience with violence, say, through criminal behavior, it is probable that the violent rioter is the most "marginal," defeated man in the ghetto. As James Baldwin said, in talking about the 1964 Harlem riot, "The most dangerous creation of any society is that man who has nothing to lose."[16] From our observations, it seems likely that many of the most violent rioters are drawn from the ranks of the defeated—those who have nothing to lose economically or psychologically. They are typified in a "hate-white" person who told a reporter during the 1967 Detroit riot, "I'm going to get me some whites tonight and you'd better believe it. I don't care if I die, so you know I don't care if I kill you."[17]

Again, according to our impressions, the most violent types come from environments characterized by utter chaos: broken, bitter, or quarreling homes; no jobs; no hope for the future.

The violent rioters—those who tend to start a riot and continue to participate until its final stages—also tend to be young men.

Our thesis, then, is that young, unemployed, marginal men tend to play a disproportionate role in the violence which characterizes a riot. But, as our research has shown, they receive the verbal support of older men and of women. Nonetheless, they differ in several ways from the person who enters a riot during its "carnival" stage.

THE CARNIVAL RIOTERS

Dr. John Spiegel, director of the Lemburg Institute for the Study of Violence at Brandeis University, has proposed a most useful prototype of the stages through which the riots of the 1960's have proceeded. In many cases, as Spiegel has pointed out, the riot enters a "carnival" period after the initial confrontation which triggered events. During the carnival time, people pour out into the streets, drink, joke, and often seem more concerned with having a good time than with starting a true rebellion. During this stage, masses of people join the riot and systematic looting begins.

The looting often follows an apparently senseless pattern. Dr. Harold Jones observed one woman in Watts lugging an armful of shoes. None of them matched. When he asked why she wanted them, the woman simply looked at him and continued running down the street.

Civility and a peculiar respect for certain kinds of laws are often maintained during the carnival period. Robert Conot reported that cars loaded with loot still obeyed traffic signals.

Houston, too, went through its carnival period before major violence broke out, but this period stretched over several weeks rather than the day-long transition in Watts. During the spring of 1967, Texas Southern University students protested a number of separate times. At one point, protesting cafeteria food, they threw food, plates, and glasses in the air— reminiscent of a Mack Sennet comedy. At another point, they objected to the fact that a major thoroughfare, Wheeler Street, bisects the campus. Civil rights leaders such as F. D. Kirkpatrick convinced the police to barricade the street temporarily and the students literally had a dance in the street. Eventually, however, the prolonged carnival period ended and a pitched gun battle between the police and students erupted.

The carnival rioters differ from the hard core of violent rioters in several ways, if our observations are correct. Most importantly, as we have indicated, the carnival period is a time when almost anyone—young or old, rich or poor, male or female, unemployed and white-collar workers—may be drawn into the vortex of the riot. The motives of the carnival rioters seem as multivarious as the masses from which they emerge, but they seldom seem motivated—except perhaps at the very deepest level—by overwhelmingly violent urges. And their actions are seldom guided by ideological considerations.

THE REVOLUTIONARY RIOTER

As we have already contended, people who hold to a consistent doctrine of rebellion, such as some of the black-power advocates, played no role in the Watts riots or even in the events of 1967 in Detroit or Newark. Yet we do not wish to deny that ideology may become a potent force in the future, particularly among college students. One of the most interesting portents of 1967 and 1968 was the fact the riots broke in previously "quiet," widely separated Negro colleges.

Thus, many motives enter into the creation of an expressive riot. For some people, the violence acts as a catharsis, for others as revenge, and for still others as a last-ditch effort to awaken the white community. As of 1967, however, we may have witnessed the emergence of a new type of violence: a class, rather than caste, riot.

Detroit: Class Riots

Daniel Patrick Moynihan has quite rightly observed that "race interacts with everything in America" but that the rash of contemporary violence in the urban ghetto was basically caused by a "large, desperately unhappy, disorganized, lower-class community."[8] Moynihan is implicitly suggesting that the riots are really a revolt of the "have-nots" against the "haves." And, of course, it happens in our society that class and racial lines interweave. The Watts and Houston evidence which we have previously cited tends to contradict the belief that the riots are really a "class war," since the white-collar classes produced some of the most militant of revolutionaries.

Nonetheless, evidence from other cities lends support to Moynihan's point. In particular, John Howard, who directly observed the riots in Detroit and Newark, discovered a lower-class, rather than racial, revolt in these cities. Not only were white and Negro stores looted indiscriminately, but, in Detroit, Howard's interviews turned up definite evidence of collaboration of Negroes and whites in rioting participation.

It seems incontrovertible that poor whites played a major role in the Detroit events. The first looter shot in the Detroit riot was a white person fleeing from a store on Fourth Street, Howard reported.

Just how did the poor whites become allied with the Negroes? Allan Van Newkirk, a resident of a Detroit area with a large concentration of poor whites, told Howard how looters from his neighborhood first got into the action: "At first they (the poor whites) hung back, but when they saw the blacks were fighting the police and not everyone was white, they went out and got into it. The feeling seemed to be to take all you could get and keep only what you needed. A fellow down the street came back with his car full of groceries and drove along the street giving them out to his friends. They don't like the cops either and so they got into it with them."

It is important to note, too, that the police can serve as a stimulus as well as an inviting "target" such as a store full of merchandise. Many whites living in slumlike conditions have "rumbles" with the police, just as lower-class Negroes do. For many, black and white, the police are a common enemy. Thus, facing law officers, a quickly formed biracial unity may emerge and result in Negro and white looting.

One other element enters into the class warfare type of rioting: dissension among Negroes has increased, and tends to divide along economic lines. In Houston in 1967, for example,

Negroes in certain areas began arming themselves against young militants who threw firebombs throughout the city. Those Negroes who secured guns did not have much to lose, but they were determined to keep it. The young militants were not aiming at Negro homes, but when they set fire to a white-owned store in a black neighborhood, the fire endangered nearby dwellings.

It appears, then, that whites and Negroes can join together in a fight against existing society. The primary conditions for such a coalition based on class rather than color seem to be these: 1) Poor whites see Negroes opposing the police, their presumed common enemy; 2) poor whites assume that ghetto Negroes have similar goals, such as looting stores or attacking the police; 3) relatively rich Negroes unite in protecting themselves against "vandals" (whether black or white); and 4) other considerations—of revenge or greed—overcome the usual anti-Negro prejudices of the poor white lower class, and they decide to join with Negroes.

During a period of class warfare, the rebels without a cause and the defeated of both ethnic groups can join together. This, we believe, will be a rare phenomenon, perhaps unique to a limited period of the 1960's. Of all groups in the urban ghetto, lower-class Negroes and lower-class whites are the most antagonistic toward each other. They can unite only in extreme situations—and their rewards for acting together in these events do not bring lasting unity. In the long run, the poor whites and Negroes compete directly for jobs and housing. Thus, the lasting coalition longed for by white radicals seems most unlikely to materialize.

Guerrilla Warfare

By the end of the 1960's, it appeared that both class and expressive riots had given way to another form of violent activity, urban guerrilla warfare. Expressive riots had disrupted hundreds of American cities; the ghetto had had its catharsis. These explosions may have had several constructive functions. For many, it led to the realization that pointless violence only destroyed the lives and livelihood of Negroes themselves. (It should be recalled that only a tiny minority in Watts believed that another riot would be useful, while Oakland Negroes— who had not experienced a riot—still believed in the utility of mass violence.) For some, particularly young activists and revolutionaries, a riot led directly to the formation of non-violent groups emphasizing black integrity, black self-help, and black political power. In Watts, for example, many former riot-ers joined indigenous groups such as US, SLANT, and various civilian protection patrols which aimed at the transformation of the ghetto.

Still others, however, learned a different lesson from the expressive and class riots. They recognized their futility and, in place of mass riots, elected to emphasize selective acts of sabo-tage, destruction, and self-defense. Organized in small, some-times highly localized, groups, these new militants held pitched gun battles with police, planned to blow up the Statue of Lib-erty, and successfully blacked out much of the San Francisco area by bulldozing major power lines.

Our research has shown that movements such as the Black Panthers have little support from the ghetto masses. Yet how-ever minuscule, the sources of support for the guerrilla war con-cept are diverse and potentially powerful. Two groups seemed to provide the major base of membership: former rebels without a cause who found redemption in a new movement, and potential achievers (particularly college students) who had lost faith in "the system." Further, unlike the traditional activ-ist organizations, the revolutionary groups found their leader-ship in lower- rather than middle-class people. Individuals such as Malcolm X and Eldridge Cleaver (often with records as rebels) took the lead. This change in leadership may have great significance, since lower-class leaders can "speak the language" of the ghetto and may be able to mobilize previously with-drawn groups such as the cool stoics and the defeated.

If, in fact, guerrilla leaders can achieve real prominence in the ghetto and if increased action replaces their rhetoric, the magnitude of this change of pace could hardly be overempha-sized. In a tender urban society like our own, a few revolutionaries can utterly disrupt a city. Unlike the past, a hundred well-trained men can now cripple the utilities, seize the radio stations, and poison the water supply of a city—thus sending America into a tailspin. We are not predicting that any such action will take place. We wish only to warn that the possibility exists—despite the number of National Guardsmen or police, armed with guns and nerve gas, who eventually arrive at the scene of a holocaust.

These plans for disrupting the entire American social system are discussed only by small groups, a tiny minority of the Negro community. Yet the idea of guerrilla warfare is but one of the many concepts spawned by the black-power ideology, and a vastly greater number of people favor black power in general. Because it is the most important ideological development in the American ghetto during the past decade, the program of black power deserves consideration.

BLACK POWER

Perhaps the most significant change in Negro styles of life in the last decade has been the transformation of many activist leaders into revolutionaries. People like Stokely Carmichael, H. Rap Brown, and James Forman—all well-educated, middle-class, "bourgeois" leaders—have abandoned both the legalistic approach of the NAACP and the nonviolent protest tactics of the old SNCC. Instead, they have adopted black power as their slogan, with all of its apparently revolutionary meanings. James Forman symbolizes this radical change of style.

I* first encountered James Forman, a courageous leader of SNCC, in Greenwood, Mississippi, during the "long, hot summer" of 1964. We had a clear-cut goal in that town: to register Negroes as voters. Forman led the effort; I ferried people from their churches to the courthouse. We failed temporarily. During that July "Freedom Day," 115 people went to jail while hundreds of others waited vainly to gain admittance

*William McCord.

to the voting booth. As police rushed men and women and children into custody, only two leaders remained. In the style of a nonviolent activist, Forman politely but stubbornly argued with town authorities. He struggled, too, with the decision as to whether all of us should go to jail, thus creating another confrontation with southern police power. As the marshals of the potential voters disappeared in police vans, it fell to me to keep the line of protesters in order and to feed them. Eventually, Forman decided that the jailings of even more hundreds would serve no purpose.

We withdrew. But, as was usual in those days, we later clasped hands, formed a circle, and sang "We shall overcome . . . black and white together."

I, a white, drove back to Jackson, Mississippi. I was frightened (my car had been smashed by white thugs and it carried California license plates—two sure signals to the KKK of the nature of my activities). Nonetheless, I felt proud of our work and, indeed, it had accomplished some purpose. Among many other factors, the Greenwood incident eventually led to federal intervention and the registration of thousands of previously disenfranchised Negroes.

Forman and I dropped out of each other's lives until almost exactly three years later. In May of 1967, as we have noted, Houston experienced a riot at Texas Southern University. Negro students exchanged gunfire with police. One man died and others were injured. (I spent some of my time at the riot lying under a police car with its motor running. Since my nose was up against the exhaust pipe, a policeman next to me felt prompted to comment that I had only two choices: being gassed or shot. Ten minutes later a bullet wounded him.) The events which triggered the riot were hardly as clear as the Mississippi denial of Negro voting rights. Earlier in Houston, people had protested the treatment by the Northeast Houston Independent School District of Negroes in one part of town. Another group demanded the removal of the city dump from the middle of a Negro section. On the campus, police had arrested one Negro student that night and (false) rumors circulated that a white person had shot a Negro boy.

About a month later, James Forman came to Houston to address a rally about the riot. We met and talked in a brief and friendly fashion. Yet he and I and the times had changed. SNCC had replaced "Black and White Together" with "Black Power" in its repertoire of slogans—and Forman echoed the change. In his speech, he presented theories of world events, rather than speaking on concrete domestic issues. He expounded, for example, a unique explanation of the Arab-Israeli War of 1967. According to Forman, the Rockefeller brothers had started it since they owned oil land in Venezuela and wished to end the flow of Mideast oil. Forman's proof of this contention was that McGeorge Bundy, president of the Ford Foundation, had been appointed as assistant on Mideast affairs to the President, and, "as everyone knew," the Rockefellers "really" controlled the Ford Foundation. Rap Brown, successor to Carmichael as SNCC chairman, followed his speech with threats that Negro maids would poison white families and that the Chinese army would lend active support to black power. Later in the evening, whites had to leave the rally.

The transformation of James Forman illustrated all too well the changes in "The Movement." White liberals had fallen into disrepute, Negritude had become the favorite theme of some Negro intellectuals, and, unhappily, no one truly seemed to know what to do about the immediate problems of urban Negroes. As Lerone Bennett, editor of *Ebony*, observed in 1965, the Negro leadership was in a state of complete dismemberment. No single group, nationally or locally, could command the allegiance of any significant part of the masses. Our surveys have clearly borne out this judgment.

Progress had admittedly been made, but too often it had touched only the lives of the black bourgeoisie rather than the urban masses. The consuming problems of the urban Negro—economic insecurity, bad housing, inferior education, family fragmentation—had not been resolved by the civil rights movement. It is this impasse which has changed many of the most articulate activist leaders into apparent revolutionaries.

As we have indicated, the black-power ideology appeals primarily to young, well-educated blacks, the potential achievers of their generation. The college riots of 1967, for example, had a distinctively ideological tone. In April of 1967, Nashville suffered from three nights of violence. Many attribute this explosion in part to the ideological proddings of Stokely Carmichael. Carmichael arrived in town to address the student body at Vanderbilt (a predominantly white university) as well as at the overwhelmingly Negro Fisk University and Tennessee A & I. *The Nashville Banner* had previously demanded that Carmichael not be allowed to speak. Carmichael capitalized upon this attempt at suppression when he told a Fisk audience: *"The Banner* says we have come to Nashville to stir up trouble. They lie all the time—but this is one time they spoke the truth."[9] Later, when addressing students at Tennessee A & I, he said: "You have to go for the honkies who are keeping you in the ghettos. . . . Victims should never, ever, apologize for the use of violence."[10]

Violence ensued. Carmichael alone could not, of course, have initiated the riot unless a great deal of black-power sentiment already had permeated the students.

Whatever igniting effect the black-power ideology had, it is quite clear that its refrain was heard in each of the six college riots of 1967. It is also evident that Negro students—who led the original sit-in movements—had abandoned nonviolence as their method of protest.

The reasons for this change are many and varied. Some of them have been outlined in the previous chapter, concerning the revolutionary; some may simply reflect the same motives which prompt student outbreaks on mostly white campuses, such as Berkeley. Nonetheless, it is an ominous sign for the future of our society that the youngest, best-educated Negroes have now expressed their grievances in an ideologically tinted, violent fashion. If the past repeats itself, many in the ghetto—the rebels, the stoics, the defeated—will follow the lead of middle-class militants. Even the Negro exploiters could gain. As the school disputes of 1968 in New York City indicated, black-power leaders can easily mobilize many of the stoics (particularly women) behind a specific cause.

What does black power mean to its proponents? Rap Brown,

chairman of SNCC, summed up the basic tenets of his movement during a private conversation in 1967. For Brown and many of the revolutionaries, the slogan of black power seemed to have this content:

• Negroes, by themselves, must assert their political and economic power through such methods as the creation of all-Negro political parties such as the Black Panther Party. Coalition with whites is either impossible or undesirable, for it would undermine Negro dignity.

• Integration with whites should not be a paramount goal. Rather, Negroes should strengthen their own separate culture and society: "black is beautiful." At some future date, if a Negro so chooses, he might integrate with whites.

• Negroes must affirm their unique identity, learn of their African heritage, and identify with the "colored" peoples throughout the world.

• White society is both oppressive and decadent. Negroes should not fight "the white man's war" in places such as Vietnam.

• Violence, at least in self-defense, can and should be used by Negroes to achieve their goals.

• While Negroes are a minority in America, they can count on the support of Asian and African peoples.

Beyond this minimal credo, some ideologues have added other touches. On at least one occasion, for example, Stokely Carmichael attempted to put more content into the black-power slogan by specifying that Negroes in Houston ought to receive 23 per cent of the political power, 23 per cent of the land, and 23 per cent of the wealth in the city—exactly in ratio to their proportion of the population. Black Muslims, of course, add on a number of ideological flourishes, including a demand for a separate state.

Novelist John Oliver Killens, in his book *Black Man's Burden*, is perhaps the most eloquent intellectual spokesman for the movement, although he is not particularly identified with any organization. Killens movingly describes the Negroes' plight in America, restating in other terms what Richard Wright, James Baldwin, and Claude Brown have been telling whites.[11] He addresses his book to a "You" whose identity alternates between that of an American white and that of a generalized representative of Western society. Killens repeats familiar themes. He tells of the emasculation of Negro manhood in America, the ambiguous situation of the Negro writer, and the presumption of American leaders in assuming direction of the "free world" while allowing Mississippi and Harlem to exist.

While Killens can hardly be considered an original social critic, he does express an ebony mood (labeled by James Farmer, former head of CORE, as the ideology of the "new Jacobins") which we must consider now, and increasingly in the future. In only slightly veiled terms, Killens advocates violence: "If you [the whites] practice violence against me, I mean to give it back to you in kind. . . . Maybe this will help whip some sense into your head."[12] Unfortunately, Killens neglects to specify the type of violence he condones. Self-defense in Philadelphia, Mississippi? A Watts riot? Or an Armageddon confrontation?

Coupled with Killens' hatred for American whites is an almost total contempt for Western civilization in general. He maintains that outside Africa, the old world of the West is dying. It is a civilization, he believes, oriented to gadgets and materialism, while in Africa new societies designed to fulfill the needs of man are being created. Black and brown men will survive to write the West's obituary, he predicts. The white minority in the world has only one choice: to humanize itself through an alliance with the colored majority. "We black folk cannot wait another moment. The tide is with us. The black commander beckons. We must put boats to sea. Git on board, little chillun, git on board."[13]

While one can sympathize with the bitterness which produced this book, one can hardly respect it as an intellectual contribution to resolving the Negro dilemma. Killens, for example, never explains *why* the wave of the future will overwhelm Western man; he simply proclaims it. His prescription for violence delineates neither the means nor the goals. He has no suggestion for national policy except an exhortation that Negro children become acquainted with their ancestors' role in America and with the great civilizations of ancient Mali and Ghana—and even here he admits that this would amount to inventing myths as a way of restoring Negro dignity.

At their best, black-power advocates do not espouse racism but call rather for Negro leadership in a fight to defend all human rights. As Stokely Carmichael has written in "What We Want," blacks should fight to uphold civil rights for all.

Whatever its virtues, the black-power program in its entirety simply will not work. Economically, the plan would entail the creation of separate institutions; Negroes would take over the businesses of the ghetto, either by starting their own or by boycotting white stores. Even if this were possible, as Fred Powledge (author of *Black Power, White Resistance*) has pointed out, the ghetto would become even poorer: "Black institutions, built alongside existing white ones, would be poverty-stricken by comparison. Whites not only would not support them, they would do what they could to destroy them. And if black people took over the existing white-run institutions that presently serve the ghettos and the slums, they would find themselves the proprietors of large chunks of decaying real-estate—schools in the process of decomposition, hospitals that are little more than morgues."[14]

Politically, the assertion of black power alienates potential allies. Its connotations of racism appall white moderates and strike white liberals as ethically obnoxious—as evil as proclamations about white supremacy.

The violence implied in the black-power plan can hardly help ghetto residents. Watts and the other riots of 1965 did indeed bring some economic benefits, for they alerted the federal government and local officials to the grievances of urban Negroes. Yet further violence in American cities will, in all probability, merely stiffen white resistance. The logical next step for those who advocate violence would be to attack white neighborhoods. Conceivably, black nationalists could follow a policy of selective assassination of Negro moderates or racist white politicians, or they could raid white business areas, or, as Rap Brown openly suggested in June of 1967, they could poison the drinking supply of a city, perhaps with a dosage of LSD.

If this holocaust did occur, the reaction of the white community is quite predictable. It would respond with black genocide.

Finally, as has been pointed out, most urban Negroes simply reject the black-power ideology. The achievers, the exploiters, and even the stoics have basically the same aspirations and values as other Americans. Thus, the advocates of a black revolution find great difficulty in securing mass support. Events may push Negroes into extremism and some ultimate confrontation with whites, but in the 1960's most Negroes seem concerned above all with political and economic, "bread and butter," issues.

THE SEARCH FOR ECONOMIC IMPROVEMENT

As our research and that of others has amply demonstrated, most urban Negroes want more and better jobs above any ideological goal. While some differences appear among those whose lives are of different styles—achievers, for example, place more emphasis on education that do stoics—all groups agree on the primacy of a search for economic improvement.

The reasons behind this demand for "green power" are hardly difficult to fathom. The gross statistics on the extent of urban black poverty need not be restated, but one incisive study has particularly revealed the nature of Negro poverty. Economist Alan Batchelder has clearly demonstrated that the Negro dollar is second-class money.[15] Operating in a market of "restricted supply," the Negro pays relatively more than the white for his housing, durable goods, and food. Thus, $3,000 in "Negro money" buys only the equivalent of $2,500 in "white money." Further, measures such as urban renewal, which benefit whites who are on the margin of poverty, have often damaged the Negro. When a typical city erects a housing project, 60 per cent of the families who are dispossessed are Negro.

Many of these must cram even more densely into the ghetto since, on the average, urban renewal projects which displace 190,500 families result in a net loss of 75,000 housing units. In the job market, changes which have benefited the general public have either left the Negro untouched or have hurt him. Between 1950 and 1960, the number of southern factory jobs rose by 944,000. None of these went to Negro men, Batchelder asserts, and only 12,000 went to Negro women. And clearly, as automation eliminates unskilled jobs, Negroes suffer the most.

This last factor has caused a polarization between the ghetto resident and, particularly, members of the black achieving class. For example, as Walter Williams has shown, economic conditions in the Hough area of Cleveland got *worse* rather than better in the five-year span between 1960 and 1965. The city as a whole prospered, but "the gap between haves and have-nots widened strikingly; and the most rapid widening was among Negroes—between those outside the slums who were rising, beginning finally to cash in on the American dream, and those still in the hard-core ghetto, on limited rations of income and hope."[16] As industry moved to the suburbs, families with male heads, men with usable skill, and the achievers apparently followed, leaving behind an increasing number of "poor Negro young people in the economically weak female-headed homes—young people whose bondage becomes more oppressive as the rest of the city grows more prosperous."[17]

The conclusion is inescapable: "Those with economic strength can flee the Crisis Ghetto. The more able Negroes should continue to widen their lead until they too become part of the symbols of success that make failure ever more visible and disturbing."[18]

Almost exactly one year after the special Cleveland census occurred, the Hough section of Cleveland exploded in the July riot of 1966.

Massive, consciously planned measures to alter the structure of Negro poverty have notably failed.

• Welfare measures, including some form of a guaranteed annual income, would obviously aid many of those counted in the ranks of the stoics and the defeated (particularly fatherless families). Yet most black households would be left untouched.

• The antipoverty program of the last decade has emphasized education while ignoring motivation. The Job Corps, Head Start, the Neighborhood Youth Corps, and even the Community Action Program have assumed that sufficient doses of education (and "community participation") will change the nature of the ghetto. Such a position overlooks white (and black) interests in preserving the status quo, and ignores the fact that Head Start children have to enter ghetto schools and thus lose whatever drive toward achievement they possessed, and that it costs one $1,000 a year in America to have black skin. Further, disparities in income *increase* as education of blacks increases in relation to that of whites. Why then should a "cool stoic" abandon his way of life when he sees few rewards for his sacrifice?

• Strategies to improve the situation of Negroes must consider the vast differences in the life styles which we have described. A simple welfare program might be of aid to the defeated group, but utterly irrelevant (or distasteful) to the revolutionaries. Further, political considerations have drastically hampered attempts to reach the "rebels without a cause"— potentially, as Malcolm X's history shows, one of the most creative groups in the ghetto.

• The slogan of "black capitalism" has a nice ring to white ears. Reality, however, will frustrate President Richard Nixon's goals. Black capitalism posits a degree of entrepreneurial talent which, as we have seen, does exist in the rebels, the achievers, and the exploiters of the ghetto. But such a policy makes other assumptions which cannot be fulfilled. White—even tax-subsidized—capital will not enter a ghetto environment where even insurance companies fear to tread. Negro capital investments cannot be raised in such an impoverished area. Even if they could, where are the skilled black men to operate automated industry?

The primary fault with the programs of the 1960's does not lie in their objectives, for, as we have seen, even the black stoic can be roused from apathy. In its assault on poverty, America must raise its sights. A. Philip Randolph has suggested a "Freedom Budget" which, if expanded, might indeed cure urban Negro poverty. The resources exist, if America had the will to the imagination of most Americans—despite our enormous expenditures for power in Vietnam and glory in space.

There is no question that America could afford to end urban Negro poverty. The resources exist, if America had the will to utilize them. As one concrete example:

Currently, we are racing to get to the moon. The estimated cost of putting a man on the moon is $30 billion. If we wished to use this money for other goals we could accomplish the following:

• Provide $10 million to each of 200 cities for funding of antipoverty programs.

• Finance seven-year fellowships (freshman through graduate school at $4,000 a person) to produce 50,000 more Negro doctors, teachers, and scientists.

• Underwrite guaranteed annual incomes of not less than $5,000 a year for three years for all the poor people in the United States.

• Create three new foundations of the scope of the Rockefeller Foundation to aid the urban black.

• Build ten new medical schools.

• Allow a 10 per cent increase in salary over a ten-year period for every teacher in the United States.

. . . And the Government could still remit $100 million in tax monies to all Americans.

These programs and many others could be implemented on one condition: that the American people wanted them. "The only thing that stands between America and integration," as Lerone Bennett has pointed out, "is the decision to integrate."[19]

It seems tragically evident, at this moment in history, that Americans do not wish to make this decision. On the one hand, as our study suggests, Negro stoicism impedes concerted drives to end segregation. On the other hand, numerous events have testified to increasing white opposition: the election of obscurantist politicians, the passage of laws such as California's Proposition 14, the failure of Congress to act on civil rights legislation, the white mobs that attacked Martin Luther King, Jr., as he tried to end housing segregation in Chicago, and, of course, King's assassination in Memphis.

We must return again to the question of power, for, as Kenneth Clark has succinctly stated, "The new American Dilemma is one of power. The dilemma is a confrontation between those forces which impel a society to change and those which seek to maintain the past."[20] No one can question that forces for change exist: every type of power, from court decisions to riots, has already been manifested. The real issue is how to channel the latent power of Negro urban masses into constructive action.

THE POLITICAL WAY

The only answer to ghetto problems, we believe, lies in the political realm. Blacks must exert political power and the socioeconomic structure will change. Admittedly, there are great obstacles which impede the exercise of the Negro's political potential: white manipulation of growing Negro political power, the isolation of Negroes in economically impoverished central cities, or the total alienation of whites from Negroes. Smart white politicians can use many devices to curtail Negro power. They can, for example, extend central city borders to swamp Negroes with white votes or, as in Cleveland, they can suddenly grant tenure to many white officials when it appears imminent that Negroes will gain political control of the city.

Further, on the basis of past history, Negroes have little reason to expect tangible gains from political participation. To determine the utility of political activity on the municipal level, for example, we have looked at two sets of cities. In the first set, Negroes held a substantial number of city council seats; in the second set, they did not. We then compared these cities as regards the social and economic status of Negroes within them.

NEGRO REPRESENTATION ON CITY COUNCILS OF
SELECTED NONSOUTHERN CITIES (MARCH 1965)

	TOTAL CITY COUNCIL	NEGRO COUNCILMEN	% NEGRO ON COUNCIL	% POPULATION NEGRO
High Representation				
Cleveland	33	10	30.3	28.6
St. Louis	29	6	20.7	28.6
Los Angeles	15	3	20.0	13.5
Chicago	50	7	14.0	22.9
Low Representation				
Detroit	9	0	0.0	28.9
Boston	9	0	0.0	9.1
New York	35	2	5.7	14.0
Cincinnati	9	1	11.1	21.6

In none of the cities did we find a Negro majority on the city council; but one might expect that Negro council members could exert a broad influence over a whole range of affairs, such as the allocation of community resources, municipal hiring practices, and the allocation of contracts. In that sense, it is not unreasonable to ask whether there were any discernible differences between cities where Negroes had high city council representation and those where they had low city council representation.

A comparison of the two sets of cities suggests no differences between them. Three of the four low-representation cities have had riots, as have three of the four high-representation cities. Apparently, having Negroes on the city council did not give ghetto Negroes in Cleveland, Chicago, and Los Angeles a sufficiently keen sense of representation "downtown" to deter them from rioting. The fact of the matter is, however, that it is by no means clear that representation downtown makes that much difference in the condition of life in the ghetto. The unemployment rate is high for all of these cities and has been for over a decade. In Chicago, Cleveland, Detroit, and Cincinnati the nonwhite unemployment rate has been over 10 per cent since at least 1950. Welfare rights organizations have been in conflict with the authorities in high-representation cities (Cleveland) and low-representation cities (Boston). Police action was the proximate cause of rioting in high-representation Los Angeles and low-representation Detroit. *In other words, it is not at all clear that there is any measurable difference in ghetto conditions between cities in which Negro representation on the city council is roughly proportional to their numbers in the population and those in which they are under-represented.*

Despite this record, there are reasonable grounds for optimism that Negroes will soon begin to reap some of the spoils that traditionally result from political participation. First, the level of Negro political action, particularly in cities, has risen to unprecedented levels. Second, recent studies have contradicted the usual assumption of social scientists that apathy, especially among the stoics, prohibits political activism. In some cases, political scientists have shown that Negroes voted in larger percentages than either lower-class or upper-class whites.[21] Thirdly, urban Negroes have recently demonstrated remarkable political flexibility and sophistication: alerted to a candidate's stand on civil rights, they have shifted their votes with uncanny accuracy.

These facts have led the most brilliant of Negro political tacticians, James Farmer and Bayard Rustin, to propose a strategy of coalition politics.[22] Bayard Rustin has argued strongly for a political coalition between Negroes and other elements in American society. Rustin recognizes that drastic economic reforms, such as the Freedom Budget, can be implemented only by government: "The young Negro who would demonstrate his way into the labor market ... will end up having to favor a great expansion of the public sector of the economy. At any rate, that is the position the movement will be forced to take as it looks at the number of jobs being generated by private economy, and if it is to remain true to the masses of Negroes."[23] Thus Rustin contends that Negroes should join with other progressive forces to bring about reform. He argues that only a political challenge will result in economic change and, further, that Negroes, by themselves, cannot win sufficient political power: "We need allies. The future of the Negro struggle depends on whether the contradictions of this society can be resolved by a coalition of progressive forces which becomes the *effective* political majority in the United States."[24]

Rustin emphasizes the critical importance of the Negro "swing vote" in various urban centers and looks forward to a period when Negroes will wrest the leadership of city machines from whites. But, he adds: "We must also remember that the effectiveness of a swing vote depends solely on 'other' votes. It derives its power from them. In that sense, it can never be 'independent,' but must opt for one candidate or other, even if by default. Thus, coalitions are inescapable, however tentative they may be."[25]

Rustin envisages a coalition that could enlist Negroes, labor, liberals, and certain religious groups in a drive to guarantee civil rights, end urban decay, and handle the problems created by automation.

If the Negro political potential is to be realized, two conditions must exist. 1) The rate of Negro political involvement must be such as to make full use of their potential. Because Negroes are a minority it becomes that much more important that there be no waste of political resources through failure to vote, voting the wrong way, etc. 2) The Negroes' status as a minority makes coalition politics mandatory if they are to realize their goals. The Negro cannot swing enough political clout by himself to get what he wants.

Let us enlarge on each of these conditions.

As regards full use of the Negro political potential, we have discussed the modes of adaptation found among various types of Negroes: the stoics, "the rebels without a cause," the exploiters, the defeated, the revolutionaries, and the achievers. Obviously, some of these orientations are accommodating to political activity and others are not. One would expect, for example, that achievers, and, in a certain way, exploiters (in terms of the spoils of politics), could be involved in the political game. The key question regarding the utility of politics and Negro modes of adaptation is one of the relative proportion of the Negro population found in each category of adaptation. Without going so far as to generalize from the proportions we have in our sample, we feel it can probably be said that fewer Negroes are in the achiever, exploiter, or revolutionary categories than are in the stoic, defeated, or "rebel without a cause" categories. In other words, it is not clear that a majority of Negroes have modes of adaptation which would lead them readily to seek a political solution to their problems.

How then can we suggest a political solution? Several factors indicate that the most apolitical Negro can be subject to political mobilization. For example, in our chapter on stoics we indicated that many persons in this category seek solace in religion and in the church. In that sense, they are deflected away from politics. The whole history of the contemporary civil rights movement indicates, however, that a religious orientation is not incompatible with a political orientation. The Negro church was probably the most effective instrument available in giving the civil rights movement of the early 1960's a broad base of support among southern Negroes. Indeed, one can say that the Negro church was the only mechanism available for gaining such support for the movement. One would expect the religiously oriented stoics, those who are members of various fundamentalist churches, to be subject to mobilization under certain circumstances.

As regards "rebels without a cause," there is some evidence in the wake of the Watts riot that young Negro males who were previously apolitical and oriented to petty criminal activity as a mode of adjustment are now more attuned to conventional politics. Tom Hayden, in his article on Newark in *The New York Review of Books* (August 1967), even suggested that people such as Tommy Jacquette may be building the equivalent to a viable political organization in the ghetto. Jacquette is himself a product of the streets who was politicized by the riots.

To summarize, then, as regards the Negro political involvement: On the one hand, it could be doubted that a major portion of the Negro population could be mobilized to engage in conventional politics. In that sense, it would be unrealistic to call for a political solution. On the other hand, there is some evidence that the most apolitical types can and have been mobilized.

Recent history suggests that Negro political mobilization may come about in unusual ways. That is, there may be unusual vehicles of mobilization. The church and street-corner boys rather than the reform-oriented, high-minded civic clubs may play the major role in getting the Negro into politics. On balance, then, one cannot say that the orientations we have described place a major barrier between the Negro and the acquisition of political power.

As regards coalition politics, the obvious difficulty with Rustin's position is that organized labor, in particular, often strongly opposes Negroes in their demand for better jobs and better housing—precisely because Negroes are "encroaching" on labor's domain. Even granting this problem, it is still conceivable that Negroes may form coalitions with labor behind certain candidates. Indeed, Negroes have effectively allied themselves even with the richest white classes on several occasions. The aristocrats of Atlanta, for example, welcomed Negro support in defeating a candidate for mayor who both was a segregationist and, in the view of business leaders, projected a bad image of the city.

The Atlanta situation illustrates dramatically how coalition politics between the oddest of bedfellows can pay off. In 1961, Ivan Allen (a moderate who later was the first southern politician to testify in favor of the civil rights bill of 1964) ran against Lester Maddox (the devout segregationist who finally became governor of Georgia) for mayor of Atlanta. Higher-income white districts give Allen 76 per cent of their votes and Negro precincts voted 94 per cent in favor of him. In contrast, lower-class white districts gave Allen only 40 per cent of their votes. If Negroes had not joined with moderate whites, Maddox would have won, since, in fact, he gained a majority of white votes in the election. Such examples could be multiplied at all levels of government but the lesson seems clear: under certain circumstances, in alliance with whites, Negroes can exercise their political power effectively by electing either a person of their own group or a white politician sensitive to Negro interests.

While admittedly difficult to achieve, coalition politics seems the only viable way to advance the Negro cause. Two additional facts lend support to this position. First, our own studies and the 1966 research of investigators such as William Brink and Louis Harris indicate that the majority of both Negroes and whites still subscribe to a politically liberal center. As Brink and Harris put it: "There is every indication that Americans are not about to panic into a crusade behind George Wallace to maintain the racial status quo. In an odd way, the Wallaces serve as the leaveners to the Stokely Carmichaels politically. The old coalition may be changing beyond recognition, but the essential stability of the center in American political life is likely to remain intact."[26]

Secondly, once Negroes assume political dominance in many of America's central cities—a trend which hardly seems reversible, even by the cleverest of racist tactics—the white power structure will react more sensitively to Negro demands. As Powledge has observed: "The hidden, scattered power structure in New York City might respond, for example, to the threat of an all-Negro delegation to the City Council from Manhattan or to the declaration by a newly-chosen set of political leaders in Harlem that they no longer will play ball with the majority. Certainly, there would be a response to a Negro police commissioner who decided to enforce the parking laws on the East Side, or to a Negro housing commissioner who decided to prosecute slumlords."[27]

Is there any reason to believe that whites will participate in a coalition movement which (at least temporarily) seems to threaten their own housing, jobs, and status? In all probability, certain groups, particularly minorities who feel immediately and intimately challenged by Negroes, would actively oppose any trend toward "black and white together." Yet in the long run, certain objective factors might push even the most recalcitrant group into reluctant cooperation. "One answer," as Powledge has commented, "is that the cities are universally awful, not only for Negroes, but for whites as well."[28] It stands to reason, then, that improvements in urban housing, transportation, sanitation, schooling, or jobs would, in the long run, aid whites as well as Negroes. Further, the crisis in American

cities is so profound that the only alternative to racial cooperation seems increasingly to be a racial holocaust. To quote Powledge: "Would it not be better (for whites) to join in such a
movement, and take a chance on its success, than to live out
the rest of one's life (and know that one's children would live
out the rest of theirs) in fear of, and in flight from Negroes?"[29]

There is only one lasting solution to the racial dilemma:
that whites and Negroes work together to improve their
common lot as Americans. The spirit of reconciliation and
good will seems moribund. If this spirit cannot be revived, we
face a new civil war. As *The Ethics of the Fathers* wisely
observed: "The time is short, the hour is late, the matter is
urgent. It is not incumbent upon us to complete the task; but
neither are we free to desist from doing all we possibly can."
We know the answers. The sole issue is whether Americans will
have the compassion and reason to act before the clock strikes
midnight.

REFERENCES

1. Quoted in Robert Samuelson, "Riots: the More There Are,
   the Less We Understand," *Science*, August 11, 1967, p. 664.

2. *Ibid.*

3. Quoted in *Newsweek*, August 21, 1967, p. 20.

4. *Ibid.*

5. Graham Blaine, *Youth and the Hazards of Affluence* (New
   York: Harper & Row, 1967), p. 87.

6. Robert Conot, *Rivers of Blood, Years of Darkness* (New
   York: Bantam Books, 1967)

7. Cited in *Newsweek*, August 12, 1967.

8. Quoted in Samuelson, *op. cit.*, p. 664.

9. Quoted in *Newsweek*, April 24, 1967, p. 28.

10. *Ibid.*, p. 20.

11. John Oliver Killens, *Black Man's Burden* (New York: Trident Press, 1965).

12. *Ibid.*, p. 175.

13. *Ibid.*, p. 209.

14. Fred Powledge, *Black Power, White Resistance* (Cleveland: World Publishing, 1967), p. 261.

15. Alan Batchelder, "Poverty—the Special Case of the Negro," *American Economic Review*, May, 1965.

16. Walter Williams, "Cleveland's Crisis Ghetto," *Trans-Action*, Vol. 4, No. 9, September 1967, p. 33.

17. *Ibid.*, p. 41.

18. *Ibid.*

19. Lerone Bennett, *Confrontation: Black and White* (Baltimore: Pelican Books, 1965), p. 256.

20. Kenneth Clark, Introduction to *The Negro American*, Talcott Parsons and Kenneth Clark, eds. (Boston: Houghton Mifflin, 1966), p. xi.

21. See, for example, Jack Walker, "Negro Voting in Atlanta," *Phylon*, Vol. 24, 1963.

22. See James Farmer, *Freedom—When?* (New York: Random House, 1966) and Bayard Rustin, "From Protest to Politics," in *Negro Protest Thought in the Twentieth Century*, Francis Broderick and August Meier, eds. (Indianapolis: Bobbs-Merrill, 1965).

23. Rustin, *ibid.*, p. 414.

24. *Ibid.*, p. 416.

25. *Ibid.*, p. 420.

26. William Brink and Louis Harris, *Black and White* (New York: Simon & Schuster, 1966), p. 116.

27. Powledge, *op. cit.*, p. 280.

28. *Ibid.*, p. 280.

29. *Ibid.*, p. 281.

Annotated Bibliography

No one could hope to list all of the important books and articles about American Negroes; a complete bibliography would run to thousands of pages. Therefore, we have mentioned just a handful of the more representative writings on the subject. We hope that it will be useful as an introduction.

Gordon Allport, *The Nature of Prejudice* (Boston: Beacon Press, 1954). The clearest compilation of evidence on the topic.

Edward C. Banfield and James Q. Wilson, eds., *City Politics* (Cambridge, Mass.: Harvard University Press, 1965). An insightful discussion on new trends.

Edward C. Banfield, *Urban Government* (New York: The Free Press, 1965). A discussion of the increasingly important problem of how to avoid anarchy in American cities.

Alan Batchelder, "Poverty: The Special Case of the Negro," *American Economic Review*, May 1965. The best summary of the relative value of "Negro money."

Lerone Bennett, *Confrontation: Black and White* (Baltimore: Penguin Books, 1966). A stirring analysis of contemporary events.

William Brink and Louis Harris, *Black and White* (New York: Simon & Schuster, 1967). A comprehensive survey of Negro and white attitudes about the "American dilemma."

Leonard Broom and Norval Glenn, *Transformation of the Negro American* (New York: Harper & Row, 1965). A compendium of knowledge.

Claude Brown, *Manchild in the Promised Land* (New York: New American Library, 1965). A probing autobiography by a man who saved himself from the ghetto.

David Capolvitz, *The Poor Pay More* (New York: Crowell-Collier, 1963). A revealing study of the costs of poverty.

Chicago Commission on Race Relations, *The Negro in Chicago* (Chicago: University of Chicago Press, 1922). A report which perceptively anticipated many of the issues which confront contemporary America.

Kenneth Clark, *Dark Ghetto* (New York: Harper & Row, 1965). A dissection of urban life by a brilliant psychologist.

Jerry Cohen and William Murphy, *Burn, Burn, Baby* (New York: E. P. Dutton, 1966). A graphic recount of the Watts riot.

Robert Coles, *Children of Crisis* (Boston: Atlantic-Little, Brown, 1965). A sensitive description of whites and blacks in the "New South."

Robert Conot, *Rivers of Blood, Years of Darkness* (New York: Bantam Books, 1967). A day-by-day, person-by-person revelation about the Watts riot.

Edmund Cronon, *Black Moses: The Story of Marcus Garvey* (Madison, Wisc.: University of Wisconsin Press, 1962). The history of one of the first and most influential Negro militants.

Bradford Daniel, *Black, White, and Gray* (New York: Sheed & Ward, 1964). A well-written survey.

John P. Davis, ed., *The American Negro Reference Book* (Englewood, N.J.: Prentice-Hall, 1967). One of the more useful encyclopedias of American Negro life.

John Dollard, *Caste and Class in a Southern Town* (New York: Doubleday, 1937). One of the first and best analyses of American Negroes.

St. Clair Drake and Horace Cayton, *Black Metropolis* (New York: Harper & Row, 1962). The most intensive analysis of urban Negroes ever written.

St. Clair Drake, "The Social and Economic Status of the Negro in the United States," *Daedalus*, Fall 1965. A revealing portrait of the Negro in America.

Francis Drodwick and August Meier, eds., *Negro Protest Thought in the Twentieth Century* (Indianapolis: Bobbs-Merrill, 1965). A comprehensive compilation of writings.

W. E. B. DuBois, *The Souls of Black Folk* (Chicago: A. C. McClurg, 1903). One of the more important books by the greatest of Afro-American intellectuals.

Editors of *Ebony, The Negro Handbook* (Chicago: Johnson Publishing, 1966.) A useful compilation of information.

Stanley Elkins, *Slavery* (Chicago: University of Chicago Press, 1959). Perhaps the very best historical account of this sad era in American history.

Robert Erhest, *Immigrant Life in New York City* (New York: King's Crown Press, Columbia University, 1949). Adds historical perspective to contemporary issues.

James Farmer, *Freedom—When?* (New York: Random House, 1966). A realistic assessment of the nation's condition.

John Hope Franklin, *From Slavery to Freedom* (New York: Alfred A. Knopf, 1954). One of the first and perhaps most lasting contributions to the history of American Negroes.

E. F. Frazier, *Black Bourgeoisie* (New York: Collier, 1962). A devastating and classic analysis of the Negro middle class.

E. F. Frazier, *The Negro Family in Chicago* (Chicago: University of Chicago Press, 1932). The first analysis of a controversial topic.

J. C. Furnas, *Goodbye to Uncle Tom* (New York: William Sloane Associates, 1956). Dispels myths concerning the American Negro.

Harold Gosnell, *Negro Politics* (Chicago: University of Chicago Press, 1935). One of the seminal works on an increasingly important topic.

Oscar Handlin, *The Newcomers* (Cambridge, Mass.: Harvard University Press, 1959). An excellent appraisal of the problems facing Negroes and Puerto Ricans.

Abram Kardiner and Lionel Ovesey, *The Mark of Oppression* (New York: W. W. Norton, 1951). A lasting contribution to the psychoanalytic study of American Negroes.

John Oliver Killens, *Black Man's Burden* (New York: Trident Press, 1965). A representative sample of black protest.

Elliot Liebow, *Tally's Corner* (Boston: Little, Brown, 1967). An enlightening report on Negro street-corner life.

Raymond W. Mack, *Race, Class and Power* (New York: American Book, 1968). An extensive anthology aimed at a systematic elucidation of minority-group relations with the dominant group.

Roscoe Martin and Frank J. Munger, *et. al, Decisions in Syracuse* (New York: Doubleday Anchor Books, 1964). An analysis of how big-city leaders actually cope with urban problems.

Gary T. Marx, *Protest and Prejudice* (New York: Harper & Row, 1967). A nationwide study of Negro attitudes.

Louis H. Masotti and Don R. Bowen, *Riots and Rebellion* (Beverly Hills, Calif.: Sage Publications, 1968). An interdisciplinary survey of urban violence.

Donald R. Mathews and James Prothro, *Negroes and the New Southern Politics* (New York: Harcourt, Brace & World, 1966). Nicely dissects the influence of the Negro vote.

William McCord, *Mississippi: The Long Hot Summer* (New York: W. W. Norton, 1965). A social history of the civil rights movement in the southern context.

August Meier and Elliot Rudwick, *From Plantation to Ghetto* (New York: Hill & Wang, 1966). An excellent historical sketch of Negro transition.

R. K. Merton and R. A. Nisbet, eds., *Contemporary Social Problems* (New York: Harcourt, Brace & World, 1961). An anthology which illuminates many of the problems Negroes face today.

Herbert A. Miller, *Old World Traits Transplanted* (Chicago: University of Chicago Press, 1925). An important contribution from the "Chicago School" of thought.

Henry Lee Moon, *Balance of Power* (New York: Doubleday, 1948). A good discussion of the Negro voter's influence.

Daniel Patrick Moynihan, "Employment, Income and the Ordeal of the Negro Family," *Daedalus*, Fall 1965. A controversial, enlightening analysis of psychological impairment.

Florence Murray, ed., *The Negro Handbook* (New York: Macmillan, 1949). A good if dated discussion of various aspects of black life.

Gunnar Myrdal, *An American Dilemma* (New York: Harper & Bros., 1944). An original call to action by a Swedish social scientist viewing America.

Seymour Parker and Robert Kleiner, *Mental Illness in the Urban Negro Community* (New York: The Free Press, 1966). The definitive work on the problem.

Talcott Parsons and Kenneth Clark, eds., *The Negro American* (Boston: Houghton Mifflin, 1966). A fine anthology by some of the best thinkers in America.

Thomas F. Pettigrew, *A Profile of the Negro American* (Princeton, N.J.: D. Van Nostrand, 1964). A distinguished achievement in unifying psychological and sociological perspectives.

Fred Powledge, *Black Power—White Resistance* (Cleveland: World, 1967). A moving statement concerning the black-white confrontation.

Lee Rainwater, "Crucible of Identity: The Negro Lower-Class Family," *Daedalus*, Winter 1966. Gets to the core of what many believe to be the center of Negro dilemmas in America.

Report of the National Advisory Commission on Civil Disorders (Washington, D.C., 1968). A far-ranging analysis of contemporary urban riots.

Charles Silberman, *Crisis in Black and White* (New York: Random House, 1964). An extremely well-written analysis of Negro conditions.

George E. Simpson and J. Milton Yinger, *Racial and Cultural Minorities* (New York: Harper & Bros., 1953). An excellent summing-up of minority problems.

R. L. Sutherland, *Color, Class and Personality* (Washington, D.C.: American Council on Education, 1942). An important early discussion of a complex issue.

W. I. Thomas and Florian Znaniecki, *The Polish Peasant in Europe and America* (New York: Dover, 1958). A basic book on the transition to urban life.

Robert Penn Warren, *Who Speaks for the Negro?* (New York: Random House, 1966). A noted historian of southern birth examines the "American Dilemma."

William F. Whyte, *Street Corner Society* (Chicago; University of Chicago Press, 1961). A near-classic description of Italian-American adjustment to urban life.

James Q. Wilson, *The Amateur Democrat* (Chicago: University of Chicago Press, 1966). A careful assessment of the "game" of big-city politics.

James Q. Wilson, "The War on Cities," *The Public Interest*, No. 3, Spring 1966. An outstanding appraisal of historical trends affecting slum residents.

Louis Wirth, *The Ghetto* (Chicago: University of Chicago Press, 1928). A lasting contribution to the study of trends within the Jewish community.

Louis Wirth, "Urbanism As a Way of Life," *American Journal of Sociology*, 44, July 1938. A classic discussion of urban life.

Nathan Wright, *Black Power and Urban Unrest* (New York: Hawthorne, 1967). A persuasive attempt at defining and defending the concept of black power.

Violence in the City, Governor's Commission Report on the Los Angeles riots (Sacramento, 1965).

Malcolm X, *The Autobiography of Malcolm X* (New York: Grove, 1966). A passionate statement by the patron saint of black militants.

Harvey W. Zorbaugh, *The Gold Coast and the Slum* (Chicago: University of Chicago Press, 1929). A major contribution to the theory of urbanism.

Questionnaires

In all the questionnaires used in this study, we asked basically similar questions and, of course, gathered the usual demographic information about age, sex, occupation, etc. In addition to the core questions, however, others were added to fit the particular city or group which was being interviewed. In some instances, other questions were added for particular samples (*e.g.*, queries concerning new Oakland civil rights groups). We have not fully presented the results of this additional data in the book since often we did not have proper control groups for comparison. We hope in future publications to report on such specialized matters as participation in the civil rights movement and its relation to psychosomatic problems.

The four questionnaires included in the appendix are the following:

1. *Houston Questionnaire 1* was used to probe the nature of the various selected types ("defeatist," "stoic," "activist," etc.) between the spring of 1967 and the summer of 1968.

2. *Houston Questionnaire 2* was used to analyze the attitudes of a random sample of Houston Negroes. Canvassed were every census tract in which there was 90 per cent or more Negro representation (nineteen neighborhoods). The interviewers knocked at the door of every middle house on the right-hand side of each block. If there was no answer, they chose the house next door. The interviews were conducted both during the day and at night to insure a proper representation of men.

3. *The Watts Questionnaire* was administered in bars, buses, streets, pool halls, and other places which the interviewers (all lower-class Negroes, many of whom had taken part in the 1964 riot) regarded as representative of that particular community. Since

the interviewers did not say they were conducting a survey, the responses were recorded on cards after each informal conversation. A later check of the interviews with census maps of Watts indicated that the interviewers did indeed manage to talk to a good representation of the various occupational, age, and other groupings in Watts. This technique was developed by Dr. Blair Justice. These interviews were conducted in the fall and spring of 1967.

4. *The Oakland Questionnaire* was again administered by lower-class Negroes after a period of training by John Howard. A check with census maps again indicated a fair representation of various Negro groupings in Oakland. The interviews were made in the fall of 1967.

HOUSTON QUESTIONNAIRE 1

Q1. In the attempts of Negroes to gain their civil rights, have things been going too slowly, about right, or too fast?

0. No information
1. Too slowly
2. About right
3. Too fast
4. Both

Q2. What groups in Houston have been effective in helping matters?

0. No information
1. NAACP
2. Religious
3. Federal poverty programs
4. Houston Council on human relations
5. Student groups
6. Demonstrations in general
7. PUSH
8. HAY
9. CORE/SNCC

Q3. What do you think are the main problems for Negroes in Houston?

0. No information
1. Jobs (money)
2. Education (schools)
3. Housing (living conditions)
4. Police
5. Discrimination in general
6. Negro apathy
7. Lack of Negro leadership
8. Communication with government

Q4. Is anything going to be done to improve the situation?
    0. No information   1. Yes
    2. Perhaps something   3. No
    4. Hope so

Q5. Do you think the riots in Watts helped or hurt the Negroes' cause?
    0. No information   1. Definitely helped
    2. Possibly helped   3. Possibly hurt
    4. Definitely hurt   5. Both helped and hurt
    6. Neither helped nor hurt

Q6. What do you think about the police in your neighborhood?
    0. No information   1. Bad/bigoted
    2. Some bad   3. OK/fair
    4. Good   5. Excellent
    6. Too few/not there when 7. No contact
       needed

Q7. Some groups in America think it would be a good idea for Negroes to have a separate state. What do you think?
    0. No information   1. Definitely help
    2. Possibly help   3. Definitely hurt
    4. Possibly hurt

Q8. How actively have you participated in the civil rights movement?
    0. No information/none 1. Protested
    2. Picketed   3. Boycott of stores
    4. Politics

Q9. (Depending on previous response) If you were asked by people whom you respected, would you:
    0. No information/none 1. Protest
    2. Picket   3. Boycott a store
    4. Do political work

Q10. In what situations, if any, do you think violence is justified in defending Negro rights?
    0. No information   1. Self-defense
    2. Gain attention   3. Attack
    4. Never (religion)   5. Never (tactics)
    6. Never

Q11. Do you think anything like the Watts riot could occur in Houston?

0. No information	1. Yes
2. Probably	3. Maybe
4. No	5. Hope not

Q12. If yes, what might cause it?

0. No information	1. External forces
2. Internal forces	3. Mixture

Q13. Are your parents living together?

0. No information	1. Yes
2. No	3. One or both deceased

Q14. In your own lifetime, what has changed most?

0. No information	1. General characteristics
2. Situation of Negroes	of modern world
4. Nothing	3. Personal change

Q15. Do you think your children's lifetime will be better, worse, or just about the same as yours?

0. No information	1. Better
2. Worse	3. The same
4. Both	

Q16. Of all the people whom you know or have read about, whom do you admire the most?

0. No information	1. Personal
2. Local Negro leader	3. National Negro leader
4. White politician	5. Sports, music figure
6. Other	

Q17. (If person in religious) How important is religion to you?

0. No information	1. Very important
2. Somewhat important	3. Not important

Q18. Does the minister of your church have much influence over the members of the church? In what ways? Does he have much influence generally in Houston?

Influence over members

0. No information	1. Yes
2. No	3. Some/maybe

In what ways

0. No information	1. Communicates ideas
2. Communicates to out-	from outside
side	3. Other

Influence in Houston
  - 0. No information   1. Yes
  - 2. No   3. Some/maybe

Q19. Do you think human nature (man's basic qualities, good and bad) can be changed? If yes, for the better or worse?
  - 0. No information   1. Yes, better
  - 2. Yes, worse   3. Yes, both
  - 4. No

Q20. Some people say that man will some day fully understand what causes such things as floods, droughts, and epidemics; others say that such things can never fully be understood by man. What is your opinion?
  - 0. No information   1. Yes
  - 2. No (general)   3. No (religious)
  - 4. Perhaps

Q21. Many things are changing in the world nowadays—in our daily life and in the society in which we live. Do you think that you could have a personal influence on the changes that are taking place?
  - 0. No information   1. Yes
  - 2. Maybe   3. No

Q22. When you meet someone for the first time, what should you do?
  - 0. No information
  - 1. Trust him until he proves untrustworthy
  - 2. Be cautious until you know him better
  - 3. Distrust him

Q23. Some people think that there is very little that a man can do by his own efforts to change his destiny; others think that a man can do much by his own efforts to change his destiny. What is your opinion?
  - 0. No information   1. Can do much
  - 2. Can do some   3. Can do little
  - 4. Maybe   5. No

Q24. Do you know who is the Governor of Texas and what do you think of him?
  - 0. No information   1. Claims knowledge, positive opinion
  - 2. Claims knowledge, negative opinion   3. Claims knowledge, no or neutral opinion
  - 4. No knowledge

Q25. Do you know who is the Mayor of Houston and what do you
      think of him?
          0. No information   1. Claims knowledge, posi-
          2. Claims knowledge, neg-   tive opinion
             ative opinion   3. Claims knowledge, no
          4. No knowledge   or neutral opinion

Q26. Do you know who is on the City Council and what do you
      think of them?
          0. No information   1. Claims knowledge, posi-
          2. Claims knowledge, neg-   tive opinion
             ative opinion   3. Claims knowledge, no
          4. No knowledge   or neutral opinion

Q27. Do you know who is running for the legislature in your dis-
      trict and what do you think of them?
          0. No information   1. Claims knowledge, posi-
          2. Claims knowledge, neg-   tive opinion
             ative opinion   3. Claims knowledge, no
          4. No knowledge   or neutral opinion

Q28. Do you know who is running for State Senate in your dis-
      trict and what do you think of them?
          0. No information   1. Claims knowledge, posi-
          2. Claims knowledge, neg-   tive opinion
             ative opinion   3. Claims knowledge, no
          4. No knowledge   or neutral opinion

Q29. Do you know who is running for Congress in your district
      and what do you think of them?
          0. No information   1. Claims knowledge, posi-
          2. Claims knowledge, neg-   tive opinion
             ative opinion   3. Claims knowledge, no
          4. No knowledge   or neutral opinion

Q30. Do you ever have trouble getting to sleep or staying asleep?
          0. No information   1. Yes
          2. No   3. Sometimes

Q31. Do your hands (or legs) ever tremble enough to bother you?
          0. No information   1. Yes
          2. No.   3. Sometimes

Q32. Are you bothered by nervousness?
          0. No information   1. Yes
          2. No   3. Sometimes

Q33. Have you ever been bothered by shortness of breath when you were not exercising or working hard?
- 0. No information
- 1. Yes
- 2. No
- 3. Sometimes

Q34. Are you often troubled with headaches?
- 0. No information
- 1. Yes
- 2. No
- 3. Sometimes

Q35. Has the idea of suicide ever crossed your mind?
- 0. No information
- 1. Yes
- 2. No
- 3. Sometimes

Q36. What makes you maddest?
- 0. No information
- 1. Personal traits or acts
- 2. Discrimination
- 3. Acts of others (regardless of race)
- 4. Passive (dumb) Negroes
- 5. Uncle Tom
- 6. Rioting Negroes

HOUSTON QUESTIONNAIRE 2

Q1. In your lifetime, what has changed most?
- 0. No information
- 1. General characteristics of modern world
- 2. Opportunities for Negroes
- 3. Personal changes
- 4. Nothing

Q2. Do you think your children's lifetime will be better or worse, or just about the same as yours?
- 0. No information
- 1. Better
- 2. Same
- 3. Worse
- 4. Nothing/Neither

Q3. Of these world figures, whom do you admire most?
- 0. No information
- 1. Dwight Eisenhower
- 2. Roy Wilkins
- 3. Malcolm X
- 4. Bob Hope
- 5. Sammy Davis, Jr.
- 6. None of above/other

Q4. How religious are you?
- 0. No information
- 1. Very
- 2. Some
- 3. Little or no

Q5. In what ways does the minister of your church influence the members of his congregation?

0. No information   1. Capacity as member
2. Civil rights   3. Personal counselor
4. Little or no influence   5. Behavior model in other
6. Other negative   ways/dress, teacher, etc.

O6. In what ways, if any, does he influence people generally in Houston?

0. No information   1. Leader in city
2. Civil rights specifically   3. Personality
4. Little or no influence   5. General model

Q7. Do you think it would be possible for a Negro to become Mayor of Houston?

0. No information   1. Next election
2. In five years   3. In ten years
4. Never

Q8. Some people say that those who are successful in life have generally made plans and arranged things in advance so they turn out well. Others say that those who are successful in life had better luck than others.

0. No information   1. Luck
2. Planning   3. Both

Q9. When you meet someone for the first time, what do you do?

0. No information
1. Trust him until he proves to be untrustworthy
2. Be cautious until you know him better
3. Not trust him because he may take advantage of you

Q10. Please give us your opinion on this situation:

You buy something in a large department store, and discover after leaving that you have been shortchanged 75 cents. You go back to the sales clerk and ask for your money. Do you think you will get it back?

0. No information   1. Yes
2. No   3. Maybe

Q11. In the attempts of Negroes to gain their rights, have things been going too slowly, about right, or too fast?

0. No information   1. Too slow
2. About right   3. Too fast

Q12. What groups in Houston have been effective in helping matters?

o. No information   1. NAACP
2. Religious   3. Nonactive Nationalists
4. Local (PUSH, HAY)   (SNCC)
6. Civil rights in general 5. Government

Q13. What do you think are the main problems for Negroes living in Houston?

o. No information   1. Jobs
2. Schools   3. Housing
4. Relations with power 5. Discrimination in general
  structure   eral
6. Internal with Negroes

Q14. Do you think the riots in Watts helped or hurt the Negroes' cause?

o. No information   1. Helped
2. Hurt   3. Both
4. Neither

Q15. What do you think about the schools in your neighborhood?

o. No information   1. General approval
2. General disapproval 3. Disapproval (racial)

Q16. What are the causes of any racial tension in Houston today?

o. No information   1. External to Negro community
2. Internal to Negro com- munity
  munity   3. Both
4. No tension/doesn't apply

Q17. What do you think of the police in your neighborhood?

o. No information   1. General approval/neutral
2. General disapproval tral
4. No contact   3. Disapproval (racial)

Q18. Some groups in America think it would be a good idea for Negroes to have a separate state. What do you think?

o. No information   1. Good
2. Bad   3. Mixed

Q19. How actively have you participated in the civil rights movement?

  0. No information   1. Any one
  2. Protests   3. Any two
  4. Pickets   5. All three
  6. Boycott of stores

Q20. In what situations, if any, do you think violence is justified in defending Negro rights?

  0. No information   1. Self-defense
  2. Never   3. Defense of property
  4. General justification

Q21. Do you think anything like the Watts riot could occur in Houston?

  0. No information   1. Yes
  2. No   3. Maybe

Q22. If yes, what might cause it?

  0. No information   1. External forces
  2. Internal forces   3. Mixed forces
  4. Doesn't apply

Q23. In what ways are Negroes and whites the same?

  0. No information   1. Human
  2. Other

Q24. In what ways are they different?

  0. No information   1. No ways
  2. Money/education/op-   3. Skin color
    portunity
  4. Other (attitudes)

Q25. In what ways are Negroes better than whites?

  0. No information   1. No ways
  2. Other

Q26. In what ways are whites better than Negroes?

  0. No information   1. No ways
  2. Opportunities   3. Other

Q27. How much time do you spend with white people? Doing what?

  0. No information   1. Over 4 hours working
  2. Under 4 hours working   3. Other than working
  4. Not at all

Q28. What do you think the average white person thinks about Negroes?
- 0. No information
- 1. Ignorant/inferior
- 2. Aggressive against whites
- 3. Bad in general/crazy
- 5. Good and bad mixed
- 4. Good in general

Q29. When you were growing up, did your parents live together?
- 0. No information
- 1. Yes
- 2. No

Q30. As a child when you did something your parents thought was wrong, what did they generally do about it? (If say "punished me" ask how)
- 0. No information
- 1. Physical punishment
- 2. Scolding
- 3. Withdrawal of privileges
- 4. Combination including physical
- 5. Combination not including physical

Q31. Approximately how many different jobs have you held in the last five years?
- 0. No information
- 1. One
- 2. 2–4
- 3. Over 5

Q32. Do you think jobs are easy or difficult to find?
- 0. No information
- 1. Easy
- 2. Difficult
- 3. Depends

Q33. Are you satisfied with your present job? (If no) what are your chances of getting a better job?
- 0. No information
- 1. Yes
- 2. No
- 3. Mixed
- 4. Unemployed

Q34. Where in Houston would you like your children to go to school?
- 0. No information
- 1. Negro
- 2. White
- 3. Integrated
- 4. Choice of kinds
- 5. No Houston school
- 6. Neighborhood school

Q35. Who is the governor of Texas and what do you think of him?
- 0. No information
- 1. Good
- 2. Bad
- 3. Bad racial
- 4. OK/neutral

Q36. Who is the mayor of Houston and what do you think of him?
- 0. No information
- 1. Good
- 2. Bad
- 3. Bad racial
- 4. OK/neutral

Q37. Who is Barbara Jordan and what do you think of her?
- 0. No information
- 1. Good
- 2. Bad
- 3. Bad (racial)
- 4. OK/neutral

Q38. Who is on the school board and what do you think of them?
- 0. No information
- 1. General positive
- 2. General negative
- 3. Favor some
- 4. Against some
- 5. Both in favor and against
- 6. Names mixed and favor

OAKLAND QUESTIONNAIRE

Q1. How would you evaluate schools in the Hills as compared to schools in the Flatlands? Would you say that the Hill schools are:
- 0. No information
- 1. About the same
- 2. Better
- 3. Worse

Q2. (If better) In what ways are schools in the Hills better than those in the Flatlands?
- 0. No information
- 1. Better teachers
- 2. Better facilities
- 3. More courses and special programs
- 4. Other

Q3. (If worse) In what ways are schools in the Hills worse than those in the Flatlands?
- 0. No information
- 1. Need for better teachers
- 2. Other
- 3. Doesn't know

Q3. a—Is there any segregation by race in the Oakland school system?
- 0. No information
- 1. None
- 2. Not much
- 3. A fair amount
- 4. A great deal

Q4. Does Oakland have any provision whereby a minority group child may transfer to a school with a smaller minority enrollment?

    0. No information   1. Yes

    2. No   3. Doesn't know

Q5. How may this be done?

    0. No information   1. Open enrollment

    2. Bussing   3. Other

    4. Doesn't know

Q6. Have there ever been public protests over the schools (pickets, marches, demonstrations)?

    0. No information   1. Yes

    2. No   3. Doesn't know

Q7. What groups that you know of have been active in terms of attempting to improve the schools?

    0. No information   1. AD HOCK

    2. WRO   3. Other

    4. Doesn't know   5. None

Q8. Do you have any children or other relatives going to school in Oakland at this time?

    0. No information   1. Yes

    3. No

Q8. a—(If yes) How many?

    0. No information   1. 1–5

    2. 5–10   3. Over 10

Q9. (If yes) At what level of education are they currently (what grade)?

    0. No information   1. Elementary school

    2. Junior high school   3. High school

    4. All levels

Q9. a—How many are in the above grades?

    0. No information   1. Under 3 children

    2. 4–5   3. 6–8

    4. Over 9 children

Q10. How much effect can the average citizen like you have in terms of improving the schools?

    0. No information   1. None at all

    2. Very little   3. Some

    4. A great deal

Q11.　(If 2, 3, or 4) In what ways can he be effective?
　　　0. No information　　　　1. Group action
　　　2. Demonstrate　　　　　3. Doesn't know

Q12.　How would you rate relations between the Oakland police and the Negro community?
　　　0. No information　　　　1. Excellent
　　　2. Good　　　　　　　　3. Fair
　　　4. Poor

Q13.　(If 3 or 4) Who is principally to blame for the poor relations?
　　　0. No information　　　　1. Police
　　　2. Negroes　　　　　　　3. Both

Q14.　Do you personally know any Negro who has been abused by the police?
　　　0. No information　　　　1. Yes
　　　2. No

Q14.　a(—If yes) Explain the circumstances. What happened?
　　　0. No information　　　　1. Police brutality
　　　2. Police harassment　　　3. Other

Q15.　What might improve relations between the Negro community and the police?
　　　0. No information　　　　1. Civilian review board
　　　2. More Negro police　　　3. More respect by Negroes
　　　4. More respect by police　　　5. Other

Q16.　Why, in your opinion, has there not yet been a riot in Oakland?
　　　0. No information
　　　1. There has been one
　　　2. Hasn't started yet (mounting tension)
　　　3. Leaders keep peace/don't really want to riot
　　　4. Fear (of losing job, of police, etc.)
　　　5. Other
　　　6. Doesn't know

Q17.　In the attempts of Negroes to gain their civil rights how have things been going?
　　　0. No information　　　　1. Too slow
　　　2. About right　　　　　3. Too fast

Q18. What groups in Oakland have been effective in helping matters?
    0. No information
    1. NAACP
    2. AD HOCK
    3. Other local organizations
    4. Don't know any
    5. None

Q19. Rank the following in terms of their seriousness as problems facing Negroes living in Oakland?
    0. No information
    1. Jobs
    2. Housing
    3. Schools
    4. Other

Q20. Is anything being done to improve the situation?
    0. No information
    1. Yes
    2. No

Q21. Do you think the riots in Watts and other cities have helped or hurt?
    0. No information
    1. Helped
    2. Hurt
    3. No effect
    4. Doesn't know
    5. Both

Q22. Have you ever participated in any demonstrations, boycotts, or picketing?
    0. No information
    1. Any one
    2. Any two
    3. All
    4. None

Q23. Some groups in the United States think it would be a good idea for Negroes to have a separate state. What do you think?
    0. No information
    1. Yes
    2. No
    3. Doesn't know

Q24. In what situations, if any, do you think violence on the part of Negroes is justified?
    0. No information
    1. Self-defense
    2. Never
    3. Other

Q25. Which would you be willing to take part in as part of a civil rights protest-political campaign: picket; march; rally; boycott; riot?
    0. No information
    1. Any one
    2. Any two
    3. Three or more
    4. All
    5. None

Q26.   Which of the two major parties do you favor?
    0. No information   1. Democrats
    2. Republicans   3. Neither

Q27.   Whom did you favor in the 1964 Presidential election?
    0. No information   1. Johnson
    2. Goldwater   3. Other

Q28.   If the Presidential election were being held now for whom would you vote?
    0. No information   1. Johnson
    2. R. Kennedy   3. Other

Q29.   Do you recall the name of the present Mayor of Oakland?
    0. No information   1. Correct answer
    2. Incorrect answer   3. Doesn't know

Q30.   Whom do you favor in the gubernatorial elections?
    0. No information   1. Brown
    2. Reagan   3. Neither
    4. Doesn't know

Q31.   Which word would you use to describe the job the War on Poverty has done so far?
    0. No information   1. Excellent
    2. Good   3. Fair
    4. Poor   5. Doesn't know

Q32.   What things do you like about the War on Poverty?
    0. No information   1. Nothing
    2. Attempt to help poor 3. Various organizations
    4. Doesn't know

Q33.   What things do you dislike about the War on Poverty?
    0. No information   1. Too slow and not com-
    2. Nothing   prehensive enough
    4. Doesn't know   3. Other

Q34.   What are your feelings about the War in Vietnam?
    0. No information   1. Unjustified and un-
    2. Justified   necessary
    4. Other   3. Doesn't like it

Q35.   Do you recall the name of your city councilman?
    0. No information   1. Correct
    2. Incorrect

Q36. Do you recall offhand the names of any members of the school board?

    0. No information   1. One
    2. Two   3. Three
    4. Four   5. Five
    6. Six   7. Seven
    8. Eight

Q37. Do you belong to any of the following kinds of organizations?

    0. No information   1. Trade Unions
    2. PTA   3. Church organizations
    4. Other   5. None

Q38. (If a member) How often in the period of a month do you get to meetings?

    0. No information   1. 0–2
    2. 3–6   3. 7+

Q39. (If a member) Are most of your friends inside or outside? the organization?

    0. No information   1. Inside
    2. Outside   3. Both

Q40. In the event of an emergency is there any friend or relative in Oakland to whom you feel you could turn for help?

    0. No information   1. Yes
    2. No

Q41. Do you consider yourself a religious person?

    0. No information   1. Yes
    2. No

Q42. How much influence do you think ministers have in the Negro community?

    0. No information   1. A great deal
    2. Some   3. Not much
    4. None at all

Q43. How much influence do you think ministers should have on the Negro community?

    0. No information   1. A great deal
    2. Some   3. Not much
    4. None at all

Q44. How would you rate your relationship with your next-door neighbors?
- 0. No information
- 2. Know both but not friends
- 4. Know one but not the other
- 1. Good friends with both
- 3. Friends with one but not the other
- 5. Doesn't know either

Q45. If you could, would you move from this neighborhood?
- 0. No information
- 2. No
- 1. Yes

Q46. How do you rate this neighborhood as a place to live?
- 0. No information
- 2. Good
- 4. Poor
- 1. Excellent
- 3. Fair

Q47. Where would you move if you could go where you wanted to?
- 0. No information
- 2. Another part of Flat-lands
- 2. Another state
- 1. The Hills
- 3. Another community
- 5. Other

Q48. In your lifetime what has changed most?
- 0. No information
- 2. Not much/nothing
- 4. Other
- 1. People and society
- 3. The Negro
- 5. Doesn't know

Q49. How do you rate the chances your children will have as compared with those you had?
- 0. No information
- 2. About the same
- 1. Better
- 3. Worse

Q50. Of these famous figures, whom do you admire most?
- 0. No information
- 2. Wilkins
- 4. Johnson
- 6. Sammy Davis, Jr.
- 1. R. Kennedy
- 3. Gandhi
- 5. Malcolm X
- 7. Other

Q51. What qualities make these figures attractive to you?
- 0. No information
- 2. Attempt to help poor
- 4. Fair/honest
- 1. Leadership
- 3. Principals
- 5. Other

Q52. Who in this community do you admire most?
    0. No information   1. No one
    2. Friends and neighbors   3. Relative
    4. Other

Q52. a—Why?
    0. No information   1. Work in advancement projects
    2. Personal qualities   3. Other

Q53. Do you think white people have more hostility toward Negroes now as compared with a year ago?
    0. No information   1. Yes
    2. No

Q53. a—(If yes) Why?
    0. No information   1. Negroes attempting to better themselves
    2. Fear   3. Reaction against Negro riots
    4. Other   5. Doesn't know

Q54. Do you think white people are any more likely to start race riots than at any time in the recent past?
    0. No information   1. Yes
    2. No

Q54. a—(If yes) Why?
    0. No information   1. Negro attempt to better himself
    2. Fear   3. Hate
    4. Other   5. Doesn't know

Q55. Taking Chicago summer of 1966 as an example, do you think white people are justified in striking out at Negroes or heckling them for marching through all-white neighborhoods?
    0. No information   1. Yes
    2. No

Q55. a—(If yes) Why?
    0. No information   1. Basic rights of whites
    2. Other

Q56. Considering yourself now as compared with a year ago, would you say, as regarding achieving equal rights, that you are:
- 0. No information
- 1. More patient
- 2. Less patient
- 3. About the same

Q57. In seeking equal rights do you think Negroes would be:
- 0. No information
- 1. More aggressive
- 2. Less aggressive
- 3. About the same

Q58. Have you ever heard the term "White Backlash"?
- 0. No information
- 1. Yes
- 2. No

Q58. a—(If yes) What does it mean? How do you interpret it?
- 0. No information
- 1. White turncoats
- 2. Reactionary and extremists
- 3. Bad attitudes and race prejudice
- 4. Other
- 5. Doesn't know

Q59. Do you rent or own your home?
- 0. No information
- 1. Rent
- 2. Own

Q60. How many people live here with you?
- 0. No information
- 1. 0–5
- 2. 5–10
- 3. Over 10

Q61. What is their relationship to you?
- 0. No information
- 1. Wife and/or children
- 2. Husband and/or children
- 3. Children only
- 4. Other

Q62. When you were growing up did your parents live together?
- 0. No information
- 1. Yes
- 2. No

Q63. What kind of ending do you think it will all have?
- 0. No information
- 1. Happy
- 2. Unhappy
- 3. Some of both

WATTS QUESTIONNAIRE

Q1. Attitude toward present job.
    0. No information   1. Good
    2. Fair   3. Bad

Q2. Thinks most jobs open to him.
    0. No information   1. Most
    2. Some   3. Very few

Q3. Thinks salary provides decent living.
    0. No information   1. Always
    2. Usually   3. Never

Q4. How often do you think you are turned down for a job because you are a Negro?
    0. No information   1. Always
    2. Usually   3. Never

Q5. How often do you think you are denied a promotion because you are a Negro?
    0. No information   1. Always
    2. Usually   3. Never

Q6. How actively have you participated in civil rights movement?
    0. No information   1. Not interested
    2. No chance yet   3. Protested

Q7. In what situation is violence justified for Negro rights?
    0. No information   1. Always opposed
    2. If attacked   3. To gain attention
    4. Only way to get desired results

Q8. Opinion of quality of schools.
    0. No information   1. Good
    2. All right   3. Poor

Q9. Opinion of integration of schools.
    0. No information   1. Doing it fairly
    2. All right   3. Not doing it fairly

Q10. General integration of schools.
- 0. No information
- 1. Too fast
- 2. About right
- 3. Too slow

Q11. Los Angeles police treatment of Negro.
- 0. No information
- 1. Fair
- 2. Some OK, others not
- 3. Abusive

Q12. Attitude toward black power.
- 0. No information
- 1. Against
- 2. Never heard of it
- 3. In favor of
- 4. All right/neutral

Q13. How important is religion to people today?
- 0. No information
- 1. Very
- 2. Not so important
- 3. Not at all

Q14. Opinion of War on Poverty in Watts.
- 0. No information
- 1. Good
- 2. Fair
- 3. Bad

Q15. Opinion of Watts housing.
- 0. No information
- 1. Good
- 2. Fair
- 3. Bad

Q16. How have riots elsewhere in 1966 affected tension in Watts?
- 0. No information
- 1. Not at all
- 2. Somewhat
- 3. Very much

Q17. What effect have the talks by the Mayor had?
- 0. No information
- 1. Good
- 2. Bad
- 3. Never heard

Q18. What causes of racial tensions in Watts today?
- 0. No information
- 1. Lack of jobs
- 2. Police brutality
- 3. White supremacy and racism
- 4. Reckless youth
- 5. Poor housing
- 6. Other

Q19. What can be done to reduce this tension?
- 0. No information
- 1. Provide jobs
- 2. Improve police
- 3. Bring understanding
- 4. Stop pushing people around/give fair break
- 5. Improve housing
- 6. Other

Q20. What is the worse problem in your own neighborhood?

    0. No information   1. Police abuse

    2. Unemployment   3. No problem

    4. Troublemakers   5. Poor housing

    6. Other

Q21. What local leaders do you admire?

    0. No information   1. Don't know

    2. None   3. Other (specify)

Q22. What national leaders do you admire?

    0. No information   1. Roy Wilkins

    2. Stokely Carmichael   3. Martin L. King

    4. None   5. Other

Q23. What do you know of Negro gangs in Watts?

    0. No information   1. None

    3. Very little   3. Other

Index

327